GUCCI

A
HOUSE
DIVIDED

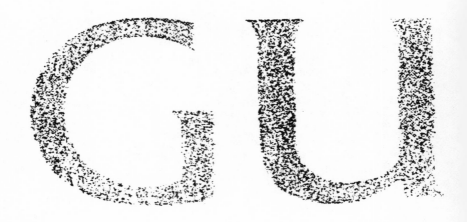

GERALD McKNIGHT

A HOUSE

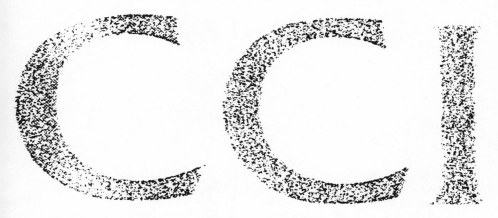

DIVIDED

DONALD I. FINE, INC.
NEW YORK

Library of Congress Cataloging-in-Publication Data

McKnight, Gerald.
  Gucci: a house divided.

  Includes index.
  1. Gucci (Firm)   2. Clothing trade—Italy.
3. Clothing trade.   I. Title.
HD9940.I84G86   1987   338.7'687'0945   86-46390
ISBN: 1-55611-037-5 (alk. paper)

Manufactured in the United States of America

10   9   8   7   6   5   4   3   2   1

This book is printed on acid free paper. The paper in this book
meets the guidelines for permanence and durability of the Committee on
Production Guidelines for Book Longevity of the Council on Library Resources.

DESIGN: Stanley S. Drate/Folio Graphics Co. Inc.

The secret . . . is the vendetta, the family ties incomprehensible to Englishmen and Americans. Much that has been interpreted in lofty terms, fate, religion, etc. is only blood and the tribal survival within the family.

—Arthur Miller
(Notebook entry for his play, *A View From the Bridge*)

CONTENTS

ix

AUTHOR'S NOTE

Wherever possible, the author has restricted himself to direct quotations and often has so indicated in the text. He also has records to document these quotations. Obviously the author was not at hand during the various meetings among the family and others, and so has had to rely on what he has been told by those who were present or by those who were told by those who were present. At all times the author's paramount intent has been to achieve a fair, accurate and objective account, playing no favorites, taking no sides, perceiving no villains or heroes. If unavailability of some of the players in the drama has created any other impression, it is unintentional and to be regretted.

The story of the Gucci family is, the author feels, a colorful and even important part of mercantile history and popular culture—if not sociology and psychology as well. To capture as much as possible of it, in an evenhanded fashion, has been the author's challenge.

ACKNOWLEDGEMENTS

It is never easy to find one's way into a family story as intimate, complex and explosive as the Guccis', and without the help of those I mention below, and others whose names I need to keep to myself, the book most certainly would have been stillborn.

My thanks are a small reward, but I offer them to those members of the family, including Dr. Aldo Gucci, who chose not to be interviewed in person by the author, but did, nevertheless, speak to him several times over the telephone, Grimalda and Giovanni Vitali, Dr. Maurizio Gucci, Patrizia, Roberto, Paolo and Jenny Gucci, who helped so materially, to Maurizio's secretary Elena and his assistant Franco Crudeli, to my interpreters Susan Fraser Becchi in Florence and Carey Pizzigoni in Milan, and for patient and accurate translations by Jim Backhouse in London, to my friend Mimi Wise in New York for invaluable research beyond the call, to my then agent, the indefatigable Roger Schlesinger, to Alexandra Murkowska, Vicki Mackenzie, Ewart and Hilda Price, Ronald Singleton in Rome and Paul Rossiter in London. To all of these who helped, and many more, let me say that I appreciate their assistance and hope the result will not be a disappointment.

—Gerald McKnight

THE GUCCI FAMILY

Gabriello m. Elena

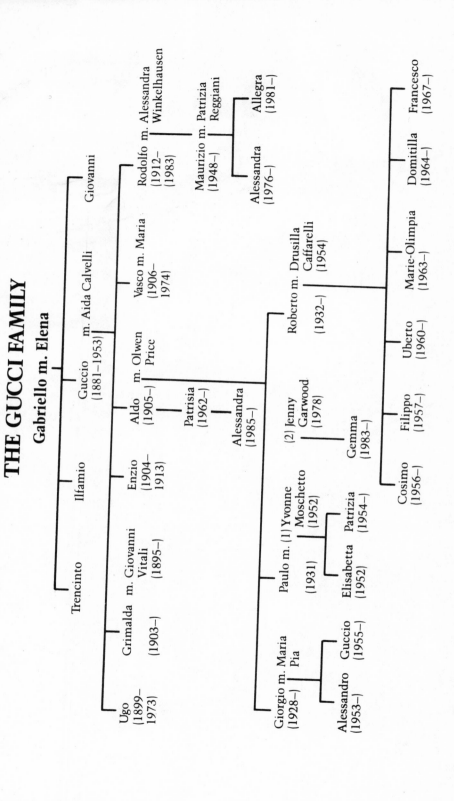

1

RAGS TO RAGS

Giuseppe Bandini, a taxi driver who stopped to let his passenger out of his cab in the via Tornabuoni, was probably the first to see it happen. One hot day in July of 1982 he had parked at the curb of the fashionable Florentine street, site of some of the most elegant and expensive shops in the Western world, in full view of the palatial Gucci establishment spread across two buildings. Giuseppe was fumbling for change when a small, dapper man clasping a blood-stained handkerchief to one side of his head pushed open the heavy glass Gucci doors and ran out in the street.

As the astonished taxi driver watched, the injured man jumped into a car, which speeded off in the direction of the hospital, as Giuseppe later told his wife.

The man looked just like one of the Gucci family. Perhaps he was one of the sons of the great Gucci *presidente* himself, Dr. Aldo Gucci. There had been rumors circulating in Florence and in the gossip columns of the world press for some time about bad blood in the family, but the shocking

1

incident he saw, as Giuseppe told his wife that evening, outdid any of the rumors.

Blood was running down one side of the man's face and no doubt stained his Gucci tie, his Gucci shirt and only the Heavenly Father knew what other items in the expensive Gucci line.

The man who had run out of the House of Gucci and sped away was Paolo Gucci, who gives this disputed account. His face under the bloodstained handkerchief smarted painfully, but the bruise to his pride hurt more. What possible right did his father, Aldo, his uncle Rodolfo, his cousin Maurizio and his two brothers Giorgio and Roberto, have to do this to him? The last few moments in the boardroom came back to him in a montage of furious incidents.

Someone, as he recalls it, had seized him from behind. He had been tussling with Giorgio over the tape recorder and had just told them all—his family and the other board directors, mostly lawyers—how, if they persisted in refusing to hear his questions or put them into the minutes, he would put them on record using the tape recorder he had bought for the purpose.

Giorgio was seated opposite him on the other side of the long boardroom table. Paolo says he saw him jump up and run around the table in his direction. He depressed the recording button just as his brother tried to grab the machine. While they both tugged at the instrument, someone's arm circled his neck from behind his back like an arm clamp. It must have been then, too, that he felt the sting of whatever it was that had cut his face and saw the first spatter of blood on his jacket.

With his own hastily summoned doctor beside him and the driver racing them toward the doctor's clinic, Paolo had time to reflect that what had just happened could—and with any luck would—grow into an international scandal. This fracas would, for the first time, tear away the mask of superior breeding and refinement that had characterized Gucci representation in public for half a century. No more would his father be able to pretend to the world that the quality of any of their "GG"-embossed products, from tie-clips to the leather trim of a Cadillac, was matched by the quality of family character.

He was glad.

The scene that had startled the cab driver did not, as Paolo expected, go unnoticed. Newspapers and radio and television in nearly every capital city ran the story. On the breakfast tables of the rich and famous it caused much more than just a mild shiver of astonishment and amusement. This gossip was juicy enough to keep the rumor mill going for several days in the world's most expensive hairdressers' salons. More was to come.

For shopkeepers to quarrel and fight in Florence, city of the Medicis, was understandable. For a Gucci to quarrel, well, that was a much more delicious bit of scandal. From New York, Jacqueline Kennedy Onassis cabled one word to Paolo's father, an old acquaintance who had helped her make uncounted purchases in his descreet Fifth Avenue *galleria*. It expressed succinctly what the titillated world of the fashionable felt about the brawl.

Jackie's cable simply read: "Why?"

She was only giving voice to society's universal cry of alarm. From Monaco, Prince Rainier telephoned the Florence headquarters to express sorrowful condolence. The prince had long esteemed Gucci's galaxy of tooled leather and gold symbols. At his wedding to Grace Kelly on April 19, 1956, he reportedly had ordered Gucci scarves by the gross and presented each female guest with one. The world press did nothing to suppress the general feeling of astonishment. In America, *People* magazine headlined a three-page, illustrated report, "Move over *Dallas:* Behind the Glittering Facade, a Family Feud Rocks the House of Gucci."

In fact, the shock wave radiating from Florence's via Tornabuoni was threatening to destroy Gucci's reputation for

punctilious service to the fashionable and the mighty that
had taken three generations of Guccis' infinite pains and
labor to create. Certainly this was no back-street incident.
The via Tornabuoni has an established air of elegance about
it unmatched in all but a few of Europe's shopping thor-
oughfares.

When the reasons for the family's infighting became
known, it was soon clear that this was not any sudden emotional storm that would blow away on the Mediterranean
breeze. Behind the explosion the alleged assault on fifty-one-
year-old Paolo was, it seemed, a long fuse that had been
sputtering and burning for over ten years.

It was known, of course, that the Guccis had been suffering serious differences of opinion over how to run their
multimillion-dollar empire of shops and boutiques around
the world, and that they were anything but a united and
happy family. Passionate, deeply loyal in their own way, they
were known to be true to the ancient traditions of this north-
ern Italian city of Florence that had given them birth, where
vendettas and family feuds flourish like weeds. But up until
now their most intimate family traits and characteristics
had lain discreetly hidden.

For example, the chauvinist edict that no female Gucci
could inherit any part of the business: this had been an iron
rule of the family since it was ordered by the founding
Guccio Gucci. The male line was all-important, and histor-
ically it had been as natural for a male Gucci to dominate his
women as for him to expect total obedience from his children and more distant relatives. Persuaders and miraculous
salesmen though they were, when opposed or forced to make
constraining or disagreeable conditions, any Gucci could
switch (as Paolo discovered) from warmhearted cama-
raderie to threats and more with a snap of his fingers.

Yet, as history showed, they had absolutely no equals
when it came to weaving the magical spells under which the
richest, most powerful people allowed themselves to be be-
witched into paying small fortunes for the luxury and es-

teem of that cherished "GG" symbol. Commercially, the Guccis had established an unrivaled key to status. Hérmes in
Paris, perhaps, came a close second. In England, whom
could one compare them with? Aspreys? Who in America?
Nieman Marcus? There were few similar dynasties.

How had they done it? If one believes their press agents,
the family were aristocratic saddle makers to royalty for
centuries before they became leather merchants. As a family
they could—and their press agents did—claim direct descent
from titled, landed nobles related to the Medicis, with their
own coat-of-arms. The less glamorous truth is that the great
Gucci empire grew more recently from a waiter's dream.

The first step into the world of upscale marketing was
taken by Guccio Gucci, who, having stoked coal to come to
England during the last days of Queen Victoria, found work
washing dishes at the new and glamorous Savoy Hotel and
was elevated to the position of waiter. He was struck by the
opulence and ostentation of the hotel's wealthy patrons and
astonished by their taste for expensive, elegant leather. When
he returned to work in a leather-goods store in Florence to
learn a trade, the dream of one day supplying this luxury
stayed in his mind.

It became a reality mostly because Guccio's vision satisfied a universal craving, a longing, especially powerful
among the nouveau riche, to flaunt their money and class,
whether or not it was real wealth and genuine class. And also
because the woman Guccio married shared his dream and
had as much drive as he had, if perhaps not more. They both
sensed that between the world wars a new class had
emerged, one that aspired to raise its social status and actually was judging and being judged by its shoes and luggage.
These "yuppies" of the twenties wanted a hallmark of pres-
tige to indicate their good taste and ability to spend on what
was out of the reach of the masses.

Gucci offered just such a recognizable badge—his "GG"
on all his leather goods—the discreet symbol of an elite club.
Identifying his products with his initials made their cost and

quality apparent, signifying the status of the wearer. To achieve this, to take the Gucci name from a humble leather-goods shop to a symbol of the highest quality, required an extraordinary blend of psychological talent and industry.

More than once Guccio found himself in financial difficulties. Only the fact that he possessed natural ability, perseverance and an innate sense of good taste gave him his remarkable edge in a viciously competitive trade.

The nurturing and maintenance of impeccably fine quality had become a carefully protected Gucci asset that Paolo's harrowing episode threatened to destroy. His grandfather would have been furius at the damage it could do to the reputation he had taken such great care to establish. Disclosure of the family's internal war threatened a multi-million-dollar livelihood for them all.

It was assumed that Guccio had passed on to his three sons and their offspring the same sense of discipline and respect for appearances that he and his wife Aida shared. So what could explain this astonishing behavior?

Never before had there been a breach of this sort. The stories whispered about the womanizing antics of the male Guccis were no more than enjoyable risqué asides by comparison. Could it be, malicious tongues asked, that fame and eminence had at last gone to the Guccis' heads? After the alleged "dastardly assault" the London *Daily Express* reported "nothing but fireworks from the worldwide multi-million-dollar business which is run with all the chaos of a Rome pizza parlor." It was remembered that Paolo's father, the founder's son Aldo, claimed to have been awarded an honorary doctorate by the city's university for his "distinguished service to the economic life of Florence." A report in the New York *Times*, referring to the assault as "a climactic move," suggested that a medical doctorate might have been more appropriate.

The eldest living Gucci, Guccio's daughter Grimalda, aged eighty-four in 1987, knows only too well what such a scandal would have cost her father. She and her husband gained least of any in the family from the Gucci success story, but she was deeply distressed by the conflict among her nephews and even more so by the publicity that followed the Paolo episode, horrified that it showed her family to be so fiercely divided.

In her eyes, the bloodstained Paolo Gucci being whisked away in the speeding car was as responsible as any for the years of struggle and conflict. It was he, she felt, who had provoked more scenes and squabbles than any of his relations—always, let it be said, in the belief that his creative plans for the company were being unfairly rejected, his position in it treacherously undermined.

Paolo Gucci, a grandson of the founder, believed that he was being prevented from trying to assert his professional, never mind his constitutional rights. Beside him in the car Dr. Nepi, his physician, made reassuring noises, telling him that the cut on his face was little more than a deep graze. But it was not the wound that bothered Paolo Gucci. For him, the more painful injury was to be denied authority as a director of his family company, and then to have his only recourse to the record snatched at, as if wresting a toy from a naughty child. The insult, the indignity felt unbearable.

Well, there was one course of action open to him. He had used it before and was no stranger to its ways. If the days of daggers in the night were no more, he held at least one sharp weapon in his hand: the law. He would sue.

In New York Paolo Gucci's lawyer, Stuart Speiser, was familiar with his client's recourse to legal action. Speiser is a disarmingly mild man who manages to provide a course of action promising comfort and security for even those among his clients who have the least hope of winning their cases. Paolo's suit against his family charged breach of contract, infliction of severe emotional stress and assault and battery.

It followed other actions the attorney had fought for him in the recent past. If the Guccis could grow fat on the fruits of their commercial flair, Speiser felt no reluctance in taking on the legal family feuds of this warring clan. The Gucci name was just one jewel in an already star-studded, highly successful roster of clients. His law practice in his suite of luxurious offices in the Pan Am Building on Park Avenue gave him daily satisfaction.

In a preface to one of his books, Speiser quotes his favorite wit, Ambrose Bierce, whose *The Devil's Dictionary* is known for its unvarnished definitions. "Litigation," Bierce wrote in 1911, is "a machine which you go into as a pig and come out as a sausage." The only sure impunity, he suggests, is wealth. And a litigant is one who is "about to give up his skin for the hope of retaining his bones."

Paolo Gucci had not seen himself as fodder for a sausage machine, but there was little doubt that he had paid dearly for his legal fencing with the family. In Speiser's opinion, a conservative estimate of the costs to date of the Guccis' legal skirmishes would be on the order of five million dollars. For their part, the Guccis appeared to regard lawsuits as no more disturbing than buzzing insects or stinging nettles. Stuart Speiser referred to them with philosophical detachment.

Even so, when Paolo faced him with details of the boardroom battle, Speiser was surprised at the intensity of feeling that lay beneath his client's well-groomed surface. "The Guccis don't seem to know how to compromise," he would say later.

Paolo wanted blood. He knew Speiser's firm, Speiser & Krauze, would advise him how best to strike back. The case Speiser prepared would do that if successful. It claimed that the attack on Paolo had been unprovoked and unexpected, that having been fired from the family business but remaining a shareholder, his client was merely trying to exercise his right to question the board's "conspiratorial and malicious conduct" in running the company.

By introducing papers into a previous lawsuit, Paolo had

already revealed a number of alleged setups involving Panamanian companies arranged by his father and uncle in Hong Kong to divert monies that he said should have been declared as taxable income in the United States. With Speiser, he now brought these to the attention of the Internal Revenue Service. It was done, Paolo says, only to try and force his father's hand and never with the intention of letting the incriminating papers stay on file in the case. But when Aldo refused to withdraw the company's objection to Paolo trading under his own name, which he regarded as his right after he had been fired from the company, the die was cast. The court refused to return the papers and Aldo had to face trial.

Ironically, Paolo's action was subsequently dismissed by the New York State Supreme Court for lack of material evidence. But the damning papers remained. And if his father's trial did nothing else, it clearly showed the deep rift dividing the house of Gucci. Later, flowing from Paolo's initiative, in September, 1986, his eighty-one-year-old father, Aldo, was jailed for a year and a day, fined and ordered to pay over seven million dollars in back taxes.

At his trial in a Manhattan court Aldo Gucci became emotional and admitted that fradulent "devices" had been used to divert income from his family's international chain of shops to accounts he and his brother controlled outside the United States. Aldo, however, pleaded that he was not personally guilty of tax evasion. The frauds, he said, had been perpetrated without his knowledge or consent by an accountant for the firm, who in the meantime had died. And, as part of a plea-bargaining agreement, Paolo's father handed over a check for one million dollars toward his back taxes. A further six million was offered.

In court Aldo said, "Some of my sons have done their duty. But some sought revenge and only God may judge them. I forgive anybody who wanted me here today." It seemed the old man's words would hang over the family like a curse.

But the Guccis can smite one moment and kiss the next.

Aldo's brother Rodolfo had died three years before the sentence. At that time his nephew Maurizio presided over Aldo's dismissal from the company's presidency, the man who had done more than any of his generation to build the business to its half-billion-dollar-a-year turnover peak. It was clear then that a gulf the size of Grand Canyon had split the two factions, the descendants of the two brothers Aldo and Rodolfo. Paolo's boardroom scuffle was only one symptom of the rift.

To the onlooker it seemed almost farcical. Every male Gucci already had more wealth than most men could earn in a dozen lifetimes. Their motivation: at least in part, unsatisfied lust for power, for supremacy. If it was a quality more common to the televised fictions of *Dallas, Falcon Crest* and *Knot's Landing*, it was no less dramatic or deadly in real-life Florence. To be the grand panjandrum of Gucci worldwide, the godhead around which the whole machinery of the business revolved, was a sufficient motive, apparently, for each of the family shareholders to wage war on his most intimate relatives, even when he had nothing but love and admiration for them all his life.

So it had merely come to a head on that July day in Florence. "They went berserk," Paolo says in retrospect. "My own family shouted me down. Ask your father, they screamed at me, as if I was still a child. What nonsense was that, I wanted to know? I don't have to go to my father to ask these things. I am a director and shareholder of the company. It was then that I saw that the secretary taking the minutes was not making a note of what was going on and I pulled out my tape recorder."

Of course, more than pride and lust for power had brought the Guccis to this bitter clash, and it would certainly be nonsense to suggest that such conflicts do not flourish behind the trademarks of many successful merchant families. But the vigor and venom of the Gucci battle was truly astonishing if not unique.

Perhaps the old saying "Rags to rags in three generations" was familiar to Guccio Gucci. He might have heard it
during his months at the Savoy Hotel. But he could not have
known then that he was destined to make one of the world's
greatest commercial fortunes. Or that his descendants, down
to the third generation, would fight over it like medieval
barons. If he had had even the slightest suspicion of the
trouble that would follow the realization of his dreams,
would he not have somehow tried to prevent it in his lifetime?

2

SAVOY DAYS

The London Guccio Gucci came to in the late 1890s was attracting visitors from all over the world. Anyone and almost everyone who could afford the fare was dazzled by the splendor of electricity, engineering excellence and trains that ran punctually. Earlier manners and customs imported in Britain by a sovereign dynasty of Hanoverian Georges had been cramping the city's style: it had taken the triumphant progress of Queen Victoria's reign to put color, however artificially induced, back into its cheeks, even though the monarch herself stood as the paragon of respectability.

The men and women in Victorian drawing rooms rejoiced in the full pleasures and rewards of belonging to a rich and successful nation. Those who came to visit marveled at the ostentation of the day as well as at the hypocrisy of an elitist aristocracy publicly upholding moral standards an archangel would have found impossible to maintain while at the same time supporting a vast number of prostitutes. They gossiped with relish behind pale hands and fluttering fans about scandals far more shocking than any encountered in Rome or even Paris.

One of its most renowned and brilliant statesmen, Sir Charles Dilke, was disgraced for allegedly having an adulterous affair with a woman who was later found to have been lying in her pretty teeth. Oscar Wilde paid the price for believing that his wit could triumph over the shocked sensibility of a nation in which the greatest sin was to be found out. The very paradigm of moral rectitude, Prime Minister William Gladstone, was curiously involved with street women in the Bayswater Road, intent, he declared, on "saving them."

It was partly, indeed largely, this charade of virtuous behavior and the reality of notorious scandal that tempted shiploads of newly rich "porkers" from Chicago, railroad barons from the American midwest, celebrated entertainers and musicians as well as highly skilled con men and predatory women to put up in the frequently fog-bound capital.

All sought the comfort and service of a hotel where they could behave in this urban Eldorado as befitted their often unfamiliar and recently acquired stations in life. They craved to be where, with luck or persuasion, they could rub shoulders with a duke and a countess or two, perhaps even with the lesser members of the royal family itself. And they were more than ready to pay for the privilege, outdoing each other in their lavish spending for whatever was "continental" and therefore chic.

By installing Cézar Ritz, a leading Swiss hotelier, as manager of his newly built Savoy Hotel, Richard D'Oyly Carte made sure of luring the cream of international society to his doors. Ritz was known not only for his excellent management but also for his genius in finding the best, the most fashionably accomplished and the most talked-about chef in existence. Ritz brought Auguste Escoffier to tantalize and satisfy the most jaded palates in the world. And with Escoffier came his celebrated cooking range of copper ovens.

All this, and the arrival of a rather frightened young

man from Italy, became part of the great hotel's early history. D'Oyly Carte's Savoy had taken its first gold sovereign less than ten years before, on August 6, 1889. The opening night's celebration was crowned by Harry Rosenfeld, one of the guests from Chicago, buying a bottle of champagne. That this event was reported in the press indicates how uncertain the Savoy was of its future, years in which magnums would be rumored to have been drunk from silver slippers almost every night.

Such luxurious excesses exposed and enjoyed above stairs in the plush electrically lit salons of D'Oyly Carte's new hotel were unknown below stairs. Fellow countrymen of Guccio's were already slaving in the hot basement kitchens and sculleries on that day when the seventeen-year-old, in spite of complete ignorance of the English language, talked his way into a job as a dishwasher. His desperate need to earn his own living, to free himself from a father who had become a bitter and angry man as a result of the business failure, forced Guccio to leave Italy.

Gabriello Gucci was facing bankruptcy. A partner in his brother-in-law's straw-hat factory, he had struggled helplessly against the pressures of Italy's domestic and military conflicts, the poverty and ravages of republican Garibaldi's uprising at home and the Italian army's costly invasion of Ethiopia abroad. When in 1898 his brother-in-law, Signor Santini, who had handled the running of the small business, died of tuberculosis, it left Gabriello in an impossible situation. He was quite unable to manage the paperwork or the invoicing and accounts. It was not long before his employees realized his incompetence and took over the company and made it a worker's cooperative, which ruined Gabriello.

By all accounts—excepting those gilded by subsequent generations of press agents and favor-seeking journalists—it was therefore neither an illustrious nor a happy home that his son Guccio wrote to from London whenever his swollen and weary hands could find time and his meager resources afforded the necessary pennies for stamps. Tales of Guccis royally appointed to make saddles and bridles for Tuscan noble families, Guccis whose leather work was more an art, a semi-precious adornment of the mighty, have since been invented and embroidered into the legend of business. Aldo Gucci, the honorary chairman, has enjoyed perpetuating the myth.

In March 1974 the American trade journal *Women's Wear Daily* reported Aldo's claim to "trace his family history back five hundred years . . . Yes, members of our family about twenty-five generations ago made leather riding boots and pouches and stirrups for royalty . . . Guccis have also been priests, cardinals, soldiers, lawyers." Gabriello's granddaughter, Grimalda, tells a different story: "I want the truth to come out. We were never saddle makers. The Guccis come from a once-noble family in the San Miniato district of Florence. In my grandfather's day they were not peasants, just simple folk with a little interest coming in from capital saved. My grandmother, Elena Groselle, was from Signa, a small industrial town in Tuscany. If her brother had not died when he did I expect things would have gone very differently."

For one thing Guccio, Gabriello's teen-age son, would not have run away to sea and landed in the Savoy Hotel. For another his father's straw hats might have prospered sufficiently for his ambitious son to take over the business instead of founding the business he did. Whether Gucci straw hats would have taken the place of Gucci shoes and purses is another matter.

Guccio certainly showed courage. A less determined youth would not have found his way to the coast, signed on to slave in the stokehole of a freighter and disembarked in Britain. Once there, a less ambitious young man would never have spent his spare time learning languages (Guccio mastered English, Italian, French and German in his lifetime). Few would have found the life of a poorly paid scullery hand in foggy London bearable after the warm olive groves of Tuscany. Guccio not only did this, he used his dark good looks and eager-to-please manners to earn promotions out of the drudgery of the kitchens to become a waiter.

The world he entered was an astonishing contrast to the one he left. His wages were still pitifully small, less than five shillings a week, but the tips were, or could be, quite grand. The hotel was riding out a storm of staff problems and its temperamental directors—Arthur Sullivan, the great composer, was a member of the board—could only hope would subside with time and the patient diplomacy and artistic interests of Richard D'Oyly Carte's wife, Helen.

Guccio had everything to learn. The sight of wealthy guests ablaze with diamonds and precious stones, regally magnificent in full evening dress, was a revelation to him. In the Savoy's new restaurant, where mahogany paneling and crystal lighting set off a ceiling of gold and scarlet, he observed a life that seemed magical to him. Yet these people treated it as if it were their own home!

They arrived from all over the world in carriages and motorcars, some veiled and dusty from the roads of Europe. Chauffeurs and footmen carried in vast piles of luggage, and then a miracle of transformation took place. The guests emerged from their suites and rooms shortly afterward as if they had lived there all their lives. How was it done? Guccio knew that to set out on a journey in Italy to anywhere as distant, even, as Milan ensnared his parents in a panic of preparation. But these privileged hotel dwellers seemingly carried their gilded worlds with them. Wherever they stayed their everyday needs and appurtenances were always at hand.

The secret, Guccio surmised, must lie inside all those piles of baggage. Huge mountains of leather and hide, embossed with crests and initials, gleaming with protective dressing and wax and firmly locked and strapped up against any possibility of damage en route, were deposited daily in the Strand entrance foyer. Page boys, paid half a crown a week but able to pick up tips of sovereigns, lugged it piece-by-piece to the "ascending rooms," as the newly invented elevators were called. Undoubtedly what lay inside the satin-lined hatboxes, the vast cabin trunks and innumerable suit-cases and portmanteaux, was what constituted a traveling home.

And these containers of mobile living were made of leather, a material Gucci had grown up with. Here was the very same stuff that hung in its raw state in many Florentine workshops, the great skins converted into strong, lasting and firmly stitched luggage by Italian craftsmen with genera-tions of experience. Leather was something he could identify with even in this strange, splendid new world.

For the most part the guests were equally splendid, not only rich but celebrated. Lily Langtry, mistress of the Prince of Wales, kept a suite at the hotel, where she entertained guests. The great actor Sir Henry Irving was only one of a number of notable patrons of the restaurant where Guccio served, his table kept at a decent remove from those oc-cupied by lesser theatrical folk.

As maitre d'hotel as well as master of cuisine, Escoffier insisted on absolute discretion and excellence in matters of protocol. Sarah Bernhardt confessed that although she had always "abhorred" English hotels, describing their "cooking as execrable, their carpets dirty, their menus medieval and their service an insult," the Savoy under her friend Cézar Ritz was to her "a second home."

The most affluent guests without exception admired quality and show to the point of worship. They wanted not only the best, but they had to possess what was fashionable whatever it cost. If quality was expensive but gave good service and value, those with genuine taste would buy it and the others would follow.

Guccio observed that the quality of what they wore and used to move themselves and their personal possessions around the world was their badge of social eminence. The most vulgar among them, the *arriviste* colonials, the socially ambitious from the New World, demanded at least a replica of it. They wanted it in craftsmanship, in everything they had so that the world would be aware of the magnificence of themselves and their possessions. Providing them with something immediately recognizable in this category, Gucci shrewdly observed, was a sure way to secure their patronage.

But England was a cold, dark country whose climate would keep anyone accustomed to Mediterranean warmth hunched over a gas fire for long periods of time. Guccio's memories of days spent in the country around Florence, with a dog and a gun, were haunting reminders of what he had left behind, and after three years, when he had saved enough money, he went back home. The tips had been hoarded. He was about to face his family, taking gifts to his mother and father. If not the prodigal son, he was at least a dutiful youth returning from an experience that, he let the family know, had extended his horizons immeasurably.

The need to work, to find a job to support him, did not at first seem urgent. He felt entitled to a rest. In the same street as his home, now grown to full beauty, was a young seamstress three years older than himself who not only caught his eye but with whom he fell passionately and, according to his daughter, instantly in love. Aida Calvelli's father, Ernesto, had a small tailor's shop on the via Romana. Her charms seem in no way to have been diminished in Guccio's chivalrous eyes by what had befallen her. A good Roman Catholic, she was guilty of having had a love affair, Grimalda says, with a man who, smitten with terminal tuberculosis, was unable to marry her. Their four-year-old son, Ugo, was all that remained of their union.

Guccio's own recent past had not been unblemished. There had been encounters with English girls persuaded by his gently flattering demands. Now he was deeply in love, and he wanted what he had dreamed about for so many cold and cheerless nights in London. He wanted Aida, and he didn't mind about her baby. He would accept the child as his own if she would marry him.

His generosity of spirit was to be tested to the limit.

About year after his return, on October 10, 1902, Guccio

and Aida married. He was twenty-one, she twenty-four. Subsequent dates suggest that their passion proved almost immediately fruitful. During their long and unbroken marriage five children were born, only one of whom—a baby boy christened Enzio—died as a young child. Their only daughter, Grimalda, was born on January 5, 1903, less than three months after their marriage. Her birth was quickly followed by the birth of four boys, the eldest given one of his father's names—Aldo.

Details of Guccio's struggle for existence at that time, indeed until after World War One, into which he was conscripted to fight, are not recorded. But with so many mouths to feed it seems safe to assume that the family was accustomed to more pasta and minestrone than beefsteak in those days.

Guccio's son Rodolfo believed that his father's first job was in a shop selling antiques and that he then moved to a leather firm called Botto. There is little known about it today, though the owner taught him the rudiments of the trade and gave him his first promotion, and by the time Italy entered World War One he was a manager. Guccio was in his mid-thirties when he was called up. According to his son-in-law, Giovanni Vitali, he served throughout the war as a transport driver. In 1918 when the war ended he was released, unharmed, to rebuild his life in the badly depleted economy of Florence. And if trench conflict had taught little else, it had at least given Guccio time to think.

He knew that Italy's recovery was to be a long time coming. He also realized that if he was to make use of his experiences gained in the great London hotel, it had to be now or never. First and most important was his need to educate himself in a working knowledge of leather far beyond that of his prewar experience. By good fortune there was a firm, Franzi, specializing in high-class leather goods of all descriptions, and it needed workers. Guccio got a job with them and learned the basics of their more sophisticated business in a matter of months. Franzi taught him how to discriminate in the selection of rawhides, the curing and tanning processes, as well as the many tricks and idiosyncrasies of working with different weights and types of leather.

Indeed, Guccio was so keenly ambitious to better himself that within a year he was appointed manager of the firm's Rome branch and sent to the capital with an improved salary and status. If Aida and the children had joined him there the Gucci legend might well have never been created. But she refused to do so. Giovanni says: "She was the one with the drive. Nothing could persuade her to leave Florence."

So Gucci went alone to taste the pleasures of postwar Rome with its seductive street cafés and jazzy nightclubs. He would not have been a Gucci if their lure had passed entirely unnoticed. Possibly he spent more time among them than Aida was told about. But at least on weekends he dutifully traveled back to Florence and his family. It was during one of these visits that the next link in the Gucci chain was forged.

One Sunday in 1922 Guccio and Aida were out for a stroll, their usual pastime, when he noticed an empty shop on the via del Parione. For some time he had been telling his wife that he was ready to start out on his own. He had explained his reasons and the ideas he had to make a success if only he could find premises and capital for the venture. He had also told her how impressed he had been in London by the beautiful workmanship of luggage and leatherwork. What he had seen there, hand-tooled and sewn, came closer to works of art than mere commercial products. He wanted his shop to specialize in such quality, and here might be an excellent site on which to begin. The shop was ideally situated, but could they possibly risk taking it?

Aida had shown little regard for caution in her domestic life and she had no doubts about this. Guccio should take the shop immediately and set up his business. Where would the money come from? Aida was not only decisive, she was also resourceful. A man they knew, a signor Calzolari, had shown interest in Guccio's plans during their early formation. Perhaps he would put up some cash. Aida seems to have had as well-developed a nose for money as she had a shapely, if already well-rounded figure. Her belief that his prospective investor would provide what was needed was soundly based. Gucci and Calzolari became partners, Gucci providing the brains and experience and Calzolari the cash.

It was not a great sum. Signor Calzolari put only twenty-five thousand lira into the business. Added to Guccio's small savings, this just made a beginning possible. If Calzolari had been content to be no more than a silent partner, his investment would have made him wealthier than the Medicis.

As it was, the new investor took an interest in the budding business so seriously that Guccio had to put up with a partner who poked his nose into the cash desk at the end of every working day, counting, subtracting and criticizing. Grimalda, by now in her early twenties, worked behind the cash box in the shop. She still smarts at the memory of her father's nosy partner. "He wanted to know exactly how much we had taken each day. It nearly drove me mad."

It had much the same effect on Guccio. Soon after the first Gucci nameplate went up on his shop in 1923 he made up his mind to get rid of Calzolari as soon as he could afford to buy him out. It was quite enough having to operate as buyer, salesman and general factotum without being obliged to satisfy the petty demands of a man who had contributed no more than money. Except money was something Guccio still lacked, so for the time being Calzolari had to be tolerated.

Meanwhile Guccio was not alone in the business. He had a young sales assistant behind the counter with him, Romolo Nidiaci. Romolo was the first of a long line of staff who would come to regard Gucci as a family to which they owed special allegiance, putting their sons and daughters into the business to follow them. Despite this, and the help provided in varying degrees by his three sons, Guccio's enthusiasm was needed in several other directions at once.

At first the wares were unexciting. Defeated Germany's goods were cheap, and Guccio bought leather goods from them in wholesale quantities. Tourists, among them wealthy war-profiteers, were coming to Florence to enjoy the treasures of the great Uffizi Gallery, to worship or gaze in awe at the splendid thirteenth-century Duomo cathedral used by Michelangelo as a model for the dome of St. Peter's in Rome. Gucci offered sturdy, well-made luggage at reasonable prices and an attractive variety of straps, bags and trunks made from the softest of his imported skins. Soon he was seeing a small profit, but the debt to Calzolari and his persistent interference continued to irritate.

There was much to do. Repair work had unexpectedly become a profitable sideline. Luggage of the period took such a battering in the holds of great liners, and when piled in the guards' vans of trans-European trains, that the stoutest threads and buckles frequently failed to stand the strain for long. It was something Guccio had to allow for. He began accepting repair work as a favor to customers, then found that it paid well. By employing local craftsmen in a small workroom behind the shop he managed to build up a name for helpful service. Furthermore, repairs were done with speed and care, rare commodities in the postwar world. Long before Gucci was recognized as a hallmark of fashionable excellence, Guccio had made an essential aspect of his business service coupled with first-class workmanship.

Running the shop was also an escape for him. He lived well, enjoying the comforts of a household in which plentiful good food and wine were everyday staples. Aida was a devoted cook who felt insulted if her food was not eaten down to the last olive or mouthful of ravioli (both she and Guccio became almost pear-shaped in later years, as photos show), but this did not suppress his appetite for young women. The favors of one or more of the shop assistants were requested and seldom refused.

During its first year the Gucci shop did quite well and Guccio risked opening a small workshop in the heart of the city converted from a warehouse in the Lungarno Guicciardini district. Work went on there until late at night in preparation for important events. The boys, and even Grimalda sometimes, would be sent on their bicycles to deliver parcels or pick up orders. Guccio himself rode everywhere on a bike. The cobblestoned streets of Florence made for bumpy ridding, but as a form of transport it was both cheap and efficient.

Before their first Christmas the shop proudly introduced several new lines, attracting local people as well as the seasonal tourists, yet Gucci's commitment to quality never relaxed. Indeed, his faith in it grew as he saw that it was the ideal accompaniment to sound business management, the rules of which he was picking up as he went along. The lesson he had learned from the wealthy patrons of the Savoy had taught him that the more expensive the goods, the more they were prized.

Calzolari, however, was still checking and cross-checking each week's costs, accounts and earnings, demanding to be told why this item had cost so much, why that one had not been marked up to provide the profit his avarice required. Exasperating as it was, Guccio's credit was so stretched that he had to suffer it. But a determination to buy his interfering partner out and become wholly independent grew steadily. When he did, only the Gucci family would run the business.

The boys were also growing. Aldo, approaching twenty and the eldest, was the strikingly handsome image of his father, but slim as a rake while Guccio's stomach kept expanding. Aldo's brother Vasco was little more than a year younger, and both had shown a keenness for entering the business, which delighted Guccio. Only his youngest, Rodolfo, was outside his father's sphere of influence, having been swept up into another occupation that, though it gave Guccio pride to mention it in the café where he took his morning cappuccino, was not altogether to his liking. Spotted by the director Mario Camerini in the foyer of the Hotel Plaza di Roma where he had been delivering a small case for his father, Rodolfo at the age of seventeen had been offered a part in a film and was soon making a name and following for himself as a star of early silent pictures (among them *Rotaie*, one of the masterpieces of the Italian cinema).

The Gucci star indeed seemed to be rising. By the end of 1923 it was beckoning Guccio on to risk expansion, to keep putting all his energy and material into the building of the business. He had proved, to himself and others, that the son of a bankrupt hatmaker, an ex-dishwasher and waiter, could rival the greatest storekeepers of Florence. Among the city's gentry he was becoming known as a craftsman of distinction. For a good Roman Catholic, one of the faithful, the omens had never been better. He prayed during each Mass for a continuation of his miraculous success, and he saw it as no accident when his prayers were at last answered for him to be able to stand on his own that it was one of his family who provided the means to do it. Next to divine intervention, the loyalty of his sons was his most cherished of expectations and rewards.

3

GOOD AND BAD SONS

The one sadness in Guccio's life was Ugo, his adopted son. He gave him his name and treated him no better, no worse than his own sons. But Ugo lacked Guccio's drive and used his height and strength, both of which were superior to the others, for avoiding rather than doing work. By the time the shop opened he was in his twenties and married. But it seemed that the last thing Ugo wanted was to help build the business or to contribute usefully in any way.

The other Gucci boys, his half-brothers Aldo, Vasco and Rodolfo, nicknamed him "the bruiser" because he affected a swaggering, bullying style and enjoyed intimidating his cronies in the cafés where he gambled and drank. On the rare occasions when he was persuaded to help out in the shop he disrupted everyone, including the customers.

Guccio solved the problem, or so he thought, by persuading one of his wealthiest customers, a big landowner named Baron Levi, to take on his adopted son as assistant manager of one of his farms on the outskirts of Florence. The job was ideally suited to the muscular young man who boasted that he could lift heavier loads and endure greater hardships than the brawniest farm laborer.

Guccio, busy with his business, went to great pains to get Ugo the job. He was to feel ill rewarded.

To find the money to buy out the aggravating Calzolari, Guccio approached Ugo, who was now making a good salary. Could he lend him the twenty-five thousand lira needed? It was, after all, a family matter and better kept within it. And Ugo was always saying that he had plenty of money, so perhaps the loan would not be too hard for him?

Ugo appeared to have been caught out in one of his exaggerations. Ashamed to confess the truth that he was already in debt as a consequence of lavishing money on an extravagant girl friend, he promised to provide the sum. On his assurance Guccio persuaded the bank to advance the cash, thankfully paid off Calzolari and arranged to repay Ugo over a period with interest.

For some time Ugo had been living above his income so as to be generous to his mistress, a ballet dancer. In the chorus of a small variety theater in the city, she was demanding more and more costly presents from him. Without further funds he was in danger of losing her to the much wealthier manager. Now, far from providing a loan, Ugo needed one himself.

In desperation he removed twenty thousand lira from the baron's petty-cash box. Guccio received his loan in full. Ugo then took his lady friend off for a three-week holiday, staying at an expensive hotel on the coast.

Guccio's happiness at achieving freedom from his partner came to a swift end when the pilferage was discovered. Baron Levi came to him with a strong suspicion of who was responsible, but since they were old friends, before acting he wanted Guccio's advice.

At first Guccio found it hard to believe that Ugo could have done such a thing, but a check of the farm's books,

which the baron had brought with him, left no possible
doubt.

Guccio's sense of loss was almost as great as his shame.
Ugo, he knew, was no saint, but he had never thought that the
young man would descend to this.

There was only one way to remove the stain. The baron
must be repaid in full. If not immediately, because that was
now impossible, at least he would manage it somehow, and
as soon as he could.

With his friend's consent he signed an agreement to
recompense Ugo's employer in full at the rate of ten thousand
lira a month. It was more than the shop was taking in, and
his loan from Ugo, ironically, was little more than a third as
much. But it had to be done if Ugo was to avoid arrest.

Why, one wonders, did he show such consideration? Ugo
was not of his blood. He had done little or nothing to help
Guccio set up and run the business that was putting bread in
their mouths and which, incidentally, was to be left in equal
shares to all the Gucci offspring, Ugo included.

Furthermore, Guccio was a stern father, known for his
closeness with money, never showing favoritism to any of his
children. Most especially so when it was unmerited by lack
of commitment and hard work. Yet Ugo had been treated
with remarkable generosity, and all through his early life the
same indulgence marks his stepfather's attitude toward him.

A close look at the dates suggests that there may have
been a more understandable reason for Guccio Gucci's kindness, even though it is pure supposition. When Guccio ran
away to sea, although at the time unquestionably avoiding
the unpleasantness of his father's plight, he could also have
been escaping a more personal obligation. Guccio was, after
all, a lusty seventeen-year-old Florentine youth. Ugo, born on
January 24, 1899 (which is to say in the year immediately
following Guccio's departure), *might* have been his true son.
And if so, was Guccio really being so generous in giving the
boy his name and share in the business or in readily accepting Ugo's mother in marriage?

If this supposition is anywhere near the truth, it con-
stitutes a most carefully hidden skeleton in the Gucci family
closet. Neither Guccio nor Aida ever hinted at such a thing to
any of their children. Yet if Guccio's escape to sea was with
the honorable intention of earning enough to support his
future wife and unborn son, then it was nothing to be
ashamed of.

And there is one fact that seems to support the theory.
Guccio is always said to have been a lad of only fourteen
when he left home, yet his departure followed the death of
his father's partner in 1898, by which time he was already
seventeen. Was his age altered to hide his adolescent dilemma?

If Guccio took after his father, he was a precocious
youth. Gabriello, according to Paolo Gucci, was "a playboy
who had known nothing of business and lived happily off the
industry of his brothers" (One of whom, Giaccinto, was later
killed in the World War One).

So Guccio's love-at-first-sight attraction to Aida may not
have been such a novel experience after all. The pretty seamstress could easily have been an early conquest. The tale
consistently related by members of the family ever since that
(as the law indeed has decreed) Ugo was illegitimate could
be another Gucci fairytale.

Yet it was for this reason that he was subsequently
barred from sharing in Guccio's inheritance after the
founder died. If Ugo or his heirs could have proved that he
was a true son of Guccio Gucci, they would have shared
equally in the succession.

By then Ugo was in no position (even if he knew that
Guccio was his father) to fight the coincidence of his birth
having occurred four years before his mother and father
were married. And in the legal process vigorously pursued
by Guccio's three legitimate sons (who may have been igno-
rant of the facts but could certainly add a judicious two and
two together), there is no evidence of Ugo's Gucci blood. Yet
the possiblity remains.

Add to all this the fact that Ugo did not entirely burn his bridges with Guccio when he so embarrassed him. On his return from his stolen pleasures with the dancer, about whom nothing more is known, he was reinstated in the shop and allowed by Guccio to share in his succession.

The extent of Ugo's inheritance is also relevant—it appears to have been smaller than that of the three surviving "half-brothers." Yet it is astonishing that Guccio wished this ne'er-do-well adopted son to inherit anything at all.

Ugo brought nothing but pain to his parents in his youth and was to bring even more distress to them with his involvement with fascism. What his father and mother thought of Mussolini is now known, but paying lip service to the fascist cause was one thing whereas joining the Blackshirt bullies who paraded and enforced its policies was another. Which is what Ugo did.

Aldo, his half-brother, was not in the least interested in politics. It was a pastime on which the twenty-year-old second son had no time to waste. He was dealing with travelers and representatives in the shop, learning everything to do with the business. Aldo early possessed an irrepressible keenness for making money.

His father was both pleased and at times overwhelmed by his son's appetite for commerce. "He was the one I never had to push but to pull back," Guccio told his grandson Paolo years later.

The secret of Ugo's history was something the children did not talk about. "My mother told me one day when I was a little girl," Grimalda says. "It was a big shock. For all of us, I think, but especially for Ugo himself who was six or seven before he discovered that Guccio was not his father." According to her, the knowledge of it made no difference to the growing family. "Absolutely not! No horrible word was ever said to him, I'm sure."

"Ugo loved carrying a gun and showing off with it," Paolo says. "He was addicted to gambling, would spend hours when he should have been working playing cards in a small café in Florence, the Gambrino. His usual way with anyone who fancied their chances against him was to swagger in, slap his gun down on the table then start shuffling the cards. People were either too frightened to play or too frightened not to."

And that was not the only way Ugo used his gun. "No, he had another little trick, which delighted him," Paolo says. "When he found himself hemmed in behind a truck or some local farm lorry, which often happened due to the narrowness of the roads where he worked, he'd shoot out one of its rear tires. As soon as the wretched driver was forced to pull over, probably spending the next hour changing his wheel, Ugo roared past laughing and brandishing his pistol. The original cowboy!"

Known for his strength ("he could toss a man across a room"), Ugo earned almost immediate promotion in Mussolini's fascist movement—first as mayor of a Florence suburb, then as political secretary over the rural area where Baron Levi farmed. With the power this gave him, he was able to do much as he liked.

He would visit his old employer's home with a party of semi-drunken fascists and their women, demanding food and drink.

He also took pleasure in terrorizing the neighborhood that had shown him nothing but kindness and help, though so far as is known he never troubled his parents or his family.

Indeed, Ugo may have served a useful purpose as an example of Guccio's belief in bringing up his sons to value strength and competitive spirit. "My grandfather wanted the boys to show they had red blood in their veins," Paolo says. "He spared no one. Indeed, he liked to provoke arguments between them, setting one against the other. Grandfather was the only one nobody was permitted to challenge. To answer back or to question the whys and wherefores was like querying holy writ to him."

It appears to have been a rough-and-tumble sort of life for the family. Each of the boys followed a different path,

developing and vigorously defending their separate interests
and aims, whether or not these pleased their parents. Among
themselves they quarreled and sparred continuously.

As for Guccio, after some years of fidelity hs periodic
flirtations at first probably caused Aida more irritation than
anguish. After all, she had the children, and Florentine mid-
dle-aged husbands were almost conventionally unfaithful.
But Aida was a Calvelli, and the Calvellis were not ones to
suffer alone, or in silence.

Guccio's strength, his powerful frame and stern manner
were by no means qualities to oppose lightly. This did not
hold back his wife in the heat of critical moments. Paolo
remembers Aida "continuously in tears, crying, complaining
how badly she was being treated by grandfather. She even
threw plates at him." His brother Roberto prefers to remember his grandmother's strength and their happier moments together: "They both became very stout. I remember
the gold chain 'round his stomach. As a small boy, it seemed
enormous."

There is no doubt that Guccio was a stern and at times
distant father. Pocket money had to be earned either by good
conduct or hard work. He insisted on his children addressing
him only in the courteous, formal Italian *le* pronoun, corresponding to the French *vous* rather than the more familiar
tu. Mealtimes could be ordeals for his children, dependent
on the harmony or anger of their parents, the emotional
temperature and circumstances of each child and Guccio's
mood.

"He used his napkin like a small whip," Grimalda remembers. "Any playing about and we got a swift, stinging
flick from it." She, by virtue of her sex, and Aldo, because of
his industry, were less likely to earn these reproaches than
the others but they could not entirely escape the stressful
atmosphere.

To his grandchildren when they came, Guccio was
"kindly but aloof," according to Roberto. "He played with us,
but he had· little time for children," Paolo says. "He upset

you, making you wonder if you'd done something wrong. I never found him an easy man to be with." Maurizio, Rodolfo's son, has a vivid recollection of his grandfather embarrassing him during a childish game he had thought up while the grown-ups were still at table after a big family dinner.

The children were playing around the table. "I had found some gambling chips, and was offering to sell them to my uncles. They were merry and drinking a lot of wine. Everyone joined in, giving me a few coins for my cheek, except my grandfather. He called me to him—I must have been four or five at the time—at the head of the table and asked me, 'How much for the lot?' I don't know what I said, probably a million lira, something like that. 'I'll buy them all,' he said. So I handed over the chips and he gave me some money. Then, of course, I had no chips to go on with the game. So I went back and asked him for them. 'Only if you pay me twice what I paid you,' he told me. Everybody laughed."

Maurizio remembers his father telling him how thinly Guccio would slice the prosciutto. "He wanted to insure that the joint of ham lasted as long as possible." This and other stringent economies stayed deeply engraved in his children's minds long after Guccio's death. Some have remained with them.

A favorite family story, allegedly true, is Aldo's weakness for topping up mineral-water bottles (the habitual accompaniment for Italian meals) from the kitchen tap. What might indulgently be called thrift marks out much Gucci behavior, despite their wealth. Aldo's eccentricity with the mineral water has something of the same ring as multibillionaire J. Paul Getty's installation of a public pay-phone in his English mansion for the use of his guests.

Guccio's children reacted to these influences in different ways. Ugo marked out his own path, and with his departure the others developed individual personalities and characteristics seldom in close harmony with one another. While

Aldo showed almost too much zeal for business in his father's eyes ("He was afraid he'd take over," Paolo believes), his younger brother Vasco became more interested in getting away whenever possible.

Vasco had inherited the Gucci streak of artistic, creative brilliance. But he used it so sparingly that his contribution to the business and its development, while recognized by the family, was never noticeably demanding. His joy in life was hunting. A day out in the Tuscan fields with a gun dog and a twelve-bore was his greatest pleasure.

The danger of taking young nephews with him on these occasions was painfully emphasized once, when Paolo accidentally shot him. "Really, I should have known better," Paolo apologizes. "It was one of those very unfortunate accidents that sadly do happen in hunting, and I'm only too glad it wasn't more serious than it was."

From Vasco's point of view it was serious enough. They were stalking pheasant, their gun dogs—pointers—about to put up two fine birds. "I called to Uncle Vasco to shoot first," Paolo says. "His bird soared up and he got it with his first shot. Mine was flushed seconds later. It came swooping low to his right and well below the height I'd been expecting. When I fired I heard a shout. The pheasant fell, but it was my poor uncle who'd cried out. I'd winged him with the same shot!"

Fortunately, the full charge had missed Vasco, but he was bleeding freely and was almost unconscious. A horrified Paolo managed to stop a passing motorist and get his wounded uncle to a hospital in Florence. "The pellets were in the lower part of his body," Paolo remembers grimly. "Nothing lastingly serious. But I made his poor wife, my Aunt Maria, very distressed for quite a while, I believe. Uncle Vasco was, you might say, put on temporary hold!"

Though Vasco stood out as the most dedicated outdoor sportsman of the family, his indoor pleasures were less marked. Like all Guccis in the male line, a certain amount of sexual conquest had come naturally to him in his bachelor days. It seemed, though, that after marriage he kept the practice up with a German girl who became pregnant. Ironically, since his own wife was unable to have children, his mistress fathered Vasco's only child. And as it was a boy, it would have inherited in due time as much as any of Guccio's male grandchildren. But this was not to be.

In the Gucci family, such occupational hazards were customarily written off as events that had to be paid for and made good. Either you married the girl, which in this case was impossible, or you adopted the child and paid off the mistress. Vasco did neither.

Unlike Paolo, whose first wife Yvonne was pregnant with their child before he married her, and other Guccis who made proper and appropriate financial compensation for their illegitimate children, Vasco uncharacteristically chose (perhaps under persuasion from Guccio) to pay off his mistress and to legally sever the child from any participation in the family inheritance.

Paolo believes that his uncle may have done so out of fear that his wife would find out about the affair and that he therefore instructed his lawyer to offer any sum of money to the mother on condition that she disown his connection with the child. Apparently she signed a paper that legally set aside the boy from all right in the succession. Surprisingly, it seems Vasco never allowed himself to set eyes on his son, and apparently no mention was made of the boy in the family. Whatever rights he may have had disappeared with the document carrying his mother's signature.

If one can imagine the Guccis at this time as a bee colony, the workers could be represented by Aldo. To a lesser, more reluctant extent also by Vasco. The queen bee without question was Guccio (with Aida behind him in a multisex monarchy). Rodolfo, known in the family as "Folfo," was the drone. Which is not to say that he lacked ability or enterprise. Blessed with cherubic good looks, Guccio's last child fitted well into the days of early cinema. His smooth charm was also an asset in the romantic and comedy roles that director Camerini cast him in. Audiences craved glamorous settings—the rich trappings that, in real life, they seldom glimpsed. Rodolfo worked in a score of these lavishly dressed productions, his natural manner and youth gaining a following that only dwindled with the talkies.

In Paolo's view his uncle enjoyed a stature that, while giving him a taste for luxury and expensive pleasures, was "one of those experiences where you seemingly make a fortune one minute, and nothing the next." Rodolfo's success may have been erratic and risky, but as Maurizio D'Ancora (the name he chose to use as an actor) there is evidence from a private filmed record he left to his son that he won more acclaim outside his family than in it.

Guccio, sound businessman at heart, had little time or respect for such frivolities. Rodolfo's stardom made little impression on him. It did, however, provide one more triumph for the founder to boast about. Guccio's natural inclination was to emphasize success however it happened, making instinctive use of anything reflecting well on his family and its business success. Long before the Gucci business could indulge in the luxury of employing publicity agents, he had a clear notion of the fundamental rules of the game. Everything good, prosperous and creditworthy was stressed. Anything suggestive of failure, tucked away and forgotten.

This applied particularly to the indiscretions of his sons. With Grimalda, he had little to worry about. She was a sweet and pretty young girl who was well shielded by her father's and brothers' protective care during adolescence. She remembers her father's firmness now almost with affection. "He was a fine man. He kept all us children in perfect order. We were very well brought up."

She was his favorite. "Of course, being the only girl. But my mother was more taken by the boys." Helping with the huge amounts of daily cooking needed to satisfy the large family, Grimalda can still recall her father's prodigious appetite for food. "He was a gourmand, liking anything so long as it was well cooked."

Indeed, Grimalda and Aldo, Guccio's two surviving children, seem to have had little to complain about. Their father was Victorian in his home, but thrusting and forward-looking in business, blending shrewd caution with an adventurous, sometimes buccaneering spirit. The vision he originally had of what Gucci was to become shaped a golden future.

Guccio trained his sons to play an indispensable part in the growth and development of the Gucci empire. He fostered, where he could, their capacity to grow with it. What he could not prevent, or foresee, was the power struggle that was to tear them apart.

Aldo, the workhorse, gained the bulk of his father's trust. Vasco was allowed to go his own way, lacking interest in business and happiest in the hunting field. Ugo was a pain to be borne. And Rodolfo was, in his father's eyes, mistaken to have got mixed up in anything "as crazy as the film thing, where one makes a fortune in five minutes, then never works again." But he forgave him too.

With Aida's warm support, he molded, loved and corrected them all. Only when they made lives of their own, and when these ran counter to his grand design, did Guccio Gucci turn sour.

4

HARD TIMES

In post–World War One Florence it was all too easy for experienced traders and merchants to flounder into debt and bankruptcy as a result of the callousness of many of the wealthiest of the citizens, who paid their bills when and as seldom as they chose. In Guccio's case he was forced to accept the fact sooner than most, since his capital was already more than fully stretched. Had it not been for the generosity of his main suppliers he would never have got off the ground at all.

But one night in 1924, during his second full year of trading, the imbalance between incoming cash and the demands of suppliers for settlement threatened to destroy him. Only the assistance of his daughter's fiancé, Giovanni Vitali, saved the first Gucci shop from extinction.

Grimalda was now regularly helping her father, working as an underpaid, enthusiastic cashier. She had grown

attractive, a small, keen-eyed girl with a soft voice and manner, much sought after by the younger men of the city.
Giovanni felt himself to be one of the luckiest fellows alive
when she accepted his proposal. He too was short, with a
round head and hooked nose. No Adonis, his more practical
qualities no doubt appealed to Grimalda's parents, Guccio
and Aida, who gave the match their immediate blessing.

They had known Giovanni since his schooldays, shared
in part with Ugo and later Aldo at the Roman Catholic
College of Castelleti. After he left, an introduction to their
sister had followed quite naturally. He had become a friend
of the family, well liked by all the Guccis.

Giovanni was a surveyor and construction engineer, valuable trades in a city as old and revered as Florence. It was
hardly surprising that Guccio favored his daughter's choice,
especially as Giovanni was by then well established in his
career, working in his father's building business. He probably looked forward to the day when such a son-in-law would
bring his skills in shop fitting and renovating to premises
Guccio had every intention of acquiring as his business expanded.

The evening he saved Guccio's shop, Giovanni came as
usual to pick up Grimalda at the shop. As he walked the
length of the narrow via della Vigna, he was thinking con-
tentedly of the life ahead for both of them, indeed for all
Florence, in the new world which was slowly emerging from
the ashes and dust of the old.

It was a world he looked forward to sharing with the girl
he had lost his heart to. "I had no idea of the extent of trouble
her father was in. When I came to the door and found the
whole place shut up tight, I could not understand what was
going on."

Normally at that time Grimalda would have been counting the money in the cash box. A few late customers would
perhaps be still in the shop while parcels were being busily

packed for immediate delivery, often by Aldo and Vasco. Now all was still. There was an air of almost sinister quiet about the shuttered windows. He knocked.

"Come in, but don't say a word," Grimalda whispered as she opened the door to him and beckoned him inside, one finger to her lips. Mystified, he was led through the darkened shop to the little office in the back where Guccio ran the business. As far as he could see, all the staff were crammed into the room, Aldo and Vasco standing beside their father. Guccio was addressing them, his voice, always soft, barely audible. In Giovanni's recollection he looked "like a man facing sentence of death."

Giovanni had had no warning of what was to come. He knew that Guccio was having difficulties with the new shop, but with his sons and daughter to help him Giovanni had never assumed these could be overwhelming. "Grimalda did not talk about her father's affairs to me in those days," he says. "She was too loyal."

So he listened with embarrassment as Guccio tearfully outlined the crisis. "He had to close, he said, because he had no money to meet his debts." Some of the suppliers who had let Guccio have goods on credit to launch the business were demanding payment. Not enough customers had settled their accounts in response to his entreaties and demands. "Unless a miracle happens," he announced, "I can't stay open another day."

Giovanni had no miraculous powers, but he did have savings set aside for Grimalda and himself for when they married, but what use would they be if her family was ruined, he asked himself? "I offered to help out, provided Guccio would pay me back monthly, as his business picked up."

Guccio told him he had been to the bank and asked for a loan to tide him over. They had turned him down flat. "He knew I had been saving to set us up in marriage, and that I would need all the cash I had very soon, so he guaranteed repayment every month over a period during which I would lend him what I had. I agreed because, after all, I was engaged to his daughter."

Giovanni's loan was confirmed in signed promissory notes and repaid monthly. There is no doubt in his mind that it saved the business. Now approaching ninety, he wrinkles a face like a benign Punchinello. "Oh, yes, he would have been finished. There would be no Gucci today. But I saw it as my duty, and I trusted Guccio."

His own father was less sanguine. "He thought I was being very rash, even foolhardy," Giovanni says. "He didn't know Guccio as I did. Still today I think of him as a completely honest, trustworthy man. A hundred percent honorable. I hate to think sometimes of how he would have felt about some of the things that have happened since his death."

Nevertheless, Guccio risked everything, including his good name, in borrowing when business in the shop was at such a low ebb that he could not even scrape together enough to pay the staff their wages. He was lucky to have made a shrewd enough assessment of the situation to sense that he needed only a second wind to turn the most crucial corner of his life. "He was a man who never owed a penny if he could help it," Giovanni says. "I knew very well what it had cost him to ask me to help. Fortunately, soon afterward, the business began picking up and he never looked back. I was well repaid."

In that his vital, timely loan was returned to him in full and on time, Giovanni was repaid. But this benefactor has never been paid, it seems, for much of the work he did for Guccio and the family business. It was his design, he says, that built the Gucci factories. His plans that fitted out the magnificent via Tornabuoni Gucci showrooms in Florence as well as many other buildings belonging to Guccio and his descendants. Giovanni says he does not care for himself, but for his wife Grimalda, the oldest of Guccio's surviving children, he has waged long battles with the family. In those early days nobody had such an important influence on the Gucci enterprise as Giovanni Vitale.

With his new sense of financial security Guccio branched out. The trade in repairs—"putting the cheese on the macaroni," as it was known locally—was already bringing in a tidy profit. He expanded the workroom at the back of the shop to allow for additional part-time workmen (mainly skilled leather-workers moonlighting from daytime jobs with the big established firms like his old bosses at Franzi). There was little these craftsmen could not do with leather. When goods were hard to come by, or too expensive, they could make them. Increasingly, Guccio encouraged them to do so.

Why pay a wholesaler a middleman's commission, he reasoned, for goods he could make himself? Guccio knew what could and could not be profitably turned out in his backroom factory and that was all he needed. In addition he possessed a sharp eye for spotting a good workman. His ability to evaluate the first Gucci craftsmen was his greatest natural talent, and he put it to good use. He knew where the specialists in each item were to be found, the real geniuses who worked quietly in the background. To create an aesthetically satisfying article in leather needed, he well knew, far more than a craftsman's skill in punching holes or sewing seams. The men he looked for, and found, were true artists.

At Franzi he had worked with men who made everything from the lightest, softest dispatch or jewel cases to the huge cabin trunks that had so impressed him in London. His grandson Paolo believes he had studied similar workmanship in the windows of London's most exclusive shops—Asprey's, Mappin & Webb and the cream of the leather-goods traders on Old Bond Street. He brought every bit of this acquired knowledge to bear on the creations that now, increasingly, were his own.

As the business grew, Guccio was finding it easier to put something away for what he and many other Florentine merchants feared was an approaching storm. Mussolini's adventures, particularly his invasion of Ethiopia in defiance of the League of Nations, excited many younger men, but those like Guccio who had seen a world war firsthand were not so swayed by the strutting dictator and his Blackshirt followers. When sanctions were imposed on his country, making it impossible for Gucci to obtain legally all the tanned leather he needed from Scotland and elsewhere, he shook his head sadly. But Mussolini's misfortune was to provide him with good profits.

What could no longer be made entirely in leather had to be adapted. The all-leather handbag became one of canvas and leather combined. Similar compromises could save many of his best lines, and the skill with which his artist-craftsmen designed them made a lasting contribution. Even luggage could be sensibly adapted so that leather only formed the most resistant parts of the goods—corners, straps and clasps. The setback that Guccio grumbled and worried over for weeks proved one of the most fortuitous events in the firm's history. The most renowned Gucci items among the collection preserved for posterity by the Museum of Modern Art in New York is still the "Handbag No. 0633."

Gucci was becoming known for a number of attractive accessories in a variety of materials in addition to leather. In spite of the proprietor's misgivings, these ideally complemented the established Gucci lines. His heavy luggage and assorted bags earned a reputation both for quality and reliability. They were still the shop's leading items, but women could now browse through the showroom picking up small but expensive trifles to give as presents.

Such things, Guccio was discovering, could insure a steady flow of trade while giving his wares the attraction of a boutique or bazaar. Belts and wallets, small knicknacks to amuse and adorn rather than for serviceable use, were displayed in the cleverly designed windows that Aldo and his father personally supervised. In effect, it was the birth of the Gucci image, the reputation for well-made goods known to last and designed with flair, at the same time offering a delightful choice of less durable but acceptable ornaments and accessories. In such fashion the sanctions against Mussolini forced them to innovate and to do it successfully.

Aldo was the first to realize what a godsend the use of

the new materials could be. He was living with Guccio and Aida and, when not quarreling about his father's reluctance to move as fast as his son would have liked, involved himself in the planning and development of the growing business. "They fought a lot, but my grandfather respected my father's opinions," his son Paolo says. "He knew that only my father really understood the business. Uncle Vasco was working with them, but he did not have the same grasp for it. Uncle Rodolfo was still with the film company and seldom at home."

Aldo saw, too, that a distinctive badge or symbol placed on the lines, old and new, would add even more to their attractiveness. Guccio—nobody can recall when—had proposed the clever, palindromic "GG," and Aldo commissioned it. He had the design embossed in metal and fixed prominently wherever it would be seen.

It was, of course, an ideal period. All Florence was enjoying prosperity. Once the worst shock waves of World War One had passed, many of the local merchants who had escaped ruin found themselves growing wealthy in the new boom years of the early twenties prior to the Depression. Tourism was on the increase and shiploads of culture- and tradition-hungry Americans arrived in Europe almost daily during the most popular months. Everyone wanted to go around the world, and visiting Europe for most Americans was the first step toward fulfillment of their most cherished dream.

Italy was on top of their lists, anxiously sought for its ancient and historical sites but also much desired for the elegance and style of its shops. Florence was rich in both. Most illustrious of the ancient cities with its magnificent architecture, its galleries and palaces, Florence was also the place where wealthy tourists shopped for the fine handmade leather goods made by local craftsmen with centuries of experience and expertise. It was this surge of tourism that brought an endless flow of wealthy customers pouring into Gucci's shop, hungry to buy his beautiful and imaginative creations in leather.

5

ALDO'S BRIDE

Typically, once the business was on its feet Guccio became restless. He wanted to move on, to expand into bigger, smarter premises, earn greater profits and attract a higher class of trade with more opulent surroundings. When a more stylish, bigger property fell vacant in the via Della Vigna Nova he seized it, though he had to use all his persuasive charm to get the bank to put up the money for the move. It was a big step, an upward move to a world patronized by many of the most affluent and distinguished families in Florence. It was a street that attracted titled and wealthy women, despite the fact that it was so narrow that movement, other than on foot, was difficult.

Rich and famous people were beginning to come to the shop in search of its excellent, if expensive, leather goods. In such affluent society, Guccio practiced a manner that combined self-effacement, obedience to the customer's slightest whim and a careful inducement to them to spend freely. For Aldo the move meant contact with many more interesting people. He was young, unmarried and prepossessing. He had already had numerous flirtations and reveled in the conquest of the most beautiful among the younger women he served in the shop. Having the lean, well-boned face of an heroically sculpted Roman centurion was clearly an asset in these escapades, as was his magnetic air of masculine virility.

In the new surroundings he extended his amorous circle with no harm to the business. More than one lady lingered longer than was strictly necessary and bought more than she had intended. Aldo urged these admirers to feel the sensual delicacy of kid and chamois, to test the refinement of hand-sewn leather stitching; he made his goods and himself equally attractive.

Should he have let such advantages slip away? His son Paolo laughs at the thought. "My father, I'm sure, had lots of flirtations with customers. Many of them were with young women he got to know through the shop, then cultivated socially, but there were some he only knew in the shop—brief encounters in the fitting room!"

The time came, however, when these casual encounters had to stop. One day a very young pretty woman came into the shop. Her eyes sparkled and her cheeks had the complexion of a life spent in country air and open fields.

Her name was Olwen Price, a lady's maid to a Rumanian princess, and she breathed innocence and freshness. Her voice was rich with the music of the English countryside, her manner charming and unaffected. Aldo found her irresistible. Within a short time he had persuaded her to meet him secretly, without the knowledge of the princess, her mistress, who was doing her best to protect Olwen from the dangerously forward young males of Florence. In very little more time, he had made love to her. When she broke the news that she was pregnant, he at once declared his intention of marrying her.

George Price, Olwen's father, and his father before him (and no doubt many generations of Prices before that) were wheelwrights, skilled joiners and coffinmakers in the village of West Felton, near Shrewsbury.

Olwen, his eldest daughter, was born on November 10, 1908, and had left the village church school at fourteen to learn dressmaking. She and her two brothers and three sisters lived with their parents in a small house above the village. As children they kept and tended sheep and pigs, enjoyed the country around and expected little more from life than their family had known for centuries.

So people were shocked when the news came to West Felton that Olwen had found herself an Italian husband, and that they were going to be married in the Roman Catholic church in Oswestry (she having converted to his religion).

It was known, of course, that Olwen had been given the chance to travel abroad. After the dressmaking, for which she was not paid, she had been glad to go into service and was lucky, it was thought, to have found herself such a good job.

She was a bright girl, not the beauty of the family in her brother Ewart's eyes, but with more than a bit of good looks to show for herself. Fair reddish hair set off a well-boned face in which a pair of laughing eyes gave a hint of impish spirit tucked away under the self-effacing demeanor required of her position. As a housemaid to the duke of Newcastle's granddaughter, Lady Frances Hope, in Dorset she had been obliged to be respectful, but obedience came quite naturally to Olwen after her parents' upbringing. And before she left Her Ladyship, she was well liked and trusted.

She was still in her teens when Lady Hope's children's governess left to take up the same post in Italy with the then exiled Princess Catherine of Rumania. According to Ewart, Olwen cannot have been much more than fifteen when the ex-governess wrote asking if she would like to join the princess' household as lady's maid.

It has always been accepted in the Gucci family that Olwen became a lady-in-waiting to the princess. She has even been referred to in Italian magazines as "Lady Price." This came about because it suited Princess Catherine, who could afford no such luxury, to call her maid a lady-in-waiting while paying her the wages of only a servant.

Olwen's family know that, much as they love her, she
was never elevated in her working life. But it was no surprise
to them that the princess, who was later to marry King
George II of Greece and share his throne when it was re-
stored to him in 1935, treated Olwen with unusual famil-
iarity. They knew her as a helpful, companionable and attractive girl who would have adapted herself to any position.

Olwen today has little recollection of those early days. A
setback in health followed an unpleasant encounter she had
with a gang of robbers who broke into her home in one of the
best and most protected parts of Rome some five years ago.
According to her brother Ewart, "She was in the bath. They
made all the servants crowd into the bathroom with her.
They wouldn't even give her a towel or robe to hide her
nakedness." The families agree that the thugs who broke in
and forced Olwen to open her safety box rejected her jewels
when they got them. The bag containing them was found the
following day in the garden, under a bush. Strange.

As a result she is no longer the bright-eyed wheelwright's
daughter who said good-by to her loving brothers and sister
all those years ago. Her memory is clouded. She walks with
some difficulty, one leg having suffered from a seizure or
stroke that followed the apparently traumatic experience
with the thieves. An Englishwoman who stayed with her
recently in Rome says that her ability to cope with day-to-
day problems is limited and her life circumscribed. She lives
in a fine house built on sloping ground running down to a
roadway off of which stand the mansions of ambassadors
and statesmen, but she sees little of them, or indeed of life
outside the electrically locked gates of her estate.

Yet hers is one of the most romantic stories in the rising
fortunes of the Gucci family. Olwen found herself trans-
ported from a lowly position in a noble English home to a
royal villa in Florence.

Grimalda, Aldo's elder sister, remembers his delight
when Olwen accepted his proposal. He saw it, she thinks, as
a splendid romantic adventure. A princess of royal blood . . .
a blushing young Welsh maid . . . their clandestine love af-

fair in the shadows of ancient Florence, where the narrow, cobbled streets had once known the imprint of Dante and the Medicis, of Michelangelo and Leonardo da Vinci. "He was crazy about her, and told me he'd never been more in love in his life." To Grimalda, it seemed that Olwen's fear of being discovered by the princess and sent home added to her attraction for Aldo.

But Guccio was not too pleased to receive an abrupt request from the princess: "Your son has been seeing my servant. It has to stop or I shall be forced to send her home. I am responsible for the girl." Guccio had no intention of telling his son whom he should see or not see. But no customer in his book was ever wrong, least of all one of royal blood. While the princess waited in his office, Aldo was summoned.

"What is all this?" his father demanded. "Explain yourself to Her Royal Highness. Tell her, if you please, that you will do as she asks."

Aldo had never before denied his father's express instructions. But this time his heart was concerned. "You are mistaken," he told the princess. "Olwen is no longer your concern. She is mine. I am taking care of her from now on."

Grimalda remembers that her brother immediately moved his future bride out of the princess' protection and into his family's care. "He asked me to take her in and look after her, and of course I did, and also became chaperone."

There were times, Grimalda remembers now with some quiet amusement, when "Aldo would come to take her out, and tell me not to bother my head, they were only going to a café. But when he came back with her much later he had what looked like grass and mud on his jacket."

Early in the summer of 1927 Olwen went home to her family. The girls pressed their sister for details of life in the royal villa, of the great artistic treasures of Florence and above all of her love affair with the handsome foreigner whose photographs she brought with her.

Aldo soon followed. It seems that his introduction to the

Prices was a pleasure for both. "They were in love, we could see that," Ewart remembers. "And mother thought it was wonderful. Father took a more serious view, of course. He didn't much like losing his eldest daughter I don't think, and to a stranger at that."

There were reports that George Price refused to have anything to do with Olwen's future husband for quite some time, expressing strong feelings about her "going off and marrying this Italian bloke." When they married, on August 22, George Price was absent.

His son Ewart explains in this fashion his father's refusal to give Olwen away to her prospective husband in the church ceremony: "Weddings always upset father. He couldn't stop crying if he had to go to one, which was why he didn't go to Olwen's. He was very easygoing about it, leaving everything to my mother to do, but he got on well enough with Aldo, we all did."

Whatever, the twenty-two-year-old Tuscan was finding life in the English countryside much to his taste. "Give him a gun and he'd be out shooting anything at all, he wasn't particular," Ewart says. "Rabbit, pigeon, everything. Oh yes, Aldo was a jolly fellow in those days. My wife Hilda's family thought the world of him. So, too, did the local people."

With none of his own family to make the journey to Shropshire to see him marry a girl with a Welsh name and family, Aldo called on Hughie Wilcox, Oswestry's sole tobacconist, to be his best man.

The ceremony in the little church was simple and straightforward. Olwen had received instruction in her new faith from the Irish priest, Father Michael O'Reilly. She listened attentively as he stressed the Roman Catholic ruling that the sacrament of marriage, once received, cannot be broken. Her responses were audible to her mother, Elizabeth, and her brothers and sisters, since there were no Guccis present, sitting on both sides of the church.

Signing the register afterward, Olwen gave her age as nineteen, her "condition" as spinster. Her bachelor husband, now twenty-two, added his parents' address, which the registrar, Mr. I. Pughe Jones, understandably misspelled. "No. 4 Piazza Verzia," by now the Gucci family home in Florence, became "Plazza Verzinia."

The profession of Aldo's father, Guccio, was given as "merchant." Aldo, more elaborately, described himself as "leather-goods merchant." Nita, Olwen's sister and maid of honor, signed as witness under Hughie Wilcox.

Details of any honeymoon his sister and new brother-in-law may have had have faded from Ewart's memory. He remembers only that the couple was deeply and sincerely in love, as his wife Hilda agrees. "Oh yes, you only had to look at them to know that."

The troubles that later set them apart were not yet apparent. But on their return to Florence, Olwen had a surprising adjustment to make. She had, she thought, married only one Gucci, but she very soon learned that she was expected to relate to the family as a whole and to make a place for herself. Grimalda saw how difficult it was for the Welsh girl, already three months pregnant, to adapt to the Gucci family style of living.

"She didn't get on here," Grimalda says. "Not with any of us. And she was so possessive of Aldo that there were bound to be problems, because my brother was a man who needed his freedom, which she did not seem to understand.

In one way Olwen behaved like the best of so-called traditional Italian wives. She bore her husband three sons in quick succession and gave herself wholeheartedly to rearing them. Strains on the marriage began to appear only when Aldo wanted her to join him in social pleasures and outings with friends. "He loved life," Grimalda says, "but she tended to put a damper on what he wanted to do. She rarely let him take her out, preferring to look after the children."

They had very little money, though Guccio recognized Aldo's value and gave him what he thought was a fair reward for his work. In his old-fashioned way Guccio took the view that his sons should be grateful to him for having started a business that gave them all (except Rodolfo) a living. If Aldo was finding the going harder as a married man, that was his problem; he had chosen, willfully in his father's view, to get married and have a family.

Guccio had no intention of becoming a philanthropist. His early struggles and the lessons learned in the stokehole and in the Savoy kitchens had taught him that everyone in life had to fend for themselves.

Toward Olwen he showed a mixture of bland detachment and exaggerated politeness. They were never really close, though her brother Ewart believes that she admired the old man. Her son Paolo says, "I never heard her say anything nice about him." Presumably a matter of perspective.

The deepest rift was between Olwen and her mother-in-law, Aida. Either because grandmother Gucci resented Olwen's possessive hold over her son and children, or on account of an elemental clash of personalities, they found little in common. When Aldo and Olwen at last got their own home and left the bosom of the Gucci family, Aida no doubt breathed more easily.

The problems with the young couple, however, had only just begun. Olwen's reluctance to leave her growing family, her less than enthusiastic attempts to fit in with her husband's life-style, tended to set her apart. Grimalda says she watched with growing dismay as the marriage drifted from early rapture to stalemate.

"My sister-in-law refused to learn Italian, and even now it's a strain to listen to her on the phone. But I'm not saying she is not a good person, very well brought up and all that. In my opinion she sacrificed herself for her boys. There's no doubt she was a fine mother, but Aldo was not the kind of man to be held down like that."

Aldo was regularly going off on his own, according to his sister. "There were sales representatives to be entertained, and travels to other cities. He told me he would have been happy to take Olwen with him on those trips but she wouldn't leave the children." Aldo had a friend, Ugo Rangoni, who sold shoes in Switzerland and who was happy to take him along as an extra salesman. The commission he was paid added to Aldo's small salary. But it also allowed him a few nights away from his family with no questions asked.

His children saw increasingly less of their father as the years went by. "He would be there most evenings but they were often quarreling," Paolo remembers. "My mother's life, it seemed to me, was altogether different from my father's. She was shy. She didn't like people until she got to know them well, and of course she found the language difficult. Also the Italian flamboyancy upset her."

But the real trouble, as his grandmother and aunts were always whispering to each other, was that his parents had simply married too young. Aldo was still too full of beans. "He wanted to go out dancing, to nightclubs. He tried to get her to see his friends but she didn't get on with them. So at weekends, either he'd go off alone or sit moping about the house."

Paolo, right or wrong, tends to blame his mother for not trying harder to match Aldo's spirited way of living. "She wouldn't have fun. While he was the exact opposite, a man who loved pretty women, who liked to have good times. She preferred a home life, so he had to find his pleasures on his own and she was never able to understand that."

As a result, the marriage, bound by unbreakable sacramental vows, became a prison for them both. The boys witnessed hostility and more between their mother and father. Paolo remembers: "Oh gosh, yes! At times they would end up with her having convulsions, or even passing out completely! Life was never peaceful for very long when the two of them were together."

As boys, Paolo and his brothers were kept short of money. Olwen took their part at times when they would beg their father to let them have a little extra. Younger than his brother Giorgio, and less diplomatic than the youngest brother Roberto ("we called him 'the priest'"), Paolo, it seems, was the one who stood up to his father.

"I only did what he did. Whenever my father wanted to say anything to us, however unpleasant or controversial, he would say it right out loud, there and then. It didn't matter where we were, or who was present. It was the same later on when we worked for him."

His brothers would bow their heads and take it, but not Paolo. "Imagine! In front of everybody—staff, customers, it didn't matter who it was."

Paolo's defiance, his refusal to accept rebukes, was the beginning of a rebellion that was to threaten both the roots of the family tree and its golden branches. "I gave as good as I got. My gosh, the fights we had! Not physical, though quite often a briefcase or a telephone would land smack on the table between us in the heat of an argument. And I remember throwing a cup of coffee at him once because I refused to go to school. My nanny had called him, and I took this big cup and hurled it at him. He took off his belt and beat me with it. A Gucci belt, of course."

Aldo's strictness sprang directly from his own upbringing. Guccio and Aida had shown how fierce they could be as parents. Aldo and his brothers inherited the old-fashioned and accepted belief that to spare the rod was to spoil the child. Aldo's rages were matched, according to her sister-in-law, by his wife's Welsh temper.

"It wasn't all one-sided," Grimalda says. "When things became difficult between them I've seen them both go at each other. Once she broke a flower vase over his head. She threw it from the stairs and he couldn't avoid it. Not that she was normally a violent person, but Olwen had a temper in her younger days. It could flare up in an instant. That contributed to the trouble."

Aldo's contribution could also be destructive. Paolo remembers his father's domination of all around him. "He overpowered everybody." Paolo's English wife, Jenny, agrees. "His behavior when we went out to restaurants . . . I'm not surprised Olwen found him impossible."

How Guccio felt about his eldest son's public behavior

mattered a great deal more. Since Aldo, more than anyone in the family, was helping to pull the family business up by its Gucci bootstraps his father could afford to overlook a great deal, provided it did not bring disgrace on the shop.

As long as Aldo treated their wealthy customers with sufficient courtesy his private behavior was his own business. Guccio had tolerated his son's flirtations before marriage, and he understood and shared his admiration of women. An occasional outburst of Latin temperament was natural in a young man with his qualities. If he personally doubted Aldo's wisdom in choosing a bride from a people whose emotional life, he knew from his experience in London, was suppressed in public, he kept it to himself.

Vasco, as suggested, was disappointing, always ready to enjoy a day in the hunting field, seldom at his desk, when wanted, in the new small factory they had opened. Rodolfo was still wasting his time, as his father thought, in films. So Aldo was the son he relied on, the mainstay of his business.

Which did not mean that this son of his could do as he liked. No child of Guccio Gucci would ever be allowed that privilege while breath remained in the old man's body. The fires burned brightly in him as long as he drew breath—and not suprisingly his offspring inherited his often firey, uncompromising qualities.

6

WAR CLOUDS

When their first son, Giorgio, was born in February 1928, the Aldo Guccis moved to a fine house on the outskirts of Florence in the via Giovanni Prati. A quiet cul-de-sac bordered on both sides by fairly large houses, some with their own walled gardens, it suggested more wealth than Aldo actually possessed. His argument to his father was that they must live well to have a reputation for doing well. Guccio, enjoying his first taste of grandparenthood, could afford to be generous.

It was to be three years more before Olwen added to the family. Her second son, Paolo, was born on March 29, 1931, and his younger brother, Roberto, the following year. On the face of it they were a thriving and happy group, but there was little contact between Olwen and her husband's family other than in her own home or at occasional Sunday luncheons in Guccio's and Aida's dining room.

On this thirtieth birthday Aldo, according to Paolo, made a decision to extend his field of operations, and with it his freedom. The name of Gucci was making itself known around the world, but far too sluggishly for his impatient nature. If the bulk of their customers came from abroad, many from the great world capitals, then that was where Gucci should set up shop. If these visitors to Florence who so often said they had "heard about Gucci" in various parts of the world were representative, why sit at home and wait for their arrival? Why not take Gucci to them?

Aldo put it to Guccio with predictable results. Why, his father asked, should they run the risk of opening branches in cities and towns they knew nothing about? Wasn't it good enough that business in Florence was increasing rapidly? Why tempt providence abroad when they were doing very nicely at home? No doubt there would be customers in the major cities like Rome and Venice and Naples, perhaps even in Paris and London, but think of the enormous investment it would take to set up in those remote and distant places. All very well to talk, but such things cost money.

Guccio's resistance would have been more convincing if Aldo had not known that his father invariably opposed any change he suggested—though only to his face. Grimalda was as accustomed to this defensive mode as her brother. "My father would tell Aldo that he would have nothing whatever to do with any scheme costing money. 'Go to the bank and ask them to back you!' he would tell him. But then he would privately let the bank know that he was behind the scheme, so that Aldo would get his backing after all."

In this way Guccio avoided commitment. In public he washed his hands of the expenses involved, refusing to advance the money needed. In private he made the venture possible. "Then, if it failed, he could put on a long face and tell Aldo, 'I told you so. I warned you, didn't I?' On the other hand, if it came off and was a big success he would boast about it . . . 'You see what I did?'"

Aldo, nevertheless, did choose a risky time to make his move. Opening a second branch anywhere in Italy, or indeed Europe, while the threat of a second World War hung in the air was a hazardous thing to do. To pick on the country's capital city, Rome, while Benito Mussolini was beating his martial drum more and more thunderously did *seem* a form of commercial suicide. But Aldo pushed ahead.

In the city of Munich, September 1, 1938, a mere twelve months before the start of World War Two in Europe, Gucci opened the silvered doors of the store on the chic and expensive via Condotti. The cost had been great. Aldo spared nothing to make this the flagship of the firm, a shop that would rank Gucci among the leading merchants of Italy and the world.

When his father shook his head over the bills and projections that showed that the new branch would have to depend on immediate popularity and a swiftly rising turnover, Aldo reminded him that Rome was not Florence. The city was one of the world's most luxurious and lavish playgrounds. Visitors here spend in a day what the perhaps more cultured but less wealthy tourists of Florence spent in a week. Long before Rome became known for *la dolce vita*, Aldo accurately assessed its value as the glamor capital of the Western world.

Alone in the family, he supported the inevitable risk taking of expansion and its vast expenses. His vision never let him doubt that this was the future, the path they had to take. Gucci could become a supreme market leader only if such gambles as Rome were followed, as quickly as was practicable, by others.

Guccio, as usual, pretended not to listen. It was all too speculative, too much of a gamble with borrowed money and the risk that not only would these farflung ventures fail but that they would ruin all that he had accumulated and built up. Aldo's young sons witnessed the battles their father had with this dogmatic attitude, and Paolo blames his uncle Vasco, Aldo's younger brother, as much as anyone.

"He was always ready to put a damper on any scheme my father proposed, totally negative. He was terrified of losing everything we had, and tried to curry favor with my grandfather by urging caution."

Guccio saw through all this. He recognized that Aldo was working on sound principles, that he was probably right to force the pace of their development. He also probably felt that Vasco was blocking his brother's plans because he did not want to risk losing a part in a business that allowed him to do as little as possible while he enjoyed the hunting, shooting country-style life he so cherished.

In the family as a whole, Aldo was seen as the Guccio son who best sensed the full scope and potential of the business. His move to Rome was, as it turned out, a master stroke. At the time it may have seemed commercial lunacy, but in fact the timing turned out to be perfect. The war, though it was to test all Gucci resources to the limit, brought everything Aldo could have wished.

The war came. No Italian whose adult years include 1939 to 1945 when Mussolini led his countrymen to battle in the shaky backseat of Hitler's blitzkreig remembers those days without anguish. The disgrace that their strutting "bullfrog of the Pontine marshes" (Churchill's contemptuous name for the Italian dictator) made them endure in World War Two still throbs like an old wound.

The Guccis were luckier than most in having benefited from the sanctions of 1935. In their present dilemma they were not so fortunate. The war was a conflict between some of their best customers—British, French, Germans and Americans. It also clamped an immediate brake on Aldo's expansion plans. Grimalda saw her husband's building skills used only to aid the army, her father's firm losing all impetus during those years.

"They were hard times. I wonder sometimes how father managed to keep the business going. The family were all in different places, Aldo in Rome with Olwen and the children, Vasco running the factory, Rodolfo off somewhere with the armed forces entertainment unit, which he'd joined through being an actor. And all of us getting along as best we could."

Only one bearer of the family name was doing well out of the war. Ugo's position and authority had increased. He had become the appointed administrator for a whole region of Tuscany. Now married for the second time, Ugo was no longer afraid to look his parents in the eye. He paraded before them in the uniform of Mussolini's most elite corps.

Meanwhile, Guccio, by all accounts, was impressed by Aldo's initiative in keeping the Rome shop open and profitable. The ancient capital was being treated by the Allies as an "open city," hence no bombs fell on or near the via Condotti. Guccio's favorite son and three grandsons lived in safety there, the boys—Giorgio, Paolo, and Roberto—growing up in one of the few protected areas of Europe.

Aldo and Olwen lived behind the shop, which for the boys meant becoming a part of it. They went to a school run by Irish nuns, the Mata Dei, where their mother had struck up a friendship with several of the teachers. After school there was work to be done, running errands and delivering parcels for their father. Barely in their teens when the war ended, they saw it as an exciting time. "We were enrolled like everybody else at school in the youth brigade, the Italian equivalent of the Hitler Youth, and had to parade about in our uniforms," Paolo says.

Less fun was the shortage of sweets and chocolates, the rationing of petrol that prevented Aldo from taking the boys out into the country at weekends or making long trips to visit other members of the family. "But we always seemed to have plentiful supplies at home," Paolo says. "I can remember seeing stacks of butter and other food, supposedly hard to get, in my mother's store cupboard. She told me it came from God, but I knew it was smuggled out to her from the Vatican supplies."

He later discovered that it was a reward for the work Olwen was doing to help air crews shot down and taken prisoner. An Irish priest, Father Hickey, was actively helping Allied prisoners who managed to escape, passing them from one "safe house" to another.

Paolo's younger brother, Roberto, was barely thirteen when the war ended, an age when the romantic aspect of warfare could be expected to leave the strongest impression on him. As a baby he believes he was taken to live in England with his mother and only brought back to Italy at the outbreak of war. "I was born in my grandfather's house in Florence on November 29, 1932, and when I was only a few weeks old my mother took me to live in England with her. As she had dual nationality we all had to come back to live in Rome, in the via Condotti, when war broke out between Germany and England. Roberto was not even seven then, too young to retain a clear picture of actual places and events.

His memory of life in England was colored by the many visits his mother made to her old home. In prewar days Olwen traveled frequently between the two countries. She proudly showed off her three sons to her family. "After Aldo made money she bought two little houses in Oswestry," her brother Ewart recalls. "She put her sister in one. My wife Hilda and I kept the other one nice for Olwen, and she used it when she came over here as a holiday home."

So far as her brother knows there was never any suggestion that his sister would return to live there permanently. Nor does such a possibility seem feasible to her son, Paolo. "We spent a lot of time in Shropshire with mother when we were small," he says. "But our home was always in Italy."

Roberto was still very young when war put an end to the Shropshire visits. His recollection of the war years is clouded but he remembers that his mother was part of a hazardous undercover escape network organized by the Italian resistance. "Mother took the men who were sent to her and hid them in our house until the nuns could take them. It was Father Hickey who arranged everything. He and the nuns helped a lot of men to escape."

The brave Father, who would have been shot (and probably Olwen as well) if discovered, was from the Church of San Carlo in Rome and in close touch with the Vatican. Roberto talks about his mother's share in the escape organization as if it was a regular activity. "She was helping British and American prisoners to escape. And I was aware of what was going on, of course. She hid them in our house. I saw them there." His elder brother, Paolo, was less conscious of what was going on. "I thought I glimpsed a man once who looked unmistakably British, with handlebar moustaches. And I think mother hid him in the cellar but I couldn't be too sure."

As the youngest in the family, Roberto had been at home to see more of his mother's activities than his brothers. "We had a duplex apartment at No. 21 via Condotti, and that was where she hid them. There were plenty, but they only stayed about three days at most, then mother passed them on to the church of San Carlo, where Father Hickey took over. He must have had some connection with the Vatican. Mother was only a part of a chain running all through Italy, and Roman lawyers were working with her in the organization."

Roberto's most vivid recollection was of an RAF bomber being shot down over the Roman suburbs. The crew, after it had made a forced landing, came to their mother's house. "One was a Scotsman and very nice. I forget his name but I know he liked to drink. He found the Italian wine we gave him very acceptable—a little too much so, unfortunately."

The Scots airman got drunk, according to Roberto. "He left our house, went over to the Café Gréco and started ordering drinks. Then, when he'd had even more to drink, he began singing. It was obvious to everybody where he came from. Fortunately, the owner of the café knew my mother and telephoned her. 'Signora Gucci, you'd better come over *pronto*. Somebody here is going to be in big trouble if you don't get him home. Please rush!'

"My mother, with the cold blood of the Welsh, ran over right away. She took the drunken flier by the arm and said quietly, 'Come on,' and off he went. Quite an experience!" Roberto laughs now at what, when it happened, must have been closer to tragedy than comedy.

On another occasion Olwen only just escaped being herded into a bunch of random hostages who were to be shot in reprisal for a bomb that had been exploded in a dustbin, killing a group of Nazi SS men. Hostilities were coming to an end, and the defeated Nazis ordered that ten Romans— men, women, children and even babies in arms—were to be killed for each of their soldiers who died.

On that terrible day the boys were with their mother. They will never forget the sight of the city plunged into sudden tragedy, the horror stories of neighbors who had managed to survive. For long years the Italians had suffered as a result of their dictator's vain ambition. Capitulation, while Germany continued the hopeless war, had at last freed them. It was heartrending that now, on the point of libera- tion, scores of them were being murdered by their recent ally.

Paolo was told how at gunpoint the hostages were herded into trucks and driven away. The furious SS men seized anyone and everyone they could grab. His mother, he was told, had only escaped through a friend who pushed her into a doorway. For years afterward he dreamed of what might have happened if she had been taken from him.

Like his brothers, Paolo had to cope with the double standard of his mother's dual nationality. Did he want Ger- many, with Italy, to triumph? Or was the truth, as his mother quietly hinted, altogether different from the trumpeting propaganda and vainglorious utterances thrust at him by youth-group leaders and schoolteachers?

To Paolo and his brothers, their Uncle Ugo in his uni- form was a glamorous figure. He told them stories that made it seem inevitable that the combined might of Germany and Italy must eventually win. When he came to visit them from his job as political secretary of the Fascist Party, the war took on a different color. His accounts of great heroic deeds made the boys' eyes shine with wonder. But it was quite clear that their mother and father did not share these daydreams.

Who was right? Their father, Aldo, had always had a liking for the English. Grandfather Guccio lovingly recalled his days at the Savoy Hotel in London, showing unmixed admiration for the breed of Englishmen who had been his comrades, fighting alongside his countrymen in the first World War. In the family shops here in Rome, and for years before that in Florence, the elegance and wealth of visiting British society and titled aristocracy had added luster to the name of Gucci.

Now that Great Britain was gaining the upper hand in the conflict, helped greatly by the United States, now that their armies were pouring into Europe, their warplanes dominating Italian skies, Guccio Gucci saw only that the disastrous, idiotic visions of Mussolini were being, thankfully, blown away.

If Olwen's help in the escape of Allied prisoners caused the family misgivings, these did not touch the boys. They were not allowed to know what was going on. Only when the final collapse came and Uncle Ugo, shorn of his glamor, was being held in a British cage of captured Italian fascist officials, did Giorgio, Paolo and Roberto catch a glimpse of their mother's loyalty to the Gucci family.

Ugo was pleading with the family to help him, complaining that he was being ill treated and starved, lacking even the barest creature comforts. Guccio and his sons could do nothing for him, but Olwen took pity on him. She knew one of the officers guarding the camp and made a strong appeal to him on behalf of her husband's half-brother. Through her, life was made more bearable for Ugo, and eventually he was set free. Whether or not he was grateful, Ugo showed at least some of the strengths of the family by making a successful career for himself in another Italian leather firm.

Aldo's younger brothers were equally in need of help. After being drafted into the Italian wartime entertainment corps, Rodolfo had moved with the troops, playing the comedy roles he had made his mark with in early silent films and later talkies. Working with some of the better Italian and German film artists of the period, he had become infatuated with moviemaking and kept a personal record on film of his own and other achievements. In a unique full-length documentary of his life, left to his son, he hints at the difficulties of those days. There is surprisingly no mention of his sister-in-law, or of how she and Aldo saved him from some of the worst of his misfortunes.

Rodolfo had fallen on hard times. With Italy's capitulation he found himself stranded in Venice, where he had been sent with the troops. In his film he talks of being flat broke and apparently friendless, but he was still a Gucci and his family knew of his plight. Aldo persuaded Olwen to go with him to rescue his brother. They drove north in an old family Fiat motorcar that had somehow survived the war, hidden at the back of a garage. Nobody can remember how they managed to get petrol for the journey, but help probably came from Olwen's kind, priestly suppliers.

An English commander in Florence provided the necessary permit to travel across Italy, and a Welsh officer chaplain who knew Olwen went with him as safeguard. It was a hair-raising excursion, but Rodolfo was rescued by their combined efforts. They found him in a pension, when he had run up debts and was under threat of imprisonment. His career was in ruins. Aldo settled his brother's debts and together they returned to their parents, Guccio and Aida.

Vasco was all right. After a short spell in the army he was released, allowed to continue running the factory and helping the war effort as best he could. His small farm outside Florence produced vegetables, which Guccio and Aida enjoyed. He still managed to bring home game for Aida's oven. The slowdown in the business left him plenty of time for his hunting.

He was married, but his wife had suffered a miscarriage and was unable to bear children. His dispossessed son had no contact with them and they were childless. Vasco wanted to have leisure and a quiet life at a time of almost universal upheaval, and Guccio did not complain so long as his son was happy.

The final days and weeks of the war were worse than anything that had happened before. In Rome Aldo decided quite early on to shut up shop and take his family out into the country. As the war grew uglier and more ferocious he saw that it was folly to trust to the chivalrous Allied promise to treat Rome as an open city. His doubts were confirmed when American planes bombed railway marshaling yards on the outskirts and bombs fell on houses in the suburbs, killing and wounding several people. It was time to get out.

But closed shops were not what the Italian governors of the city wanted. Their duty was to show a good face to their citizens, to do everything possible to give an appearance of success. Shops, especially those such as Gucci on the fashionable via Condotti, had to keep their doors open for business.

Aldo was summoned before the city counselors and ordered to take down his shutters immediately. His family? They could stay in the country if he chose to keep them there, but the shop must reopen.

His sons were not bothered. Paolo and his brothers were enjoying their stay in the country. Too young to fight or even to put on a uniform other than the one they wore in their youth group, they had a confused notion that war was just one more restricted part of the adult world. Children, even teen-agers with a strong and confident belief in their growing strength, were excluded from it. They were happier in the country where they had stayed with their mother for some six months.

Paolo recalls: "I saw the finish of it when we got back. The Germans were pulling out of Rome. Not proud or splendid any more. They were on foot, commandeering pushcarts, anything they could get. Heading north. I heard shooting. And airplanes were diving on the roads ahead like flocks of birds, strafing I suppose. Everybody knew about Mussolini running away and being caught and strung up. His mistress had been living in the via della Camilluccia, where we went to live later on." And where Paolo's mother still lives, visited occasionally by her husband (in Paolo's words: "separated but not unmarried. He even takes her his washing!").

Rodolfo was now penniless and without a job. Grimalda was in Florence, grateful that her husband's protected occupation as a building surveyor kept him out of the firing line. And perhaps, too, that they had had no sons to sacrifice to the war. Guccio had been too old to fight.

He was also content to keep out of politics. As a merchant with two shops, one of them in the capital of the country, he had other responsibilities. For one and all, the return to peace was a joyful release.

Olwen Gucci, who had risked so much to help Allied prisoners, soldiers and airmen, to escape, was not forgotten. Roberto remembers with pride how she was treated by the liberating Allied armies. "General Alexander awarded mother a special citation to honor her work. It reads: 'This certificate is awarded to Mrs. Olwen Gucci as a token of gratitude for and appreciation of the help given to the sailors, soldiers and airmen of the British Commonwealth of Nations, which enabled them to emerge from, or evade capture by the enemy. Signed: Field Marshal, Supreme Allied Commander, Mediterranean Unit, H. R. Alexander.' Though her heart was with us in the family, my mother's loyalty to her native country had never changed."

In England Olwen's family was overjoyed to hear of her safety as the war came to an end, even more so to learn of her bravery. "We lost contact with her completely all the time it was on," her brother Ewart Price says. "The only time we heard from her was when we got a letter posted in America. It must have been brought over by one of the men she'd helped to get away."

Later, when she came home to the borders of Wales, Olwen told her family of the adventures she had had. "She and the nuns had once disguised twenty-five soldiers as peasants. They got the whole lot away in a bunch," Ewart says proudly.

Though Italy had not entered the war until 1941 and

Mussolini's capitulation brought it to an end sooner than elsewhere in Europe, these had been years—1939–1945—of privation, of upheaveal and of loss. Commercial as well as domestic life had suffered during those years. Gucci emerged with dusty and limited stock, with a shortage of staff and helpers and with little in the way of resources of any sort.

There had been hardly enough time in Rome to get established. In Florence, there was an added delay as the tide of retreating Germans gave up their hold on the country slowly and stubbornly. Guccio and Aldo faced a massive task. The cost of Mussolini's folly would have to be met.

7

RODOLFO'S RETURN

The retreating Germans and their Allied prisoners had been equally destructive, and the chaos left in their wakes was an unlikely setting for the sale of high-price, luxury goods.

The best that could be said that it represented a challenge that Aldo had fortuitously met in opening the Rome branch when he did, and for which both father and son were more than equal. It forced them to meet the demands of a trade that was hungry for good things, an influx of troops with no fighting to do and money to spend, followed increasingly by more and more visitors from countries that had suffered wartime restrictions and were now anxiously striving to make up for the lost years.

No Italian shopkeeper, least of all those like the Guccis with a living to be made from the carriage trade, could see further ahead than a few weeks at most. It was the time of the ants, when men and women stripped to bare essentials in order to rebuild their impoverished livelihoods. Assets could only be measured in terms of men, women, brain and industry. Money for merchants was less readily available.

Guccio could depend on the bank as he always had, but there was difficulty in arranging long-term loans at reasonable rates of interest. Of course, the Banco d'Italia told him sympathetically, funds could be provided against the security of buildings and trading forecasts. But naturally after such a disastrous period things would take time to settle down. Who knew what the future held in store?

Time was a commodity Guccio lacked. He was sixty-four, close to an age when the farms he had been buying before the war in the wild and lovely Castel di' Rossi district outside Florence would tempt him to retire and leave the labor of restarting the business to his sons, who had come through the conflict without even a scratch on any of them. Aldo, on whom such a large part of the weight of the business depended, had even avoided conscription into Mussolini's armed forces and had been left to carry on the business. As a family, the Guccis had been remarkably spared most of the horrors of the war.

Furthermore, Aldo's opening of the via Condotti shop in Rome, which seemed so reckless at the time, had left them better placed for a speedy recovery than many of their rivals. American troops were enjoying almost unlimited liberty in the capital. They and their officers (some with their wives) were thronging the shop, pockets bulging with seemingly inexhaustible dollars. The GIs were the least discriminating and the most generous of customers, buying anything and everything—provided it was made of genuine Italian leather and ornamental work—to take back home.

As presents for wives, sweethearts and local acquaintances, Gucci's smaller items were hard to beat. Aldo introduced a number of smaller items, accessories and ornaments. Whenever practicable he applied the "GG" symbol to add style and to "personalize" his wares. As industry recovered and life returned to normal, business in both shops was running at a healthy level.

How long it would last, nobody could guess. But the slowness of suppliers in keeping pace with the recovery was the only drawback in sight. Aldo was constantly hammering at the ones he dealt with, knowing that the revival was a race and only the fastest and fittest would survive in it.

Without Rome, Gucci would surely have been far less well equipped for the struggle. It was a period of intense competition, and Florence was taking even longer to return to its old splendor. But the chief and most frustrating enemy of progress was the corrupt and petty-minded Italian administration left in the wave of the fascist bullies.

Bureaucracy always slows things up, but military bureaucracy is many times worse. The Allied Control Commission officials behaved like overworked minor civil servants who believed that starvation would be relieved by the issue of more and more food coupons. Forms, permits, allowance regulations and returns flowed through the Gucci counting house like the Arno River so close to their door. Leather was still a controlled item vital to military and defense requirements. It took weeks, sometimes months to obtain permission for the smallest consignments of goods from old suppliers where they existed. Where they did not, as in Germany, where the devastation of Hitler's last-ditch stand had decimated industrial strength, alternatives had to be found by ingenious and exhausting means.

Aldo was not yet forty and his energy was titanic, but Vasco lacked his drive. It was Aldo, always Aldo, who had to wrestle with the problems and try to find a way around the bars and barricades. It was Aldo who had not only the energy but the vision to take all possible advantage of the postwar, GI-created boom. His first thoughts were on expansion.

Guccio opposed it. His belief was that they must first get everything in order on the home front before venturing outside to foreign cities like Paris, London and New York. He had to agree that these were where their best customers were pouring in from, that Rome had proved Aldo's contention that it was not enough to sit back and let the world come to them, that they must invade the very doorsteps of their moneyed clientele. But so much still had to be done at home, and where, he demanded, was the money to come from for these farflung schemes?

Aldo's most remarkable quality was his complete lack of economic fear. Though not a gambler in games of chance, in business he rarely bothered his head about the financial "down side" of projects. Once he had conceived and embraced them with his customary enthusiasm, the schemes seemed to him to pay for themselves. He devoutly believed that money should and would follow success, not the other way around. And now, as never before, the time had come for Gucci to spread itself across the world.

Why should his father doubt it? Let them show the banks and financiers what they were capable of by opening branches in foreign cities and winning a place in their markets. Do that, he argued, and Gucci would soon have people begging to invest in them. The markets were *there*. Aldo sensed the unending consumer demand resulting from the long years of acute war shortages, the hunger the war had created for quality goods such as Gucci made and sold. It could only be a unique opportunity.

Yet Guccio stalled. Aldo may be right, he grumbled to Aida, but what about the others? How would Vasco feel about the risk involving his position as head of the factory and a major shareholding director? Guccio already knew how Vasco felt. Anything his more adventurous and successful elder brother Aldo wanted to do he was against.

Then there was Rodolfo. He and his father had had a heart-to-heart talk. Come back into the business, Guccio advised him, forget about this play acting. If there was to be expansion (and even without Aldo's schemes the business was certainly growing fast) plenty of room would exist for another Gucci.

Now that his youngest son had rid himself of this desire to go off to Hollywood and make a fortune as a matinee idol,

Guccio felt it was time to bring him back to where he be-longed.

In the filmed biography of his life, Rodolfo glossed over his father's sensible proposals and the practical reasons he had for accepting them. It seems the life he would like re-membered is that of a successful and glamourous young Italian screen actor who not only made an impact on films but who worked with and made friends of all the major stars and producers of the period.

It is true that it was through working with her in a little known film, "Together in the Dark," one of the first "talkies," that Rodolfo met and later married a vivaciously pretty blonde Hollywood actress, Alessandra Winkelhausen, whose stage name was Sandra Ravel, and who bore his only son, Maurizio. But it is doubtful if his film career—or hers—would have supported them. Their marriage followed his return to the family fold and a seat on the Gucci board of directors in 1948.

Ugo's wartime record hardly justified branding him a war criminal, but the Allies were particularly sensitive to those who had held senior, or even modest, administrative posts in the Facist Party. It was decreed by the conquerors and ratified by the new democratic Italian government that all such persons would forfeit possessions and properties acquired as a result of their wartime activities. Ugo was officially a Gucci, Guccio and Aida's eldest son, and as such stood in direct right to succession to his father. Guccio feared that Ugo's shares in the company, due to him on his father's death, would be seized. He therefore offered to compensate Ugo with land and a large sum of money in exchange for the shares, which would then go to Rodolfo.

Ugo accepted, remarried and virtually went out of Guc-cio's life from that day. At his death in January 1974 his half-brothers sought and obtained legal ratification of Ugo's il-legitimacy, thereby making it impossible for his estate to claim any part of the Guccio fortune. Whatever the true facts of Ugo's conception were, his association with Mussolini's party was to cost him and his descendants a great deal.

But even without these family difficulties Guccio was finding it unthinkable that they should set up shop in any other country but his own. Aldo could say what he liked about the United States. His son was always ready with some reminder of American progress, of the huge wealth being created there and the unsatisfied demand for luxury-items and goods such as Gucci supplied. Guccio liked being where he was, where he could see and understand what went on.

His firmly established perch in Florence, the success of Aldo's daring Roman venture, these were far too valuable to be put at risk by mortgaging them to an unknown set of circumstances in a country that, so he had heard, prized hamburgers above pasta! Anyway, how were they to overcome the still considerable restrictions imposed on exportation? The right of merchants in the conquered nations to operate businesses, other than in their own countries, was encumbered by a forest of red tape. And Guccio doubted the victor's announced plans for encouraging their defeated foes to "get back on their feet" and become self-supporting.

Guccio's business was small, and he wanted it kept that way until it grew naturally of its own accord. Many of the ideas proposed by Aldo were, he felt, too risky, especially his belief in opening a Gucci shop in America. Some ideas he did approve, though. For instance, the creation of harmony in the lines they produced, showing there was a "Gucci concept" that linked all their products.

The idea of using a pair of linked stirrups back to back in the shape of his initials "GG" was something he was privately very proud of. That and the horsy look of many of the leather bags seemed to appeal to everyone, not only to society types who rode horses. Such products gave the shop style and class.

The colors of the stableyard and the hunting field came later, by which time Guccio had almost convinced himself that his ancestors had, in fact, been makers of courtly saddles. Bands of primary reds and greens—the same shades as flew from the nation's mastheads—were taken from girth straps. Other textiles and bamboos were designed to look like horse blankets. Still more were dyed blue and white to resemble jockeys' silks. A wide variety of ornaments in the shape or style of horse brasses and harnesses flowed through the shops to add to the image.

Later, in the 1980s Rodolfo's son Maurizio would like to shake loose of the legend but with little success. "My grandfather began the *leitmotif* of the horse. Always, everything had to do with the stable: the saddlestraps, bridles, harness and so on. His style was to suggest Old World aristocracy, which was what he lived up to in his personal life. Always the finest shirts, the most perfectly pressed clothes and so on," Maurizio said.

Pictures of the founder, proud, stout and aristocratically whiskered, suggest a merchant of supreme self-confidence who one suspects would never have approved of Maurizio's attitude toward the carefully nurtured aristocratic history of the Gucci name, his opposition to any unnecessary gilding. Nonetheless, his respect for the founder—whom he had always to address as "sir"—was in part based on yet another gilding of the facts . . . that Guccio, who was never more than a junior waiter at the Savoy, rose to become maitre d'hotel. That seems even less likely than the saddle-making story and is not to be found in the hotel's archives. Maurizio insists it is an historical truth.

"Yes, I am proud of that," Maurizio said. "But we must do away with all this kind of *noblige* about our ancestry. People today want facts. They want deeds, not words. In my own family I insist that we do not carry on as if we came from some sort of kingdom."

When publicity personnel continued to put out brochures, as they recently did, stating that the Guccis are genealogically linked to great and noble names, that Guccio started his business almost twenty years earlier than he did (when, in fact, he was a penniless shop assistant), and even that the equestrian motif was no accident of fortune but evidence of their ancient connection with courtly saddles,

Maurizio appeared to be losing the battle. No doubt he de-
plores it, but it still goes on.

"Well," Maurizio said, "people like to say, basically, that
'we are a family that comes from the Medicis.' That is, excuse
me, bullshit. It is not true. Nor must we give the impression
that we have some special right to be on top of the world. No.
The concept I believe in is that we are in the shit up to here
and we have to fight our way out."

His Aunt Grimalda apparently shared his desire to see
an end to the legend. "We always wanted the truth to come
out. My father was a great man. Aldo is a great man. We had
no need of this false history."

Nevertheless, as Aldo and his father struggled to succeed
in the postwar renaissance, the story had its place.

"I owe success to the customers who pushed us," Aldo
told British reporter Anthea Hall in the spring of 1980. "A
status symbol is not born, it becomes one when it is accepted
by a certain elite, and everyone then becomes eager to buy
it." And Aldo Gucci has not been averse to honors, perfectly
proper, that have helped to enhance his status. That goes well
with the legend he helped to create. The origin and nature of
Aldo's doctorate is unclear. According to unchallenged press
reports Florence's San Marco College awarded him a degree
for the "profitable business and reputation Gucci brought to
the city and the nation," and in June 1963 he was awarded an
honorary doctorate by the Graduate School and University
Center of the City University of New York, this time as Doctor of Humane Letters.

At the awards ceremony the school's then president, Dr.
Harold M. Proshansky, told graduates that "education . . .
has to do with values and people." Dr. Gucci, he said, had
earned his degree for "his philanthropy, and for being 'the
Michelangelo of the merchandising world.' " More modestly,
Aldo described himself to an interviewer as "number one, an
economist, number two, a philosopher."

Aldo realized that, like him, scores of fashionable merchants and manufacturers aspired to the top branches of the

marketing tree. The symbols of status, of a refined but recognizable badge of belonging to a discerning elite, were prime marketing essentials. And he temporarily suppressed expansionist aims in favor of maintaining and increasing quality and style.

Anything lacking these—an item, line or shop fitting that suggested even a hint of vulgarity or cheapness—was thrown out. The remnants of prewar wholesaling, which he had encouraged while traveling with his shoe-dealer friend in Switzerland and other European countries, were no longer suited to the new design and were dropped. The new postwar Gucci set an uncompromising standard of luxurious excellence down to its smallest detail.

Rodolfo, who had gained an addictive taste for sybaritic living and whose earnings as a film actor had for a short time been princely, shared his older brother's vision of quality and together they overrode Vasco's objections.

To Guccio, his sons' dreams may have been tempting, but they could only become reality if shown to yield profitable results. Until he could see comforting black figures in the company's books, he was suspicious of them as dangerously farfetched. Quality, he believed in. But his father's failure in the straw-hat business and the lessons he had learned in London left the seeds of doubt breeding caution. True, the wealthy London hotel guests had been remarkably profligate with their spending, but they had also been resolute in their rejection of anything they did not wish to possess and very hard to tempt with what was new and different.

However, Guccio Gucci could not deny that business was booming, and Rodolfo's return provided another lieutenant he could rely on to carry out his wishes. The strictness with which he and Aida had brought up the boys insured obedience, or so he believed. If Aldo was right, then another branch would add considerably to the already well-stuffed Gucci cash boxes. And with Rodolfo to run a new branch there would be no need for outside managers.

In Guccio's shrewd eyes, nobody could be trusted as

much as his own flesh and blood. His sad, costly experience with Ugo had not diminished that conviction. Blood was thicker than water, and it flowed where it was directed by parental influence.

Rodolfo must take the new helm, if new helm there was to be.

But not overseas, not in a foreign country. On that point Guccio was adamant. There were plenty of Italian cities opening their arms and their market places to wealthy visitors. What was wrong with those? Aldo accepted this "half loaf" as better than none at all. It was agreed that they should find a site in Milan. And Rodolfo and his new wife, the half-German blonde actress Sandra Ravel (Alessandra Winkelhausen) could manage it.

The new shop must, of course, be in the very best part of town. Ideally it should be sited in the via Monte Napoleone, as narrow and exclusive a thoroughfare as Florence's via Tornabuoni and as popular with the discerning rich of Milan as Rome's via Condotti. Furthermore, it ran parallel to the via Bagutta, which housed the internationally famous Trattoria Bagutta—the restaurant where Milan's most influential journalists and writers met and entertained, the celebrated home of the Bagutta literary prizes awarded annually.

Already the art of wooing publicity for their business (though only in the way most likely to attract the very best people) was a Gucci requisite. A beautiful new Gucci shop in this fashionable Milan street and a proximity with the Baguta would polish their image.

For the biographical film he made for his son (as a tribute, he said to Maurizio's mother) Rodolfo included film shot at Sandra's funeral. The impression is of unrelieved and irreconcilable grief at her death. Few of the family have been shown these harrowing scenes, or those that follow where Rodolfo's handsome face fills the screen, tears welling from his eyes.

For Rodolfo, turning his back on a disappointing film career (which had nevertheless become something of an ob-

session), the zest of taking charge of a glittering new establishment in one of the best neighborhoods of Milan was
sufficiently alluring to compensate for the loss of the Kleig
lights and makeup of the studio. Both he and his wife enjoyed life in the industrial city, now rapidly rebuilding itself
from the ravages of war. If he suffered pangs, they were
largely allayed when his son Maurizio was born on September 26, 1948.

Alessandra's parents, her German industrialist father
Johan and her Italian mother Marie, had separated soon
after her first meeting with Rodolfo in the film they appeared
in together. The shock of it had affected her health. Milan,
and nursing her baby who was only a year old when they
moved, proved an excellent tonic. But it was short-lived.
Alessandra died only five years later in 1954.

So it was left to Rodolfo to bring up his only son. He
proved a more than considerate father, but at times, it
seemed to others in the family, Maurizio was cosseted; at
other times the care shown for his safety and security struck
them as almost oppressive. Rodolfo never remarried, and
Guccio and Aida privately worried about the effect this
would have on their grandson. But Rodolfo showed no inclination either to find a mother for his child or to seek the
companionship of women.

One wonders, though, how this sustaining of visible private grief may have affected his son. Further, although
Rodolfo's sincerity is not in question, Paolo describes
Rodolfo's marriage as "anything but placid." Could this, too,
have had a bearing on Maurizio's upbringing? He is naturally
reticent about their lives together, but Maurizio confesses to
be going through "a period of reevaluation of my father." If
this includes Rodolfo's treatment of Sandra and hers of him,
it may help to explain his father's obsessive behavior toward
him, his only son. It could also throw light on Maurizio's
marked determination to succeed on his own.

According to Paolo, who did see them together, the
Rodolfo Guccis' married life was no bed of roses. Though

only eighteen when his Uncle Rodolfo, then thirty-seven, moved his family from Florence to Milan, Paolo says he remembers his parents talking of friction between his aunt and uncle. "She could be very fierce at times. She threw things. A very strong woman, though she was small. And my parents told me he sometimes had to sleep on the billiard table!"

Regardless of any familial strife, five years after the war the Guccis were well positioned to take advantage of profitable trade winds blowing toward and down through Italy. Gucci was in full command of his Florentine flagship, rarely bothering to make the long trips to his sons, Aldo in Rome and Rodolfo in Milan. And with four grandsons growing up he could look to the future with confidence.

The business was growing, and the family was growing with it. For the time being he had avoided the risky trend of opening new shops overseas, keeping the business in the way he liked it to be, small enough for him to know exactly what was going on where, and how much each of the three stores was taking in.

It was a contented man, bald on top of his rotund head, who drank a toast to the new decade, the fifties, at a small family ceremony to celebrate the start of the new year of 1950. He was approaching seventy. He had worked hard and lived well. Aida and he were both comfortably stout, their figures emphasizing the prosperity of their latter years. Always a neat man, Guccio now wore his gold watch-chain across an ample midriff with the air of a man who knew that, whatever was in store, the worst was over.

Gucci was on a sound business footing, and as long as there were men in the family to tend it, it should be able to hold its own against all comers. He turned to look at the third generation of Guccis, his grandsons Giorgio, Paolo and Roberto, all either in or near their twenties. These young men, his eyes told him, would surely not let him down.

And if he wanted further assurance he had only to look across the room to where his son Rodolfo was sitting with his pretty wife and their two-year-old son Maurizio. Guccis, all of them. The future, as he said raising his glass to drink to its health and prosperity, lay with them and with Guccis yet unborn. It made for a toast full of hope and warmed with family pride.

How could Guccio Gucci know that the very success he was asking the gods to bless them with would bring profound dissension as well as riches to his kin?

8

MEMENTO MORI

The early fifties was plastic money time, an age of credit, of living on loans and never putting off spending till tomorrow what you could spend today. Old values such as thrift and husbandry were discarded. Old and young alike wanted to live each minute to the full while the nuclear clock ticked in the background. If you were not wealthy enough to own a Gucci handbag or a pair of Gucci loafers, then you borrowed to buy them.

Yet Guccio remained stubbornly shy of the overseas expansion plans that Aldo, supported now by Rodolfo, pressed for. When Princess Elizabeth, soon to be queen of England, came to the shop in Florence and told the old man "we have nothing quite like this in England," he was flattered but unconvinced. After she left, Guccio confided to his son-in-law Giovanni Vitali, "I tried to avoid her. I've been told royalty never spends any money and expects you to make a present of anything they fancy." A visit by the United States' equivalent of royalty, Mrs. Eleanor Roosevelt, accompanied by film star Elizabeth Taylor, did nothing to change the old man's suspicion: "They also spent nothing!" Giovanni says, "Guccio preferred lesser people with money to spend."

But sometimes the great and the famous could be a more material asset quite apart from the publicity they brought. Jacqueline Kennedy, then America's First Lady, became a regular customer. And an even more frequent patron later when she married the so-called world's wealthiest man, Aristotle Onassis. Jackie was on hugging terms with the cuddly Guccio. Another devotee was film star Grace Kelly, even before her marriage to Prince Rainier of Monaco.

There is a story that one day Grace Kelly came to the shop in a panic, urgently in need of a last-minute gift for a friend's wedding. Did Guccio have a floral silk scarf? Gucci then had nothing floral at all. Textiles were largely restricted to canvas, burlap and coarse materials for bag linings and other hard-wearing appliances. No, but he would make her one. Which was presumably the birth of the now famous Gucci floral scarf that has since been sold to thousands all over the world.

Meanwhile in Rome Aldo was making many friends among the Hollywood film stars who came to the shops, leading to social engagements that helped to relieve the pressures of his domestic life. Though her three sons were now grown men, the youngest approaching twenty, Olwen still resisted Aldo's entreaties to join him in these visits and occasions.

Rodolfo's connection with the film world, though mostly limited to prewar Italy, was also a help. Among the earlier Gucci customers, predating the firm's opening in New York in 1953, were Bette Davis, Katharine Hepburn and Sophia Loren. The Italian star Anna Magnani, who had been a close friend of Rodolfo since her first film *Alone at Last*, in which he played a penniless womanizer, also became a steady customer. The goods Gucci made and sold had no substantive need of the allure these glamorous customers gave them— they had earned a deserved reputation for staying power—

but international names were increasingly setting styles for others to follow.

And in due course Guccio gave in. "All right," he reportedly told Aldo after one of their most heated discussions, invariably accompanied by energetic arm waving, "you and Folfo [Rodolfo] may be right. After all, I am an old man and old-fashioned enough to believe that you don't have to go abroad into foreign countries where God knows what sort of cutthroats and crooks are waiting to skin you alive, in order to grow good potatoes. The best vegetables come from your own garden. Risk your necks if you must, but don't expect to do it on my money. Go to the bank, see if they'll risk their necks with you!"

And then once again Guccio made sure that the bank would back the project, privately underwriting his sons' scheme.

Aldo, the entrepreneur of the two, did the spadework while his younger brother stayed in Milan. Aldo's first target was Paris, the chic and fashionable rue de Rivoli. Then he had his eyes on London's Bond Street. Money? Yes, it would cost, but wait and see, he told his reluctant father, what it will bring. There was also no problem about stretching himself too thin; his eldest son, Giorgio, was already in the business and doing well, and his second son, Paolo, would soon be coming to join him.

He could let go of the controls for the time it would take to find and rent the right sites, staff them, train the sales assistants in the essentials drilled into him by Guccio that "the customer, right or wrong, is always right" and attend to the launching of the stores. He had to be on the site to do it. Nobody else knew so much detail. Nobody else could so drill and charm and bully the smart-looking young men and women who stood behind the plate-glass display cabinets that had taken the place of counters in Gucci shops. Nobody else could pick them with such astuteness as Aldo did. And Giorgio was conforming nicely to the pattern his father set for all his sons, dutifully learning the business from the bottom up; Roberto was still young but showing obedience (that in his brothers' eyes sprang from fear of his all-powerful father).

But Aldo, caught up in his own busy schedule, did not notice that his middle son, Paolo, was already showing an independence of spirit that would alter the entire face and future of Gucci.

Like every other Gucci, and in time their wives and children, Paolo was expected to lend a hand whenever necessary for the business. In Florence as a small boy he ran errands for his father and grandfather. When they moved to Rome and lived "over the shop" in the via Condotti, taking parcels to hotels and the houses of their more important customers was a service he and his brothers were expected to do. By his late teens Paolo had begun to resent this role.

"I remember one day particularly. The shop was very busy and I was having to help out. In the ordinary day I wouldn't have been allowed to deal directly with customers, but all the sales staff had their hands full at the time. A man came in urgently wanting a suitcase. 'See to him,' I was told. I'd never sold anyone a handbag, let alone a suitcase, in my life. But I did know that some of our cases had hangers already inside and I thought I was being smart when I asked the customer, 'Do you want a *full* suitcase?'

"He stared at me. Was I trying to be funny? Of course I should have explained, but I was too embarrassed. I said nothing, which only made things worse. In the end, faced with my dumb flushed face, he said angrily, 'Why? Are you going to fill it up with clothes?' I felt a complete fool."

Paolo was young and proud. The often patronizing way in which sales assistants were treated by wealthy customers upset him. Clients were to be paid homage as if they were tin gods. And in Gucci, where a prince or a prima donna might sweep into the shop at any minute, an air of deferential subservience was de rigueur. "It was expected that I and my brothers should go into the firm as soon as we were old enough, but I didn't want to. The whole idea of spending my life as a shopkeeper, a retailer, went against the grain. Why should I? Giorgio was already working quite happily for my father and telling me I was stupid to have ideas 'above my station.' And I knew that my younger brother, Roberto, would do what the family wanted him to do. We called him 'the priest.' I felt I could do better for myself than sell shoes and handbags for the rest of my days."

To prove it he applied for a job with the British airline BOAC, which had offices in Rome. The job was in India, which seemed to offer both a chance to see the world—he had heard that airline personnel were given cheap travel everywhere—and an exotic life in a country out of reach of his family.

"I might have got it, too. But I was also enjoying myself at the time. There were plenty of beautiful girls in Rome, and I used to go to the cinema and watch out for one I might strike up an acquaintance with. If I couldn't pick her up right away, and I was quite shy, I'd follow her when we left the cinema and try to get her to say hello. Quite often she'd let me see her home, and in a small way I was becoming quite a Don Juan."

Rome in the fifties had something of the wild abandonment caught by Frederico Fellini in his film *La Dolce Vita*. Paolo found it an ideal playground: A long evening spent in a café on the via Veneto was as exciting as watching the romantic film performances of Hollywood movie stars. With a woman and a glass of wine, it was even better. He had only to keep an eye on the paparazzi photographers on their Vespas to know where everyone famous was spending the evening. He was star-struck, even if sometimes it meant staying out until the early hours to catch a glimpse of a celebrity, and rising late was a habit he found difficult to break.

On the morning when he was supposed to turn up for an interview with the airline he made the mistake of lying in bed until after the time it was due to take place. As a result his reception when he turned up was negative. The post was filled. "Or maybe it wasn't—anyway, they weren't very pleased. I was almost thrown out." There was nothing for it but to go to his father and tell him he needed a job.

"My father," Paolo says, "could be an earthquake and this time he blew his top. 'You silly fool,' he shouted at me. 'Why the hell are you looking for something else? This is your fortune. This is what you were born to do.' So for a salary which was only glorified pocket money I joined the firm."

It was 1952. Paolo could hardly have selected a more important and auspicious moment in the firm's and the family's chronology. His father was in top gear, at the peak of his power, his new branches sprouting under his firm hand like healthy seedlings. More than ever convinced that they must not confine their activities to the European continent, Aldo was again pressing Guccio to consider his plans to open in New York. "That is where the real money is," he insisted. "Our future is there." And, privately, he was searching for ways of crossing the Atlantic with or without his stubborn parent's approval or backing.

He had met an American lawyer named Frank Dugan who had every confidence in the project and who encouraged Aldo to make the move himself, whatever his father said. "We'll find the money," he said, "and with your track record the banks will fall over themselves to stake you. Gucci in New York? They'll lap it up."

Dugan offered to go with Aldo and set up a corporation in New York—Gucci Shops Incorporated. Grimalda and her husband recall that "Aldo went over without anyone from the family at first. He did it on his own. Then when Rodolfo and Vasco made the trip with him to open the first shop just off Fifth Avenue, Guccio got to hear of it."

Guccio was, or pretended to be furious. A cable from Florence informed his sons that they were acting like damned fools. A hint, or threat, reminded them that he wasn't dead yet. And their inheritance was in jeopardy if they insisted on pursuing these wild schemes that could ruin them all.

Aldo shrugged off the threat, but he did not realize how close they all were to that inheritance. Guccio and Aida were enjoying the respect that success had brought them. In Florence very few merchants could match the growth and profitability of Guccio's growing empire. "Oh, you don't get there without taking chances," the old man would tell his envious contemporaries. "You see, when I set my mind to it, I will risk all on a venture. That is why we have got where we have."

And Aida, sipping her vermouth, would nod appreciatively. "Your sons, Guccio," she would remind him. "And, of course, my sons," he would beam. How lucky he was to have sired such a family. But without him, would they ever have taken such risks?

Well, they were taking plenty of them now. New York, four thousand miles away, was far from his orbit. He did not understand its customs, its people or the strange way they used the English language. Persuaded to make one visit, he found it all too much for him. But Aldo seemed to thrive there. The excitement of the city heightened his zest for life. There was no doubt that the new shop, though only small, was well chosen.

Guccio came back to Florence content that the company Aldo had formed was worthy of Gucci. He could relax and he did. He was almost as fond of the movies as his grandson Paolo. It pleased him to see the great films made by Italian directors of the period in which poor men rose above their circumstances, as he had done. Films like "Open City" and "Four Steps in the Clouds" delighted him. He was looking forward to seeing one of them in the best cinema in Florence when he went to wash his hands in the bathroom for lunch on a summer's day in 1953. Aida, going to see why he was taking so long, found him dead. The doctor said his heart had stopped like an old watch.

"A fantastic death," Maurizio says. "And perhaps a good

time to die. He had seen his dream accomplished. To a large extent, anyway. And he died before all the troubles in the family that followed his death."

The old man had indeed picked a good moment. He was not by some standards fabulously wealthy. "No, but he was worth a million dollars," Maurizio says proudly. To the ex-stoker, dishwasher, waiter it had been more than enough to justify an existence of unremitting hard work. All his life Guccio Gucci had held to the rigid standards he set himself. He demanded no less from his offspring. "If he had lived to see his son Aldo in jail it would have upset him dreadfully," says his son-in-law, Giovanni. "Even a fine would have appalled him."

Grandfather Guccio never saw Gucci blood spilled by blood relations, or the costly, bitter vendetta dividing his grandchildren. "The shame of it would have killed him," Grimalda believes. But in her husband Giovanni's opinion, there was also the possibility that Guccio had been more than usually worried. "Guccio's factory had been visited by tax men a few days before he died, and I'm sure that had upset him very much. He could not bear to be under suspicion and any suggestion that he was not scrupulously honest would have struck him to the heart." True or not, it was his heart that killed him.

At his funeral his three sons and their sister shared a moment of sad reflection. Had they done all they might have done to reward this stern but strongly provident father? He had given them, in their separate ways, a business ladder to climb to almost certain lifelong success and plenty. He had also left them a spiritual legacy that could never be undervalued. He had taught them, whether or not they enjoyed the lesson, or appeared to accept the teaching, to consider others beside themselves, to expect no more from the human race than they contributed to it. As their thoughts turned from their grief to the future, which now belonged to them with all its risks as well as its bounty, the children of Guccio Gucci fully realized what a truly remarkable parent they had lost.

It is likely a certain relief, too, was excusably in their private thoughts as they stood around the open grave in the Roman Catholic cemetery in Florence. Their father had long barred the way to an advancement that could secure glittering fortunes for them all. "But in the end he had given in," Grimalda remembers. "He had lived to see that Aldo's ideas were not so crazy, after all."

Aldo's hands were now free. He had lost a parent he respected and loved, but he now had unfettered control over the business he had increasingly been taking hold of since those first days in the little shop in Florence, when it had been touch and go whether they would be able to pay their workmen their wages.

Vasco was wondering how he would now fare in the boardroom battles. With Guccio's death he had lost the one authority who had never turned a deaf ear to his pleas for caution. His bank balance was growing nicely and he was enjoying life with his childless wife, Maria. There was plenty of time for his favorite sport of hunting, and the work at the factory was not too arduous.

Indeed, he was finding a talent for design that he had not known he had. His creation of new lines was unrestricted by formal training or policy planning. Gucci had no set theme in those days. the whole direction being impromptu. So if Vasco came into his office in the morning with an idea in the back of his head, he could sketch it roughly, hand it to one of his draftsmen, and it would then go immediately into production.

Paolo, who was later put to work under his uncle in the factory, remembers it as "total, unplanned chaos. Nothing was checked in advance or test-marketed. We just went ahead and shoved the new line in the windows. At one time we had hundreds of handbags, all different."

To Rodolfo, Gucci's departure could best be described as a mixed blessing. "My father was a very special kind of person" is almost his sole comment on their relationship in his revealing (as much for what it leaves out as for what it depicts in its two-and-a-half hours of rather self-indulgent screen time) biographical film. "He always seemed slightly aloof, severe. But at the right moment he was close to his children. And, of course, he was the force that had maintained and protected them."

In the same sequence of the film, Rodolfo refers to his brothers' "delight" at his having returned to the family business. There is no mention of his rescue from dire straits in Venice by his brother Aldo and his wife, Olwen.

No suggestion that receiving the same share of the equity in the expanding business as Aldo and Vasco was a gift of considerable generosity.

Grimalda today puzzles over her father's generosity toward Rodolfo. "Aldo did everything for the company. Everything. All the others ever did was make difficulties for him. Even father opposed him because he thought the shops in Milan and Rome would make the business too big. Yet he gave Rodolfo the same as he gave Aldo. I don't understand it. And Giovanni, her husband, echoes her. "It was only Aldo's strength that built Gucci up."

As for the grandchildren who attended the funeral, Paolo could already see that there was a disproportion in the amount his father and his uncles put into the day-to-day running of the company. Yet they were equal shareholders. "Vasco was so negative, my father always had to persuade him to adopt any new tactic. Uncle Rodolfo was different. Everything Aldo did Rodolfo had to do. If my father bought a house, he had to have one like it. He was like the crown prince while my father, the elder brother, was the king."

In one most important way Guccio's death freed the house of Gucci from a major hindrance. Guccio, on his own visit to New York, had refused to agree to Aldo's request that they should buy the building now famous as Van Cleef and Arpel's fashionable jewelry store next door to the great Bergdorf Goodman store on Fifth Avenue. "Not now," Guccio had insisted. "Maybe in two years' time when we see how things are doing over here."

So instead of this fine building, with Frank Dugan, the lawyer, Aldo had formed the American company with only a small shop in the Sherry Netherland Hotel and another on Fifty-Eighth Street on the site now occupied by the General Motors Building. If he was right, and experience taught him that his instinct was reliable, then they had to move and expand quickly, or copies of their type of luxury-goods store would spring up like mushrooms in this wide-awake hungry city. This was not war-torn Italy; the Americans were aggressive dealers, quick decision-makers and daring gamblers with anything new in which they put their faith. Aldo had been depressed for so long by his father's rejection of what seemed a perfect opportunity to stay ahead of the game. Now he could do as he wished. It was doubtless a heady feeling.

9

NEW GENERATION

merica in the early fifties was as ready for Gucci as
Gucci was primed for America. Many Americans had
accumulated vast wealth during the war. The nation had
become a consumer society and the wealthy among them
were now climbing over each other to spend for status and
elegance. Gucci, by the very nature of its products, fitted the
demand like a fine leather glove.

New Yorkers in particular, it seemed, craved what had
been unobtainable or difficult to get in the U.S.A.

There was a rage for possessing at nearly any cost the
top-quality workmanship of ancient Europe. While California boasted of leading the world in innovative technical
design and production, and Detroit's automated assembly
lines rolled big American cars onto the highways of the
world, the people who profited from such things, the new
millionaires, were eager for quality marks of status to spend
their money on.

Which is not to say that Aldo found the going easy. His

early days in this unfamiliar city were teaching him that Yankee success was not just an elusive, overnight phenomenon. One word of dislike or complaint from any of the rich fashion trendsetters and the chic "GG" colophon could become a badge of disgrace. His wiles and charms notwithstanding, Aldo was on a tightrope that called for every last ounce of his skill and dexterity.

The small company he had set up with Frank Dugan in the Sherry Netherland Hotel had only limited capital. Dugan, an ex–police detective chief's son, had a rough-edged, down-to-earth way with him that was an ideal at once counterpart and complement to Aldo's Latin theatricality. Americans tended to be suspicious of foreign-sounding exotics. They preferred putting their money into something solid. As his son Paolo recalls, "Aldo was the force but Dugan opened the doors."

It helped, too, that Aldo had found a new and unusually lovely companion. He and Olwen were separated in every sense but that of the law. Having been married in England, it was the divorce law of the United Kingdom that had to be observed. Olwen refused to submit to it, maintaining her right to remain firmly resident in the grand house in Rome that Aldo had bought and, according to Paolo, had put in her name.

Aldo was now spending weeks at a time in America and was able to bring over personnel from Italy to staff the New York shop. His new favorite, the most long-lasting of a succession of ladies attracted to New York by job prospects, was Bruna Palumbo, who had the raven-haired, soulful-eyed looks of film star Gina Lollabrigida. Aldo had first seen her in the Rome shop, where she had been hired by his manager. When he offered her the job in New York, it was said that Aldo had found another companion.

There were others as well. One was Alexandra Murkoska, a slight, attractive Polish girl with soft, curling fair hair and baby-blue eyes. Her introduction to the firm of Gucci was perhaps less formal than Bruna's or any of the

other assistants. Alexandra had the luck to be picked by
Rodolfo in Milan after asking him for a job when she could
not speak a word of Italian. (Her name also happened to be
the same as his dead wife.) "I didn't know what I was getting
into," she says now. "Luck? I wouldn't call it that exactly."

This was at a time when Aldo's international experiment
was still at its testing stage, long before Maurizio grew old
enough to take a part in the business and personally redesign
the premises. He was still at school, still working under
Rodolfo's firm "guidance" to qualify for a place in the university. Alexandra apparently felt sorry for him; "Poor kid!
When he came home from school he was expected to work in
the shop, learning the business, often until nine at night. And
on Sundays he dressed the windows. No wonder he got to
university, he *had* to do well."

She herself found the job with Gucci under Rodolfo's
demanding hand a difficult experience. "It was terribly hard,
and I had to learn the whole thing from the bottom up. Six
days a week from nine till eight, and then I'd volunteer to
help on Sundays when we cleared out the shop. I could never
do it again, and at the time I told myself, 'This has got to be
for something.' "

Aldo came regularly to Milan in between flying to and
from the States. "I had seen him in the board meetings that
they had twice a year, and at other times with his father and
so on. I'd found him very attractive. He was the driving force
in the company, there was nobody like him. Rodolfo could
never have done what he did. He was always telling journalists, 'We did it together.' Bullshit! Aldo was the creative
one of the two."

Alexandra blames Rodolfo for the later rivalry among
the brothers and their sons. "Aldo never wanted it. Rodolfo
had to be the one who had the majority with him all the
time." Working for Aldo was apparently altogether different.
"He asked me one day, 'How would you like to come and
work for me in New York? I need somebody like you.' When I
arrived it was more that I could have dreamed of. Fabulous.

"Aldo and Rodolfo were alike in some ways, but very

different in how they treated those who worked for them. In New York Aldo arranged everything for me. I went first-class everywhere as a senior Gucci executive. I had an apartment and one of the staff to meet me when I went on trips. But nobody gets all that for nothing."

Her work was showing results, and she pushed the shop to move in several new directions. Alexandra, in her twelve years with the company, claims to have laid down a basic Gucci strategy that had previously never existed. "Everything in the past had been done on impulse, with no proper planning. I changed all that," she says.

Not, however, without resistance. "They switched their minds all the time, but you had to ride it. There was always another day, another project." She was becoming involved in the intimate affairs of the business through her close friendships with Aldo and, when she was in Italy or he paid rare visits to New York, with Rodolfo. So close to them both, she saw firsthand the cancer of jealousy growing between the brothers.

"God knows, I have seen fights I didn't even know what they were about. Maybe it was because I'd said I'd be at some place with Aldo, then go somewhere with Rodolfo. I really went through hell, because they had their own priorities. And things like that were very important to them. For someone who was not Italian, it could be appallingly difficult. I'd ask, 'What on earth are you fighting about?' It seemed they'd fight over the smallest thing."

The brothers tried to take out their intense competitiveness in high-speed dashes on the Italian motorways. "They had to get ahead of everyone on the road. I've had some hair-raising rides with them, I can tell you! Aldo used to say that he could make Florence from Rome [180 miles] in under two hours and I'm sure it was true, though I was too scared to watch the clock." But their personal difficulties were more deeply rooted. "In every family there is rivalry as well as love," Alexandra says. "The Kennedys are an example. It is not exceptional."

Nor was it unusual for two brothers in a highly successful family, both fired by dynamic Latin temperament, to rival one another in the inevitable buildup of separate empires and power structures. Aldo was less interested in titles and authority, partly because he was pretty much the unchallenged Atlas of the company, bearing the weight of Gucci worldwide on his shoulders. Rodolfo was striving for the same position, though his privately filmed biography presents him as a man whose one wish was to return to the rustic pleasures of the countryside, "the sweet solitude he loved so much."

A more revealing section of the narrative suggests that Rodolfo was not unaware of the looming conflict in his family's affairs. "Our fathers passed away with the assurance of having bequeathed us their fortunes, small or large as they may have been. They never knew that after them everything they believed in was to be questioned, which underlines the dubious value of an unearned inheritance." Some in the family have expressed the rather uncharitable view that the trouble was more rooted in Rodolfo's dislike of having had to descend to shopkeeping after his years as a film actor of some note.

His sister Grimalda seems especially harsh: "He was the one who got the best out of the situation. He managed to end up with fifty percent of the company after coming back from the war penniless. Before that he had never done anything for the business."

It was an opinion shared by Paolo, Aldo's son. "Rodolfo was getting his feet under the table in Milan while my father was doing all the work," Paolo says. "My uncle spent most of his time in his sumptuous villa in St. Moritz, the finest in the place. After being a movie actor, getting into an office at five past nine! That wasn't his style. When my father tried to persuade him to open a shop there in St. Moritz he always found some excuse. My father would have opened a shop from the back of a lorry, but not my Uncle Rodolfo."

True or not, there seems a certain coloration in Rodolfo's filmed life story as it treats his departure from show business to enter the family firm. "With a touch of regret he turned his back on the whole business, despite the offers that kept coming in . . . Rodolfo returned to dusting showcases, to selling bags, purses in the old store on via della Vigna Nuova." Grimalda knew nothing of such sacrifice of acting roles. She says: "When he left Venice he didn't have a bean. He was waiting for film scripts and roles that never arrived. His wife (Rodolfo and Alessandra Winkelhausen were married in Venice on July 16, 1944) said, 'We are Guccis, and we demand the right to live with the family and be part of the family.' It made Aldo so mad he gave his brother a slap across the face in one row they had, but they still clung on. They wouldn't leave until my father sent them to Milan, to the new shop there."

What Alexandra Murkoska was witnessing at first hand, and in close proximity to them both, was a struggle that could only damage the roots of the Gucci tree. Rodolfo's son was still at school. However much his father protected him, while sternly insisting on hours of "learning" duties in the shop, Maurizio could not enter the business until the late sixties. Meanwhile Aldo's three sons were maturing swiftly in various parts of the Gucci empire. Roberto and Giorgio both followed their father to New York for brief periods. Paolo was at work in the factory under Vasco's tolerant eye.

Aida had followed Guccio soon after his death. Roberto, Aldo and Vasco each inherited a like amount of shares, and their combined court actions prevented any claim by Ugo, their half-brother. Apart from Vasco's illegitimate offspring, the chips were evenly stacked. Whether, in view of their differing inputs to the business, they were stacked fairly was to be a source of lasting contention. Grimalda had expected to inherit a part of the business, which she had helped her father to create and build up. When she found there was no share coming to her, the blow was apparently as much to her pride as to her pocket. "Father had died so suddenly," she says, "that it was some time before I realized that I was to have no part in the business in spite of everything my father had led me to expect."

Guccio, she maintains, had informed her that he had put fifty percent of the shareholding of the company before he died in the names of his three sons. "He told me that they would have these free of death duties. I thought another forty percent was to be divided equally among the four of us." Presumably the additional ten percent was to remain in his widow's possession during her lifetime.

Grimalda realized that there were to be no shares for her when Aldo and the others excluded her from the running of the business. "When I saw I wasn't going to get my share, I tried to appeal to them. They wouldn't listen. I'd had nothing to do with the running of the company, they said, so I wasn't entitled to any of it. Eventually, I had to call in a lawyer."

He gave Grimalda the impression that she had a right to an inheritance. "Whereas all I had had was a small farmhouse, standing on above eleven hectares of land [about twenty-seven acres], and a sum of money, about twelve million lira, I think it was. My brothers had my parents' villa and much more land and so on." On the lawyer's advice she again appealed to her brothers. "They once more refused to listen to me. We ended up in court."

Her old eyes seem to cloud with pain as she tries to remember the outcome. "That day in the civil courtroom, here in Florence, was very confusing. The court procedure was strange to me. I did not understand what was going on. My brothers, Vasco and Aldo were asked by the judge, a Signor Pedata, 'Is this your sister?' They told him who I was and he said, in quite a casual sort of way, 'And I understand that you and your sister have reached an agreement. Is that so?' They nodded. Vasco, I remember, said 'Of course we have.' He smiled at me. And I took it that they were agreeing to give me my rightful inheritance. Then Judge Pedata turned to me and asked 'Do you agree, Signora Vitali?' I was so shocked, I nodded. 'Yes,' I said."

With that "yes" Grimalda apparently lost all chance of asserting moral right to any share in the Gucci business firm. She describes her horror when her lawyer told her what she had done and that it was not worth her taking it any further. "My acceptance had made it virtually impossible for me to gain anything more than they had given me by way of compensation for being left out of the business. Whereas what I really wanted was a part in the development of the company I'd seen grow from nothing."

The experience left her embittered for years. "I had not understood what was going on. And I was so fond of my brothers . . . I didn't want to take them to court. The night before the hearing I asked Aldo to come and settle matters with my lawyer and me in private, so that we would not have to go through all that. He said he would come. I waited until nine o'clock but he never arrived."

Yet when they meet today they seem as warmly devoted as ever. "I happened to run into Aldo in the street the other day and we both flung our arms around each other. Of course I will always love them." Which of the three does she blame? "All were equally responsible." And then, with a hint of her old bitterness, "My brothers are a bunch of shopkeepers."

Aldo probably would not have denied that last. He was flying between Europe and the United States with increasing regularity. In the States he was always on the go, bringing over his sons to help set up the first shop in New York while he went in search of new sites, new areas for expansion. At the same time he and his attractive companions were moving freely among the café-society celebrities whose nightly parties and flirtations were reported daily in Cholly Knickerbocker's, Walter Winchell's, and Leonard Lyons' newspaper gossip columns. It was a heady time, but while Aldo managed to play hard he worked harder.

Initially, to give him assistance, he brought over his twenty-one-year-old youngest son, Roberto. "I opened the first boutique at Seven East Fifty-Eighth Street," Roberto remembers. "It was November 1953, a fabulous time to be there, not just in business but for the whole life-style in general. In those days one felt part of the history of New York, which you no longer feel." Nevertheless, either the pace of Manhattan life or of working so closely with his exhaustingly dynamic father proved too wearing for him. After a brief spell Roberto went back to Italy. Three years later, in February 1956, he married his Italian wife, Drusilla Cafferelli, now the mother of their six children, one of whom has become a nun.

Aldo gave each of his sons experience in the very different style and scale of American marketing techniques. Paolo was still at his factory job, where he was dabbling in design and establishing himself as perhaps the most creative member of the family. He, too, was well aware of his father's demanding personality. "He surrounded himself with people who did his bidding. They had to do what he told them. 'Get my hat, get my coat . . .' Lawyers would be told, 'I am the client, you work for me.' And the wages he paid his sons . . . it was not altogether surprising that they found it easier back home."

By now Paolo had been married and fathered two daughters. His wife, Yvonne Moscetto, whom he married in 1952, was one of the young ladies he had followed home from a movie house. When she became pregnant it had taken Paolo five days to get the courage to face his father, who advised them to marry. Their daughter Elisabetta was born that same year, and Patrizia was born in 1954. But the marriage lasted only a few years. The couple, according to Paolo, "separated by mutual consent." Aldo then agreed to guarantee alimony payments. Nevertheless, Paolo says he had no great wish to leave Florence and the factory for New York and life under his father's thumb.

Aldo, he felt, was reacting excessively to the stress of running the now widely spread business. He seemed nearly obsessive about cooking and the cleanliness of restaurant tables. "If a waiter brought a dish he didn't like he would ask to see the chef. And when he came, all smiles, expecting a tribute, my father would ask him, 'Have you ever been on a farm?' If he had, my father would thrust the plate of food under the man's nose. 'You know what they give pigs to eat.' "

The eldest, Giorgio, followed Roberto to New York. But Giorgio, too, found New York less agreeable than working in Rome, close proximity to his whirlwind father perhaps making Rome seem preferable. In Giorgio's case, however, there were other forces pulling him back to Italy. His mother, Olwen, was increasingly alone, Aldo cut off from her in all but name, her sons now seldom at home for long. Giorgio was a devoted son who continued to spend as much of his time as possible with his mother, later taking her to his beautiful villa in Porto Santo Stefano for holiday visits, partially making up for his father's absence. As with the children of most broken marriages, Aldo's sons were having to choose between being close to their mother or their father. If they chose Aldo, then they had to accept his way of life, leaving little room to live their own lives. But Aldo's way promised power, wealth, fame.

The choice was not an easy one.

10

REBELLION

Alone since his wife's early death, Rodolfo was spending more and more time in his millionaire's villa in the Swiss mountains, skiing and relaxing with his only son. His greatest fear was that the child might be kidnapped or taken from him. The teen-age youth was never far from his father's sight without constant bodyguards. If Maurizio wanted to ride his bicycle down the little-used Swiss roads, his father's chauffeur had to follow closely in a motorcar insuring that no traffic threatened to approach too closely.

In summer Maurizio roamed his father's open farmland among the cattle and goats, but always under his father's watchful eye. And if Rodolfo's protection gave Maurizio the claustrophobic impression of being locked inside a silken cage, his father's lectures made it plain that he was no ordinary youth. His destiny was, one day, to take a leading place, perhaps the leading place, in Guccio Gucci S.p.A. (Societa per Azzioni).

At school the other boys' talk about their exploits and

holidays made him wonder why his father treated him so differently. As he says, "Yes, sure, he both overprotected and made me work hard. Which was his way of making me see that I had to fulfill a dual role in life, on the one hand dedicating myself to a full-time job and on the other of having the privilege of wealth and position."

Maurizio was expected to work in the shop during his only free time from high school, sometimes all weekend. "It seemed fantastic to me at the time, I lost a lot of my youth. My friends had far more to live for, or so it seemed, than I did. I didn't go out at night, or have time to enjoy myself. Because of that, it has since been difficult for me to have relationships. My friends often seem to be talking a different language. And now I realize what it was all about. I shall not treat my own children that way. But I honestly don't know if what my father did was right or wrong. If you ask me would I want to change it, I would say no. I didn't have many good times then, but those who did don't enjoy today. I do, very much."

According to Alexandra Murkoska, Maurizio's sympathy for his father's spartan treatment only came with advancing years. "His father was mean with Maurizio, and of course he resented it. Who wouldn't? At his private school most of the other boys were given super cars by their fathers, Maseratis, Porsches and Ferraris. Maurizio was only given a tiny car and he had to be in strictly at nine o'clock every evening."

The car, Maurizio remembers ruefully, was hardly a gift. "I had to wait for it until I was eighteen, and even then I had to pay for half of it myself."

To many, Maurizio's plight might seem that of a spoiled boy, but this was a special world. He was in his second year at Milan university, studying for a law degree and specializing in economics, when he made his first trip to New York. He was later to spend seven years learning that side of the business, working closely under Aldo's firm and, reportedly, sometimes heavy hand. At the time he was fascinated by his uncle's approach to people, so different from that of his rather more patrician father. "The difference between my father and my uncle was that my uncle was a marketing man, a developer. He was the one who handled the expansion side. He had a completely different influence on everyone. Very human, sensitive and creative. He was the one, in fact, who was building up everything in the company, and I saw how he was able to establish rapport with the people he worked with as well as the customers. What fascinated me most was how different he was from my father, who was an actor in everything he did. My uncle wasn't playing a part, it was the real thing with him."

Less than three years in age separated Aldo from Rodolfo, and in matters of work Guccio had not favored one son over another. Both had known the hard times of the early days in Florence, when money in the Gucci household was short and their father merely a poorly paid sales assistant in a shop. "Day after day my parents would wander through the streets looking for inspiration," Rodolfo's film script records. "Any idea to help end their humiliating poverty."

Aldo apparently did not feel their poverty so keenly. "My father was unable to plan ahead," he once said. "We had to do it for him. Adventure was not in his spirit." The question now was how much of these qualities lay in the temperament of his sons and nephew. And whether they would give him the same backing and support he had given Guccio, his father.

Giorgio and Roberto clearly seemed to want to. But Aldo's middle son, Paolo Gucci, was taking stock of the way the business was being run. His criticism of the "ad hoc" methods used since Grandfather Guccio's day was beginning to upset his uncle in Milan. Paolo felt that without his father the business could never have reached its position as one of the world's top makers of luxury goods. He also felt that his Uncle Rodolfo would not have achieved what he did without his father's dynamic chairmanship.

But Paolo also believed that both his father and his uncle were living in the past, that they were locked into antiquated methods of production and design, a subject for which he had a definite flair. Being either blessed or cursed with curiosity, he had not been working long in the business before he began to be critical of the company's productivity and about the Gucci concepts of marketing and planning. Paolo had his own ideas about these matters and was eager to have those ideas heard and implemented.

In a reflective moment in his film history, Paolo's uncle Rodolfo noted prophetically, "Even while I savored the calm, joyful life that revolved around me, I was aware how fragile and uncertain the most tranquil family happiness could be. And I wondered how long it would last." He, more than anyone, was in the position to doubt that it could outlast his generation, what with his talented and impatient nephew pressing those in command to move with the times as he saw them.

Meanwhile Aldo's investment in America continued. Gucci stores were opened in Chicago, Philadelphia, San Francisco, Beverly Hills and Palm Beach in a drive to satisfy a nationwide American demand for the company's luxury products.

The old factory in the via Caldaie in Florence was working to capacity. Housed in an architectural gem, a red brick two-story palazzo, no expansion was possible. Frequently the staff was overwhelmed by the orders flowing across the Atlantic, and although hundreds of part-time workers were sub-contracted to cope with the flood, delays and backups were increasing. Something had to be done, and in 1967 the firm acquired a site in the Sandicci area on the outskirts of the city.

Grimalda's husband, Giovanni, was commissioned to supervise the construction of an ultra-modern factory occupying some 150,000 square feet, and it was from here that Paolo, appointed head of design by his father, was paying critical attention to his older relatives' methods and finding them far from satisfactory.

Quite often he would come to the office in the morning

to find that one of his uncles had commissioned an entirely new line of products without consulting him. In the time-honored way of the family, everyone in authority did as he felt inclined or prompted to do without mentioning it to the others. There were meetings, held whenever the three brothers happened to be in the same city or place at the same time. But often these were casual affairs, more concerned with the cash flow and new tax laws than product lines, quality control and stock. In Paolo's view the business had no method for planning for the future. If a line ran out it was either discontinued or, if demand for it persisted, delayed while a further batch was reordered.

"My Uncle Rodolfo thought himself to be a master of organization, which in fact he had no conception of. What he did do was give orders left and right, changing his mind from one day to the next. Then he'd blame the result on his advisers."

If Paolo had shared his brother Roberto's mild temperament he would have accepted his uncle until he was in a strong enough position to challenge him. Instead, with less experience in the business than Rodolfo, he felt justified in questioning and rejecting.

"I was constantly rebelling. The whole way of running things seemed to me to be inefficient and old-fashioned. There were these clever advisers of my uncle telling me what I should and shouldn't do, on his authority. I wouldn't accept those ideas coming from people hired by him. Why should I? My opinion of my uncle was that he was a good actor, but as a businessman . . . He'd been smart enough to surround himself with good people, but he was no leader. My father, on the other hand, was a born leader with rubbishy advisers."

The biggest area of disagreement was not, however, administrative. Paolo says he wanted to secure Gucci's future through licensing. This would mean offering select merchandisers the right to sell Gucci products in return of an annual license fee to the company for doing so, thereby adding to the volume of Gucci-made product sales. Both his father and his uncle opposed this. "But Uncle Rodolfo, whom I called 'Folfo, the big bad wolf,' was the one who was most vehemently against it. He refused all such forms of expansion."

Paolo dared to question the company's share-structure. "Yes, and that made him furious with me too. I pointed out that we were a family business. He should have known that, since it was the family that had provided him with everything he now had. But, as I said, the shares and benefits in it were anything but fairly apportioned. Like my brothers, I had only three-and-a-third percent against his fifty. Was that fair? I told him, 'How can you guarantee full cooperation and collaboration with such an uneven balance? It can't be done. You can say, as in *La Traviata*, "Let's go? To the battle!" and nobody moves.'"

"And at the end of the day, when you sit down to eat, who gets the leg of the chicken? We were supposed to share in the cooking, so why not the bird? On top of which, as I pointed out, perhaps I could live with the position indefinitely, having only just had my second child, another daughter. But we had members of the family, like my brother Roberto, with five, six and seven sons. How could he share equally with all of them? And how was it possible to guarantee and equal participation in a family business unless you did at least start to distribute the shares fairly?"

Above everything else Paolo apparently wanted to be in a position at board meetings to carry some weight with his marketing ideas. His designs were being recognized in the family as an important asset. In America Aldo proudly told reporters about "my designer son." If he could contribute so much, he felt, and was a Gucci, should he not have a voice in the way the company was being run?

"But Uncle Rodolfo prided himself on his own designing ability. He had become the 'scarf man,' having found some new designs for our ladies' scarves. So he saw himself as the king of scarves, while in fact I was responsible for the entire fashion range of the company. When I dared to poke my nose into the scarf-and-tie field, which as head of design I was certainly entitled to do, oh gosh! Without any warning I'd suddenly be confronted with an idea he'd thought up for a handbag, already in full-scale production. Nobody had bothered to mention it to me. There'd been no pre-planning, no consideration of size, price or quantity. A rush into production, in the way the firm had been doing things for the past fifty years."

Paolo made his opposition to such moves very clear. "Whatever he'd put in the shop windows without telling me, I took out. When he objected, I told him, 'Look, I'm sorry, but it's my job to decide when we want new lines. We have enough already, more than enough—in fact, we've got handbags coming out of our ears.' Then, of course, he became angry."

Giorgio, Paolo's elder brother, was also causing concern. His work in the Rome shop had apparently created a similar frustration, making him want to move out on his own. "Everyone in the family is an individual, despite strong family ties," Paolo says. "Giorgio wanted to go his own way as much as I did." But in his brother's case the route lay in a seemingly more attainable direction.

Giorgio Gucci, without parental consent, found the backing for an entirely new and different development—a Gucci boutique. The attractive lower-priced items that in the main shops, were largely offered as appetizers, charming little knickknacks for the gift-shopper, were his stock in trade. Younger, cost-conscious customers were encouraged to crowd into his small premises and pick up a Gucci belt or tie-clip as easily as if they were buying a record.

It was immediately popular, but to his Uncle Rodolfo it was provocative. Having Paolo's rebellious assertion of power to contend with was bad enough, this on top of it was near-intolerable. The more successful Giorgio's venture became, the more it aggravated him. Since his wife's death, Rodolfo had become increasingly austere about what younger members of the family should do, and Giorgio's move was seen as a transgression.

No doubt Giorgio's venture would have been summarily dealt with had not the unthinkable happened in Rodolfo's circumscribed life. His son, Maurizio, fell in love. If this had happened with a girl from a family Rodolfo knew and approved of, there might have been no trouble. He might even have allowed himself to come to terms with losing his only son. But the object of Maurizio's affection was not such a girl, and Rodolfo—on what evidence is unclear—suspected her of being after Maurizio's (and hence his own) money.

Maurizio was twenty-four. Until now he had been a dutiful and obedient son. At the university, he was working hard for his degree while continuing to show a commendable interest in the business in his spare time. Rodolfo had allowed him little money or freedom, but this did not seem to bother him. When sent to New York to explore that end of the family concern he behaved well, inspite of the temptations of the city and his taste of Manhattan luxury living. His father received no complaints. Maurizio was put up in one of Aldo's penthouses, and he worked hard, learning the American end of the business from the bottom up.

There had been no hint then of the rebellion that his infatuation, as Rodolfo called it, would cause. When his father rebuked him for running up a moderately large telephone bill, Maurizio accepted it. But now and for the first time, he dared to defy his father.

As he says: "I had done everything he wanted until then. But after he lost my mother, my father had put all his love into the business. He seemed to have none left for others. So much dedication to one thing can be negative, and for me it was because I was forced to realize that he expected me to be his creature. He wanted to plan everything I was supposed to do in my entire life. Well, a young man does not always accept such direction indefinitely."

If Rodolfo had believed his beloved only son would reject the girl he loved out of his customary respect for his father's wishes, he was mistaken. Maurizio left home and was married.

"I had to define my own position, and perhaps I over-reacted. Anyway, for a year and a half I went to work outside the company."

The battle over Patrizia Reggiani's marriage to Maurizio developed into a family feud which she compares to the Montagues and Capulets of Shakespeare's *Romeo and Juliet.* "As soon as Maurizio began taking me out, I knew something was wrong," she says. "And I told the story to Aldo. But the Guccis seem to think it quite normal for a young man of twenty-three or -four to have to obey everything his father said. Never, never to go anywhere or be with anyone without his consent."

Despite his ultimate rebellion Maurizio's subservience to his father, as she saw it, during the courtship astonished her. They met through a girlfriend of Patrizia, who wanted to invite Maurizio, whom she had seen at a cousin's wedding, to a party. "I'd invented a story about a girl being at the party who was madly in love with him. He made the mistake of thinking it was me!" Before long they were going out together. And it was then that Patrizia discovered how closely guarded Maurizio was.

"I thought my own father was strict. He insisted I should be home by half past one. But Maurizio had to be home before me. And I discovered he was having to eat two dinners when we went out, one with his father and another with me!"

Rodolfo's anger over a weekend in Portofino revealed how profound his feelings could be. "Maurizio had promised to come and stay with us," Patrizia says, "but he didn't arrive. I called and asked what was the matter. He told me his father would not let him come. I said, 'We are supposed to be in love, so how can you not come and spend a weekend swimming with me?'"

Maurizio came for the day and stayed on. When he did not return home, Rodolfo telephoned Patrizia's father, Fernando Reggiani and reportedly said his daughter was after Maurizio for his money and that he must refuse to let her see Maurizio again.

Patrizia says, "My father was not a man to be spoken to like that. He told me he would do nothing of the sort, that his daughter had his complete trust and if she wanted to see Maurizio Gucci or anybody else he would not do anything to stop her."

Maurizio left home. Signor Reggiani, still smarting over Rodolfo's accusation, offered him the hospitality of his house. "I love you like a son, and you are welcome to my home for as long as you wish," he told Maurizio. "Whether or not you marry my daughter."

Patrizia was delighted, though her father made it clear that there was to be no intimacy between the young people. "While my father was very understanding and we had a large house, I found that his offer meant that Maurizio, for me, absolutely disappeared. My father hardly let us see each other."

Maurizio was on the point of finishing his law examinations. Signor Reggiani insisted that he should qualify before they married. "Also, he wanted to make sure that we both really did want to marry, so he took me around the world for a month. When I came back we were even more in love. Then he let me marry, Maurizio got his doctorate and he came to work for my father."

During the year and a half that this went on, the two families, the Guccis and the Reggianis, kept apart. According to Patrizia, Rodolfo went to the Cardinal of Milan and asked him to ban his son's marriage. On what grounds? "Because he is my only son, his mother is dead and he is all I have," Rodolfo told the Cardinal. The priest's reply was that if they were in love and wanted to marry there was nothing he could do to prevent it. At their marriage, no member of Maurizio's family attended the service, and only one sent a gift. "His Uncle Vasco gave us a large silver vase."

To his cousin Paolo the crisis between Maurizio and his father was an inevitable result of Rodolfo's control of his upbringing. "He had been throttling him. When Maurizio left home and went to work for his fiancée, Patrizia's, father it taught him a great deal, for instance that the whole world did not revolve 'round his own father."

If it had not been for his Uncle Aldo, Maurizio might never have returned to the family. It was Aldo who finally calmed Rodolfo down after Maurizio's marriage. (Similarly Aldo's powers of persuasion brought his son Giorgio back into the fold, arranging for his by then flourishing boutique business to become a part of Gucci.)

Paolo says he believes that Rodolfo sought the intercession of the Archbishop of Milan to enforce a ban on the wedding. "My cousin had to make a special confession of his sin of disobeying his father before he could receive the sacrament of marriage from the church."

Maurizio says this is an exaggeration. "Yes, but on October 2, 1972, eight months after I left my father, we were married without any difficulty. And although none of my family was present, I sensed that by then my father was regretting his opposition. I think both of us, my father and myself, realized that we had gone too far. We each had expressed what we felt, our love and other emotions, but it was time to end it."

When he made things up with his father, there were no apologies. "Neither of us said we were sorry, in fact we didn't talk about it. And in time it passed over. My father got to know Patrizia and got on very well with her in the end. But it took time."

Now, looking back, Maurizio seems to feel that the crisis was useful. "That is how I see it now, but when I was twenty-four I would not have said that. Anyway, I came back and pretty soon afterward I went to work in America, where it was a lot easier to forget the problem." And when he reflects on it now, Maurizio seems to have perspective. "You know, I think fathers always see their sons as they want them to be, not as they are. My father, I believe, realized it just before he died. He'd wanted me to be exactly his idea of the ideal son, and I'd let him down. But he came to see, I think, that I was someone else, and someone he could, if he tried, relate to."

Maurizio at least had shown that he could get along on his own. "I'd spent years away, and actually shown a special kind of character. He had to see that in my own way I was proving something. I believe he said to himself 'Look at this guy! He's able to take all this training, he can't be so bad after all.' Then, maybe, my father began to realize who his son was—both the good and the bad in me. Because I have many defects."

Rodolfo felt the pain of his son's defiance for a long while. He, more than either Aldo or Vasco, was acutely sensitive to such slights. Vasco seems barely to have noticed anything outside the hunting field, and Aldo was too busy to be bothered with such trifles. His attitude, it seems, was we're all in the family and these are only family squabbles. What seriously mattered, in Aldo's perspective, was any rift in Gucci's commercial performance. But, as events were to show, he underrated the current of deep-seated hostility that was beginning to loosen the blood-ties in his family.

Aldo also had some problems of his own. In 1965 he had planted the first Gucci flag in Japan. Canada, Australia, and South Africa were all possibilities to be explored when time and funds permitted, but he seemed to trust nobody else to sound out these untapped markets. Aldo apparently took after his father in respecting no advice or judgment more than his own. So his work took him away so much and so often that Bruna, his mistress, was demanding more attention.

With Olwen, it had been different. She often seemed to prefer his absences to his presences when he was in the wrong frame of mind, and when all they did was quarrel. But Bruna, who needed his constant support, was resenting more and more his trips back and forth across America and the world. She was becoming nervous and restless.

His excuse, as always, was that the business was like a building in process of construction. He could not leave while the roof was still incomplete, the extra floors still rising. Bruna could find no defense against this logic. Because the one undeniable fact was that it was working. All over the world Gucci's real and perceived values were satisfying a universal yearning. The most glamorous status symbol of the sixties was fulfilling the dreams of millions of women.

And in so doing it was making Aldo's own dream of Gucci an increasingly richer and more powerful reality.

Guccio and Aida in Florence. *(Martinis)*

The Gucci family at table. From left to right: Aldo, Vasco, Aida, Guccio, Rodolfo, unknown woman, Grimalda, Ugo, unknown woman. *(Gucci family archives)*

Aldo and Ugo in the uniform of the *Balille* (Fascist youth). *(Martinis)*

Olwen and Aldo on their wedding day in 1927. *(Gucci family archives)*

Rodolfo in 'Hollywood' guise.
(Gucci, Milan)

Ugo in the uniform of the Italian
Fascists. *(Martinis)*

Vasco, Aldo and Rodolfo in front of the handbags which by this time in the
1960s had made Gucci a household name. *(Martinis)*

Aldo arriving in New York for the first time. *(Martinis)*

Paolo, Giorgio and Roberto during a stay in England. *(Martinis)*

Maurizio as a boy in St. Moritz. *(Martinis)*

The old factory in via della Caldaie, Florence. *Above:* interior. (Gucci s.p.a.)
Below left: exterior. *(Gerald McKnight)*

The Gucci showrooms in the exclusive via Tornabuoni, Florence.
(Gerald McKnight)

Paolo and Aldo outside the New York store. *(Martinis)*

Grimalda. *(Gerald McKnight)*

Giovanni. *(Gerald McKnight)*

Paolo, Jenny and three-
year-old daughter
Gemma. *(Gucci family
archives)*

Patrizia with daughters,
Alessandra and Allegra.
(Gucci family archives)

Aldo outside the Court House in New York. *(New York Post)*

Maurizio in front of a picture of his father Rodolfo and grandfather Guccio. *(Gaston Jung)*

11

FLOOD AND FURY

Indeed, by the early sixties Gucci was functioning like a Formula 1 motor-racing stable. Rodolfo was the Ferrari-style manager, Vasco the pits boss, and Aldo the world-class driver. Aldo, the man in charge, put all his concentration into passing the vehicle ahead of him. There was no time, or so he apparently thought, to look over his shoulder. In all this heady excitement the friction among the younger generation passed almost unnoticed.

It was Gucci's most successful time. The Gucci moccasin was sweeping America, to the discomfort of more prosaic shoemaking merchants and manufacturers. "What did Jerry Lewis, John Wayne and Reggie Jackson have in common, other than fame and money?" The New York *Times* asked. "They were all 'constant customers' of Gucci, and fans of the slip-on loafer that, more than any other item, carried the company to fortune."

There were nay-sayers. Paul P. Woolard, senior vice-president of Revlon, said that "Gucci made fashion out of an established trend. It's only an Italian penny loafer. Status has nothing to do with it." He and others like him were having their business cut into by Aldo's "carpetbagging" invasion. But Joan Glynn of Wells Rich Greene, Inc., had a rejoinder for a colleague's suggestion that the distinctive, bitlike gilt chain across the shoe was not a reason for the American public's rush to be seen wearing Gucci. "The appeal is the obvious status symbol. It's an easy road—not like flashing your tank watch, which you have to raise your cuffs to do."

Whatever it was, the Gucci shops mushrooming across the States were happy to supply it. Behind them in Florence, the craftsmen worked overtime to keep pace with the flood of cabled orders from Aldo's new offices on Fifth Avenue. Industrially it was not the best of times. Italian workers protested more and more volubly about the rising cost of living and their inadequate paychecks. Vasco's calm authority was keeping the pot from boiling over, but the pressure was mounting.

Partly because of this he and his brothers made the decision to expand the new, much larger factory in Sandicci (the unlikely suburban district where D. H. Lawrence completed *Lady Chatterley's Lover*). Giovanni was to design an addition; Giovanni's building and surveying skills were proving to be a valuable family asset.

Aldo's dream of seeing a Gucci shop on the finest shopping street in the city, the via Tornabuoni, had also come within view of realization. Premises had been found there and contracts signed. But just when Giovanni was completing an elaborate and costly refurbishing of the premises, disaster struck the city.

On the night of November 4, 1966, the river Arno burst its banks and flooded the streets of the old town, destroying and damaging priceless works of art, turning the magnificent city into a sewer and flooding the shops of the whole area around Gucci in the via del Parione to a height of five or six feet. Giovanni's first thought when his nephew Paolo telephoned him the news early the next morning was of the valuable stock lying in the old shop.

"We weren't due to move for another few weeks, and everything was still there." And Gucci's leather goods, he knew, were insured for only a fraction of their value. Flood damage was arguably not even included in the policy. As he drove toward the edge of the flooded district closest to the shop, Giovanni's thoughts were on the extent of the possible damage.

Hundreds of thousands of dollars of highly priced, and in some cases irreplaceable, items were involved. At a time when the firm's credit was stretched to the limit to meet the costs of Aldo's expansion, the blow would be monumental if even a part of the stock was ruined beyond repair. And all those expensive shoes, handbags and suitcases lay in the direct, low-lying path the floods would take.

Giovanni arrived at the shop as the water was just beginning to flow into the street, its solid, stone-built houses terraced on both sides forming a canal. With relief he noted that, so far, little more than a trickle had reached the Gucci doors. But along the embankment he had seen it rising fiercely. He estimated that it would take only a few hours before the level in the street rose above the low walls under the windows of the shop and poured into the interior. How much higher they might rise after that he did not like to think.

By this time Paolo had warned his brother Roberto and his Uncle Vasco of the danger. They were the only members of the family in Florence. Aldo was abroad and Rodolfo in Milan with Giorgio. Paolo urged the others to make their way to the shop as quickly as they could.

Along the streets beside the river the waters were now waist high. A few more feet and it would be impossible to get through. In the narrow streets of the old city, flood waters were becoming a muddy torrent, carrying refuse and anything that would float on the foaming surface.

Paolo relates how he tried to reach the old factory on the far side of the swollen river, knowing that staff there were working round the clock to cope with the pre-Christmas rush of orders coming in from all parts of the world. If they were unaware of what was happening in the city they might be cut off, and he felt he had to warn them. But police guarding the bridges stopped his car and turned him back. He went instead to the shop.

It was now about nine-thirty, and Vasco and Roberto were already inside. Giovanni had let them in to the shuttered shop, their feet splashing through water up to their ankles. Vasco was in charge. "We must get everything up to the second floor," he told the others. "Just carry all you can."

For Paolo, the hours that followed were an unforgettable nightmare. "We kept looking out and seeing the water rising higher and higher in the street. It was so quick. Uncle Giovanni took a wheelbarrow and managed to get over to a place where he knew there were some bags of cement. He brought them back and stacked them in front of the shop as a protective wall."

Which was unlikely to give more than a temporary respite. By eleven the flood water was streaming over the cement bags and into the shop, making their feet squish and slither as they carried their loads. Paolo's arms felt as if they were falling off with fatigue. The smell of the flood waters was nauseating. Sewers had burst and the stream was a smelly sludge.

"Refrigerators were floating past. We saw cars being carried along in the current like huge dead bodies, smashing into shop windows and snapping off street signs like twigs. I was frightened."

All electricity and telephone services were cut off. So far, the shop's shutters had held back the worst force of the flood but the stench and darkness of the closed showroom were becoming unbearable. Paolo had the impression of being inside a doomed submarine with only a limited time to escape. The job of locating and carrying the goods up the stairs was exhausting enough without such thoughts.

He remembers "pulling, pushing, grabbing everything movable. Handbags, wallets, trunks. It wasn't easy because the carpet under our feet was beginning to bulge and bubble. When it got too bad we had to fix planks across it."

At last it was done. Everything movable had been taken upstairs and Giovanni raised the shutters. Water poured in, submerging them to their waists. Paolo remembers a loud report. "It was the doors of the baptistry, by the cathedral, bursting open. It sounded like a big gun. I thought they were dynamiting buildings.

"By now I was really very frightened. We put on long waders, like fishing boots. The current in the street was growing stronger and Roberto and I decided we should go while we could and try to raise some help. We managed to wade up to the piazza Duomo, but it was impossible to get across, the undertow was too great. I had to hold onto Roberto to prevent his being sucked away."

So they returned, soaking wet, to the shop and waited miserably until about six that evening, hoping the flood would go down. When there seemed to be no sign of a lessening in the height of the stream surging along the street, the four men made another attempt to wade their way out. It was fruitless. Paolo remembers: "My Uncle Giovanni, a small man, was very nearly swept away. We had to hold onto each other and clamber back as best we could, helping one another along. When we reached the shop we couldn't open the door leading to the upper floor because it was swollen and held by the pressure of the water. I put my backside against it and pushed with all my might. Thank heavens, it gave."

A family who lived in the rooms above the shop had heard noises coming from below and realized the danger. "They started knocking on the floorboards, terrified that we would be drowned like rats. We climbed up and they helped us to dry off, then shared dinner with us, little birds they had shot on a hunting trip."

Paolo thought they were destined to spend the rest of the night with their neighbors, but at midnight he looked out and to his astonishment saw that the water had subsided. "It had vanished as quickly as it came." Outside, the devastation was terrible. Mud, small trees, bicycles and garbage lay in mounds everywhere.

When they reached their homes, the bedraggled party heard that four elderly, bedridden Florentines had perished, swept away from their ground-floor rooms. The Guccis were the lucky ones. "My house was slightly flooded," Paolo says. "And of course the shop was a mess. But we'd saved ninety percent of the stock and we did not have to go to the expense of redecorating because the new premises in the via Tornabuoni were due to open in a few months' time. So, all in all, we got off lightly."

Certainly, without Paolo's early-morning alarm call and Giovanni's prompt action, it could have been a lot worse. By the middle of 1967 the new shop was ready.

Gucci's move into the via Tornabuoni was a major achievement. The premises were more elegant and luxurious than ever. Deep pile-carpeting and soft lighting set off the subtle, pastel-shaded decor. A discreet use of mirrors and the uncluttered appearance of the showroom's plate-glass and gold showcases flattered customers into believing that they hand wandered into a deluxe art gallery.

The main doors from the street were modeled on those of Europe's grandest hotels—particularly reminiscent of a side of London's Savoy that Guccio in his days there had rarely seen or been allowed to use. Once inside, visitors were greeted by handsome, smartly dressed assistants who gave an impression of relaxed charm, as if inviting a guest into their own homes. Aldo's "Gucci concept" of refined elegance had come of age.

With the Sandicci extension, the central structure of the organization was now complete. The firm's craftsmen and women were spaciously housed in the factory, turning out an increasing number of fine quality leather goods. Accessories that could not be made were bought in rough state and finished there. In the homes of the army of pieceworkers now regularly employed there was a constant stream of Gucci products. New equipment and machinery had raised productivity and Vasco's energy was now concentrated on making the place hum. The near disaster of the flood was soon no more than a frightening memory.

And for a time at least even the dissenting voices of the younger generation (of Paolo and Giorgio in particular) were stilled. Only one member of the family, Giovanni Vitali, was unhappy. "They never paid me for my work. I had built their factory and the shop, and I was the one who had saved their father from bankruptcy. But, of course, now that he was dead they wanted to forget that. From time to time they'd given me a sop, but nothing much. I was just good old Uncle Giovanni. Don't you think I deserved something from all the money they were making?"

He thought so, and not only on his own account, but on his wife Grimalda's as well—in their opinions they had not been given a fair share of her father's will, although in Grimalda's case there had been an adverse court judgment. "I got very angry with Aldo sometimes," the old man recalls. "I told him, 'You behaved disgracefully in the way you and your brothers treated your sister, giving her a pittance.' I said that to him, and he didn't like it. Since that day he has never set foot inside our house."

Grimalda, presumably out of her still strong affection for her brothers, would do nothing about it. But Giovanni took them on. "I fought them, legally, for both of us. She didn't want it. But I believed they had to be made to treat her properly." Not until his wife's nephew Maurizio took over the company from Aldo did Giovanni's actions bear fruit. "Maurizio came here after his father died and said, 'I want to end this matter.' He took out a file of old invoices, bills I'd sent them over the years. He said, 'I have all these accounts of yours, adding up to about five million lira, and I want to settle things.' I told him, 'Don't worry about me, what about your aunt? She is the oldest member of your family. You've got all these millions. Give her something.'"

Maurizio, he says, "agreed to have the company pay her five million lira a year. And since then Grimalda has been receiving that. She has to be on their books as an official designer, though she does nothing!"

But Giovanni, for all his rancor, has dropped the legal actions against the family. He and Grimalda had no children ("Providence has not been kind") and nobody other than the family to leave their money to. She was plainly relieved that there was no longer a battle dividing her from her relatives. She felt she had been wronged but her feelings for the family overrode everything.

"It only hurts now when people I know talk jokingly about the Guccis and their divisions as 'Dallas on the Arno.'" She smiles sadly. "We are no worse than any other family, I suppose. At the time I was sickened by it all, and very upset. Anyway, I forgave them. And that was that."

The oldest living Gucci may have come to live in peace with her family, but for the younger generation, Grimalda's nephews and great-nephews and -nieces, problems were less easily set aside. The three sons of the founder, though clearly moving in different directions, had control of the company exclusively in their hands. Paolo and Giorgio found that, as minor shareholding directors, they might as well have been called Smith or Brown; being Guccis and having some small equity in its business operation gave them no real power.

Aldo could declare, as he did in London during a publicity promotion of the new Bond Street Gucci, "I never stop thinking up ideas for products and plans for expanding the business, but it is my son Paolo who follows them through." But Paolo saw it differently. He felt he was unable to make his voice heard, either by his father during the brief meetings Aldo's globe-circling life allowed, or by either of his uncles in Italy.

Giorgio had expressed his frustration more practically by launching his own boutique, Maurizio, by marrying against his father's wishes. By their acts Giorgio and Maurizio had given clear notice of their growing independence.

There were other obvious signs that the family as a whole was growing apart. Vasco's lack of children, Rodolfo's increasing asceticism and Aldo's relationship with Bruna bred tensions that affected the children. Their loyalties were divided and heightened by mistrust of the way their elders were handling things. It may have been good public relations for Aldo to say in press interviews, "I bring a bunch of flowers to the shop every morning from my villa in Rome." But the villa he referred to was where his wife Olwen lived in increasing isolation (apart from occasional visits by her English family), and seldom accommodated him now for more than a night or two at a time and at lengthier and lengthier intervals.

He and Olwen were no longer emotionally involved, though there was no question of her releasing him from the marriage. He and Bruna, therefore, were obliged to practice a degree of discretion while Olwen remained "la signora Gucci," because under a concordat with the Vatican Italian law forbade Aldo to live openly with any woman other than his wife.

When Bruna became pregnant, Aldo no doubt would have welcomed a divorce if only for the child's sake, but Olwen knew that divorce would lose her the rights to her inheritance from Aldo. Yet, in Alexandra Murkoska's recollection, "It wasn't a real marriage. She never said a word against him and always behaved with perfect decorum, but to me she seemed not to care about his relationships with Bruna or anybody else. Maybe she was hiding her sadness, I can't say. What do I know, after all, about British ladies?"

In 1965 Bruna's child was born—a daughter named, like her half-brother Paolo's daughter and her cousin Maurizio's wife, Patrizia, but with a *c* in place of the Italian *z*. To be with her, Aldo first bought Bruna a house in England, then took her to America with him and settled her in his Palm Beach and Manhattan homes. For the first two or more years of the child's life he lived with them, introducing Bruna as "Mrs. Gucci." Then his explosive energy became a problem.

"Really, Bruna couldn't handle it," Alexandra says. "It

was too much for her. It really overwhelmed her. She's a very nice, sincere woman and I like her. But Aldo was all wrong for her. She tried, but she couldn't handle it with him."

Sometimes when she was with the two of them, Alexandra wondered how they had ever come together in the first place. "No two people in the whole wide world could have been so unsuited to one another. They simply were never made for each other. They quarreled from when they got up in the morning until they went to bed at night. She'd carry on whenever he announced that he was going off on another trip somewhere. Why did he always have to be going somewhere, she wanted to know? Why couldn't he stay with her?"

Aldo flattered Bruna with gifts and bought her wonderful clothes. She had a car and chauffeur to take her wherever she wanted. The cachet of signing for credit at the best and smartest stores in the name of "Dr. Gucci" was hers to command. If she could have tolerated his itch to be on the move, to be always working toward some new goal and the satisfaction of celebrating its achievement, her life could have been much easier. "I think he loved her very much," Alexandra says. "But he needed more than she could give him. He needed somebody who could share all that with him, and she never could do that."

The gulf between them, despite Aldo's adoration of Bruna as a beautiful and much-admired woman, was apparently too wide. "Intellectually she couldn't come up to him." Alexandra says it with compassion. "She found his life nearly incomprehensible. Why was he flying off every other minute to open a new shop somewhere? Or getting up at five in the morning to be at some stupid studio in Los Angeles? She thought he was crazy!"

And, in fact, he at least seemed driven. Bruna came close to losing her grip on things, and understandably, according to Paolo. "There were too many violent scenes, too much weight on her. And my father was so seldom with her, less and less as time went by." According to Alexandra, Bruna once took a quantity of sleeping pills. "Perhaps in a distraught state she made a mistake and took too many. But there's no doubt that she was sometimes desperately unhappy."

Paolo heard about the matter from his half-sister, Bruna's daughter Patricia. "She told me that, fortunately, it did no more than make her mother ill. But my father could never give her what she wanted. He couldn't marry her."

Paolo feels his father put the problem to one side, hoping it would solve itself. "It's the same over everything, he won't finish things when they grow too difficult. They are never over for him. If Bruna was disturbed and sad, why was she? Because of my father, that's why."

Paolo's uncharitable assessment of his father's relationship—divorced as it was from the blessing of the church—overlooks the fact that Aldo and Bruna had sought their own form of happiness. And that their daughter, as beautiful as her mother, was the personification of that search for happiness.

Aldo's extraordinary vitality would have made it hard for any woman. Alexandra, perhaps, was more capable than most of fitting in with his moods. She knew how to share exhilarating moments of celebration with him, following his succession of glittering triumphs. "He really needed someone to share those moments with," she says. "There were a lot of people he could have called on, I know, but they didn't understand his dynamic nature. And often they seemed to begrudge anything he did that made him feel good."

Jealousy? "I suppose it was that with Olwen and Bruna. And I really pitied them. They could have had such wonderful lives. The trouble was "—she shakes her head sadly—"the Guccis are all about power. Unless you share that with them, you miss an awful lot."

One has the impression that she missed very little.

Paolo, though, was not much interested in his father's need for celebration. Though his work in the factory was absorbing, he missed family life. His own marriage to Yvonne had failed and his daughters were with their mother, estranged from close contact with him. Florence was too far from Rome to pay more than occasional weekend visits to his mother. His father was seldom in Italy. His whole future seemed, during the latter part of the sixties, to be empty of love, of meaning, of challenge and of hope.

12

SHARES FOR ALL

"The children of hardworking, self-made men in Italy," Gaia Servadio, a leading Italian journalist has noted, "are prone to become spoiled and uninterested in their father's business. The fathers do not like to give power to somebody outside the family circle." In the case of the Guccis, the problem was that the younger generation was not supposed to have a say in anything to do with the business. But increasingly they wanted to do so.

Paolo may or may not have been spoiled but he was certainly not uninterested. In the family, his openly expressed criticism for his elders' conservative, cautious ways was now considered grounds for an unbridgeable breach. Rodolfo saw that before long a reckoning would have to be made with this rebellious nephew. It bothered him that Aldo, Paolo's powerful father, resisted seriously discussing the matter, tending to treat it as a passing boyish caprice.

Other weightier considerations were worrying Aldo. The

new shops he was creating were spectacularly attractive and crowded with customers from the day they opened their silvered doors. The increase in turnover they brought in was gratifying. But he knew that the capital structure of the company was strained to the limit by having to keep pace with the fantastic cost of all this expansion. He needed more and more money.

In 1971 he summoned his brothers and fellow directors to a board meeting. None of the third generation was present. His three sons had no shareholding votes, and neither did their much younger cousin, Rodolfo's son, Maurizio.

Aldo told his brothers that it was time to reconsider the basic principle established by their father, Guccio Gucci, and never seriously questioned in almost half a century of trading: that ownership of the company should never leave the family and that no outsiders be allowed to share in the management and profits. But that meant that they could never finance the expansion Aldo wanted to engage in with anything but their own funds.

He had called the meeting, he said, to propose a public flotation on the Milan stock exchange of between 20 and 25 percent of company equity. He pointed out that rivals were already beginning to threaten some of their markets. Before long if they did not move into other major territories in the world such as Japan and the Far East their competitors who were challenging them with product lines based on Gucci concepts could seal off these lucrative areas. If that was to be prevented he had to have the means to beat them to it.

Gucci credit was stretched to and in some cases beyond the limit, with little immediate hope of halting the negative cash flow occasioned by launch costs and acquisitions. A Scottish tannery had recently been added to their properties at further cost. Where was the money to come from for further activities if not from a public flotation?

Heretical though it was, the effect of such a sale of equity would have been timely. The Gucci name had achieved blue-chip status among traders and bankers. Their rivals grudgingly had to admit that Gucci was rising to dominate an enormous area of the leather- and luxury-goods market. To sell equity now, to invite public investors and institutions to participate in their glamorous success, made a good deal of financial sense; with the millions thus available, the family would be able, as their chairman said, to make many more and faster millions in the immediate future.

It all sounded like good marketing logic, and Aldo put it to his brothers with his usual persuasive power. Rodolfo however had grave misgivings. Vasco shared them. Their innate caution and conservatism balked at risking anything so drastic, so revolutionary for the family. Their adventurous brother's expansions were already causing them sleepless nights, knowing as they did that it only needed another slump (such as the one in the twenties that had so nearly written off their father) to destroy them. Above all, they resisted gambling with their comfortable livelihoods.

Rodolfo had his magnificent Swiss villa home to think of, Vasco his farms. They valued their comforts, chauffeur-driven limousines and holiday homes. Converting precious shares into cash for Aldo to play with was apparently asking too much. They rejected the proposal.

In its place they counterproposed a ban to last for one hundred years. During that time no shares in the company would be allowed to pass into other than Gucci hands. Only the family would own the company.

With two-thirds of the voting power held by his brothers against him, Aldo had no alternative but to accept and bury his plans for global expansion. The counterproposal was passed. Three years later he admitted to Samuel Feinberg of *Women's Wear Daily* that he never entirely lost interest in the project. "It is an idea I still caress, but we want to keep the stock completely in the family. We would not now consider losing the reins to strangers, to third parties." By "we," he presumably meant Rodolfo and Vasco, his own wishes having been turned aside. Had he known how soon the balance of power was to change, one guesses he would have delayed the attempt to realize his goal.

What changed Gucci history was Vasco's death in 1975. A heavy smoker, his end was quick once the tumor on his lungs was diagnosed. Ironically he was the most leisurely, the least driven of the brothers.

On his death his shares, one-third of the stock in the whole of Guccio Gucci, passed to his widow. It had been Guccio's wish that no shares in the business should pass to other than male Gucci descendants. This had never been given legal power; nevertheless, the loss of the shares to a woman faced the surviving brothers with a dilemma.

It was resolved, as most problems in the family were, by money. The brothers put together a sum believed to have been not less than a million dollars by way of compensation. Vasco's widow, Maria, accepted, agreeing that if her late husband's father had devoutly wished it, then the practice of having only male Guccis running things should not be ignored.

Greatly relieved, Aldo and Rodolfo hired lawyers to make the necessary transfers and became equal shareholders, initially on a fifty-fifty basis but with Aldo subsequently dividing one fifth of his holding, 10 percent of the shares, among his three sons. So for the first time, Giorgio, Paolo and Roberto were given a voice in company affairs.

At the time their individual equities of 3.33 percent each of the shares in the entire Guccio Gucci operation no doubt seemed too insignificant to bother about and quite unlikely to cause trouble. But since Aldo's sons could, if they chose, line up with Rodolfo—who already held 50 percent—against their father, events were to show that Aldo had dangerously weakened his position. Any one of the third-generation shareholders could now swing the balance of power.

Maurizio was the only third-generation contender to be left out, and he felt it keenly. "I had nothing. Zero. Not one share, so far as I knew, until my father died." Paolo, who had assumed responsibility for Scandicci upon Vasco's death, and for the old building in the via Caldaie where he had served his apprenticeship, thought he understood Maurizio's feelings: "His father didn't trust him, that was why he never had a single share. He knew his son was tremendously ambitious despite his relative immaturity. I think in a way, having put him through university and almost forcing him to study the business in every spare moment he had, Folfo was even a little afraid of Maurizio."

Which would tend to explain why his father had transferred his shareholding to him before he died without telling him.

"I didn't know he was having them put in my name, because my father didn't want me to know," Maurizio says. But in view of evidence given to the Italian courts (and confirmed by caligraphic experts) alleging that the transfer had been fraudulently made to avoid taxes, with Rodolfo's signature forged, he would have to prove this, indeed, was so or possibly face criminal charges similar to those against his Uncle Aldo. Losing the case would also mean that he would have to pay taxes that would have been due on his father's death if the gift had not been made in his lifetime. To meet such a cost—a sizable percentage of the notarized value of 50 percent of the entire company—he would have to sell a large part of his equity. But under the rule whereby no shares may be disposed of outside the family for a century, Maurizio would then be faced with having to sell only to his cousins, his uncle or to any other Gucci with means enough to buy them.

When it became company law, of course, nobody thought of this. Gucci was going through a period of frustrating difficulties. The astonishing speed of its expansion had forced the brothers to consolidate each foothold as quickly as possible. Consequently credit lines were stretched to the breaking point. If the list of distinguished and wealthy Gucci clients had not been so glamorous—featuring Queen Elizabeth and Princess Margaret of England, Audrey Hepburn and a host of Hollywood and international celebrities including Imelda Marcos—it would have been even more difficult to raise cash for each new venture.

In the eyes of some critics, Gucci suggested ostentatious consumption. Journalists in need of a descriptive image for the super-rich had only to mention Gucci apparel and the point was made.

Those who wore the Gucci symbol expected the family to live up to it, and Aldo and his relatives were accorded a status far above that of ordinary merchants. The Gucci legendary ancestral connections inflated their self-esteem.

Maurizio, however, believed that the modern world was growing impatient with such snobbish window-dressing. As soon as he had the power to do so he tried to abolish it. Aldo was making use of it whenever possible, alert to any fresh ideas of advantages that might come from a casual shopping visit by a member of high society likely to spend a thousand or more dollars.

His newest notion was to launch a Gucci perfume that would both add to Gucci's profitable accessories and provide a seductive note to their showrooms. He spoke to people in the trade and they were enthusiastic about the project. At the next board meeting he proposed it to his brother and fellow directors.

According to Paolo, Aldo said, "Let's do it. We are in a magnificient position to market something really expensive and desirable for women."

Rodolfo could hardly deny that their clientele included a great many wealthy women, but he was wary of Aldo's adventurous marketing. He agreed on condition that a separate company was formed to handle the perfume. It could also take other additional items and accessories in its range of products.

An American company, I. G. Magnin, which made the

Mennen range of toiletries, was approached. Aldo was assured that a suitably distinctive, expensive and appealing perfume could be blended, one that was exclusive to Gucci. A company was registered in the French name considered most suitable to their image—"Gucci Parfums."

With his sons clamoring for a larger slice of the Gucci family pie, this attractive sideline was a comforting piece of equity for Aldo to direct their way. The new company had a hundred shares in it. Why not use some of these to placate the vociferous third generation? he proposed to Rodolfo.

Rodolfo raised no objection to Giorgio, Paolo and Roberto receiving shares, but his own son was in effect no longer one of the family. It was during Maurizio's defection over his marriage. The disobedient son would not share in anything that would give him power in the company. Aldo, Rodolfo and Aldo's three sons would share in the Gucci Parfums equity; Maurizio would not.

Had either Rodolfo or Aldo sensed that Gucci Parfums would grow to become even more valuable in terms of profit-to-turnover than its parent company, one tends to doubt that anything more than titular directorships would have gone to the younger Guccis. But inasmuch as such a revolutionary notion apparently did not strike them as remotely possible, Aldo and Rodolfo each received 40 percent of the shares and Aldo's three sons partook equally of the remaining 60 percent of the shares.

If the newborn company had functioned as conceived, marketing only perfume and perhaps toiletries suited to the Gucci image of luxury, probably no difficulties would have arisen. But Gucci Parfums began to invade the entire range of accessories and novelties. Within a few years it was challenging the main company in sales, while its profit margins were considerably healthier.

Even more significantly, the relative power structure among third-generation cousins was now so unevenly balanced (Aldo's sons with 20 percent each of the perfume company and 10 percent of Guccio Gucci, Maurizio with nothing at all) that Paolo was able to use the situation against his increasingly hostile Uncle Rodolfo. "If we are to be a family unit, all of us sharing in the running of the companies, then why is there this enormous discrepancy? Why not make us all equal shareholders?" Paolo said.

Rodolfo declined to consider such a thing, no doubt viewing the suggestion as one more example of Paolo's impractical rebellion against what he and his father had established. Where, after all, would it stop?

Unable to make the slightest impression on the board of directors or to pin his father down to side with him in his campaign for a greater say in company affairs, Paolo then pulled out all the stops. He laid proposals before the board to modernize what he called the "medieval concepts" of the entire Gucci operation. They must abandon their ancient customs, he insisted, and bring in financial backers to provide the capital needed to expand more fully. Furthermore, they should no longer rely on selling exclusively through their own Gucci shops. Licenses should be granted to selected department-store outlets.

Giorgio's boutique had been successful, he argued, for exactly the reason that a huge market for lower-priced Gucci goods existed, a clientele that might be intimidated by the elegant upscale salons of Gucci itself. But where Giorgio had offered the same goods as were available in the main shops, there would have to be a clear and easily recognizable line drawn between the two.

Paolo proposed appealing more to the young with less money to spend. "I suggested extending our range of cheaper lines, like Benetton and others. If we don't want to license the operation, then why not set up a chain of these shops, on the lines of Giorgio's Rome boutique, wherever we had a Gucci shop? Provided the goods were markedly different, there would be no conflict."

He might as well have asked for the moon. The board did not have to make up their minds about a matter that Aldo and Rodolfo had already decided on.

Such concepts, Paolo was told, violated the traditional policies of the company. Also, they seriously weakened the parent shareholders' positions, since the perfume company, as natural proprietor of the proposed downscale new chain, would have increasing powers. And thereby the nonconformist third generation—in particular Paolo—would be given more scope.

It was not to be. But according to Paolo, his frustration was still not seen as a major problem in the family with his father in control. Easy reassurances were given by Aldo to Rodolfo about Paolo's ambitious demands. Paolo would be told to stay in line, to carry on with his useful designing and the management of the factory. If necessary he would be brought over to New York, where his father would be able to instill the same discipline and corporate loyalties in him that he had already passed on to his other sons and his nephew Maurizio. All would be well, he assured his brother.

But all would not be well. Aldo's optimism apparently blinded him to the widening split in the Gucci family. Behind Paolo Gucci's gentle manner, his quiet tone of voice and elegant gestures was a tough and stubborn nature.

13

HAUTE CHUTZPAH

"The rudest store in town," Mimi Sheraton called Gucci in New York magazine in November 1975. "Gucci's staff has mastered the art of the drop-dead put-down and the icy stare, flashing signs that the customer is unworthy." Not revealing that she spoke Italian, the reporter tried to buy a pair of shoes in the Fifth Avenue store. "The foppish Italian salesboys perfected a quality of rudeness, Gucci-style, as polished as their astronomically priced leather goods. In Italian they made insulting jokes about customers, dubbing anyone who did not buy a *cafone*, a coarse and vulgar lowbrow."

She asked for a particular color in her size. "The boy who was oh-so-patiently waiting on me said, in Italian to his colleague, 'When I ask you if we have brown in thirty-six say you know we do not.' Neither seemed at all miffed when I told them, also in Italian, not to bother and left."

At the time (a practice later discontinued) Aldo was closing the shops for lunch, an unheard-of custom in the

United States. Miss Sheraton said she questioned twenty-five regular Gucci customers. "Only three said they had been treated pleasantly and courteously at Gucci's." Her experience, she said, was almost widely shared and astonishingly tolerated.

Yet nine thousand customers a day were paying tribute to the lure of Gucci in America. Aldo's grasp of the psychological mores of the wealthy had cleverly incorporated their apparent liking for the same sort of manners many practiced on their servants and perceived social inferiors. "When the article appeared, he was delighted," Alexandra Murkoska, who was working for Aldo in the Fifth Avenue store, remembers. "Aldo sent the writer flowers that must have cost five hundred dollars. He regarded it as fabulous publicity."

But was it true? "Oh, yes," Alexandra says. "The salesgirls, remember, were not all professionals. Quite a few were princesses and movie actresses. They were doing it just for kicks. Aldo knew that. He used them as window dressing."

If the sixties had given Gucci world status, the mood now insured even wider acceptance. Gucci shoes with their identifiable double G-strap were the "in" thing. Casual, jacketless clothes offered ideal showcases for Gucci belts and accessories. Luggage wrapped in broad stripes and symbols, which a few years earlier would have been thought *outré*, was envied and copied. The mood and style of the seventies had made Gucci even more popular.

To be on the wrong side of the generation gap was distinctly non de rigueur. The new young needed all that Gucci offered at any price put on it. It would have been difficult to avoid making money from the stream of well-made, high-profit, beautifully designed goods flowing from the Scandicci factory south of Florence.

At great cost Aldo had enlarged the Fifth Avenue premises to handle only women's and men's apparel, shoes and textiles, while his corner store on East Fifty-Fourth Street was wholly given over to luggage, accessories and gifts. Together they were now, at twelve thousand square feet, only slightly smaller than the Florence flagship. In Chicago he was expanding and adapting to ride the soaring wave of popularity.

On the debit side he had lost more than one lawsuit brought by an irate customer. A lady who had had her arm seized by one of the sales staff when she tried to leave, having been delayed, she claimed, beyond patience while her sales slip was being corrected, won a thousand dollars. According to Paolo, Gucci offered the customer half the money in gift certificates usable only in the store.

A drama student, Dierdre Scher, claimed to know the key to Gucci's more accommodating ways. "I used my newly perfected upper-class British accent and the results were terrific. Gucci saleswomen fell all over themselves to wait on me and actually smiled . . ."

An ex-saleswoman, Gail Gitlen, alleged that Gucci did not discriminate in its treatment of staff. "Before leaving at night we all had to pick a marble out of a jar. If you got the color-of-the-day marble, then your bag was searched. I guess the Gucci people thought that everyone was just dying to rip them off." But there was some justification for this. The industry in fake Gucci had spread to the Far East. In Japan and Korea deft hands were manufacturing exact look-alikes of the distinctive buckles, the "GG" symbol, the color-striped belting. The Gucci board was being forced to approve hundreds of thousands of dollars to bring actions against such prepetrators in each country they appeared in.

At home Aldo filed suit in the New York State Supreme Court against Federated Department Stores and Picture Pies Company for selling a loaf of bread in Bloomingdale's under the name of "Gucci Gucci Goo." Trade-journal writer Samuel Fineberg observed, "One day I fully expect to come face to face with a lovely pink and rose toilet paper labeled 'Gucci Gucci Goo.' " It seemed not so improbable.

But imitations could not offer Gucci's lasting quality.

Snob-appeal aside, the centuries-old Florentine leather workers coupled with the skills of several hundred local part-time workers in homes and workshops, produced unmatchable excellence. The sweatshops of the Far East could not begin to approach the Gucci standard. A genuine Gucci was obviously superior, and the older the article the more obvious and authentic was its pedigree.

Few social gaffes were more humiliating than to be caught with a fake. Aldo enjoyed telling a story about the wife of a wealthy if parsimonious New York banker known for his penny-pinching meanness that he met at a Park Avenue party. "Oh, Dr. Gucci," said she, "how fascinating to meet the man who created my husband's absolutely favorite gift store. He buys just everything he ever gives me there, and all your things are so gorgeous." Aldo saw at a glance that the woman's purse was a fake. "I had to tell her so, for the sake of my reputation," he laughingly explained, "but you should have seen the look she gave her husband."

It sometimes paid, Aldo believed, to make his wares less than readily attainable. Rosemary Kent, a New Yorker transplanted from Texas, who had saved up to buy the acme of perfection in a pair of Gucci "pumps with horsebits across the instep," felt rejected by a Fifth Avenue Gucci salesman. "I prepped myself by clipping my toenails and wearing clean hose and a well-polished pair of shoes because I had heard rumors of salesman intimidation. I wanted the salesmen at least to think I could afford Guccis." Whether she convinced them or not the visit was not exactly a success. "Salesmen flew around me but no one landed. Finally one approached me and looked at my foot. 'I don't think we're going to be able to fit you,' he said. 'That's a thirty-nine and a half, double A, a European size, and your instep looks too high.'"

Could they not try, she asked? "I'd always thought that long, narrow feet were fashionable. After all, I'd read of Jackie Onassis' size tens." But when the young man returned he handed her a shoe that was too small. "See," Miss Kent says he told her, "I told you your instep is too high for Gucci."

When she asked if there were other styles she could try, he told her: "Our shoes are all handmade and they don't make your size now. I don't know if they ever will."

She gave up. "I marched out of Gucci's and went next door to Chandler's. For half the price and one hundred percent of the fit I got what I was looking for."

Aldo may privately have been amused by such tales of customer relations, as Alexandra Murkoska declares he did, but in staff meetings he distinctly was not. "My father came from the real school of shopkeepers," Paolo says, "where the customer is always right. He was a stickler for that, and drilled it into my brothers and me when we were small." Later, when working for his father in New York, he saw an example that he believes typified Aldo's attitude to even the most unruly customer.

"One of the girls working in the shop was serving a customer when a woman tried to distract her. She wanted to exchange a handbag she'd bought and was in a tearing hurry. It wasn't enough to be told she'd be helped in a minute, she took the handbag and threw it at the girl so hard it broke her nose and she had to go to hospital and have four stitches in the cut on her face."

Paolo was with his father in the office when the salesgirl was shown in, her face bruised and bandaged. "He was sorry but he told her, "I understand what happened, and another time you must try and allow for customers like that. We have to serve all sorts." He knew, of course, that some of the customers would come in under the influence of alcohol, others behaving rudely, but he would not change historic policy. We had to be nice to all of them, and at all costs avoid bad publicity." It was the traditional retailer's policy of the customer, right or wrong, is always right, though perhaps carried to an extreme.

For the same reason Aldo refused to let any hint of the assault leak out to the press. "His belief was always 'no fuss, no publicity' for that kind of thing. He wanted the world to see him as a sort of good fairy godfather."

Aldo's tears in court when later convicted and jailed by an American judge may have at least in part been because that so important image had been sullied.

Six hundred people were on the Gucci payroll in the United States, and nearly two hundred of these were in the New York headquarters. Aldo ruled over a multinational monarchy, on which the lives and careers and often happiness of more than a thousand individuals worldwide depended. He was treasurer of a business that in America alone had increased twenty-five times over the preceeding ten years.

Yet there never seemed to be enough money. Behind the bewildering columns of figures produced for annual meetings of the main Gucci board of directors, behind the smoothly rounded explanations of "expansion costs," "loan interest charges" and other symptoms of the firm's galloping development, all the millions known to be pouring into the firm's tills and checking accounts remained nearly invisible.

Unable to fathom the reason for this, Paolo Gucci was becoming increasingly concerned. On paper it seemed that all the family should have been millionaires, their equities in the company placing them among the world's wealthiest men. In practice he says his monthly paycheck amounted to little more than that of a middle-echelon manager, and he wondered if his father's explanation for keeping him and his brothers on such salaries ("You must not expect to earn more than you are worth.") might not be related to questionable financial management and control.

"They were spending millions on properties and boats, but when my father invited me, as the chief designer of the collection, to attend a Gucci fashion show in London and I took Jenny, my brother Roberto, who was in charge of administration, refused to pay for the two tickets. I had to explain that it was necessary, since I was to meet the Italian ambassador and Jenny was an important asset and adornment. He would not budge. In the end, my father had to tell him to pay it."

From his newly elevated position as director of the factory, it made little sense to Paolo for his father to keep sowing Gucci seeds around the world but for no fruit to come from the tree. Above all Paolo still wanted to move more extensively into the lucrative marketing of licenses by which selected stores would be allowed to sell Gucci products on a royalty basis.

Aldo and Rodolfo rejected his proposals out of hand. To do anything of this sort, they said, would weaken their exclusivity, the valuable image of their product line. Paolo came out of board meetings in a fury at these repeated and apparently implacable arguments. His impotence against the two brothers who, between them, now held total power, angered and embittered him.

"Big Bad Folfo was the worst, he was dead against it. But my father thought any idea from juniors was useless. He was always far too strict with us all, utterly dominating the younger members of the family."

Perhaps. But Aldo was also aware that he needed their support. He never fought openly with his sons, or with his nephew Maurizio. Instead he took them to New York, under his wing. First Roberto, then Giorgio and his first wife Orietta, then Maurizio. In Paolo's eyes "he pushed them into the ground."

Paolo had yet to enter Aldo's Manhattan training school. His memories of working with and under his imperious father seem a blend of admiration, love and resentment. "He was one of those who frustrated people. He didn't reprimand or scold, he didn't ask questions. He just called them insulting names," Paolo says.

An unpleasant experience of making a trifling mistake

stood out in his memory. Customers were all around him, able to hear every word. His father came over, the anger in his eyes warning Paolo that he was in for it. "Look what you've done. What the hell good are you?"

Paolo was sure he was good but he was not able to convince either his father or his uncle of his competence. He, in turn, was far from sure that the way they were running things was good.

Paradoxically he saw Aldo taking infinite pains to defend and elevate the Gucci public image. If dressing down his grown-up offspring was a habit he could not break, he kept it well away from company policy. "He wanted to keep us on our toes and firmly in our places," Paolo said.

Certainly Aldo's manner in the shop on Fifth Avenue, New York, never exposed the least savagery in his makeup. There he was all charm, in the words of a surprised woman interviewer, "an effusive, ebullient, vigorously well-preserved seventy-year-old." He was also, says Alexandra Murkoska, with admiration, "very, very attractive to women." She also says, where necessary, he could treat wealthy customers with lofty disdain.

Aldo also did not believe in becoming involved in his sons' behavior toward wives and women friends. If asked to put a word in on their behalf, he would point out that this was a personal matter between the lady and whichever of his sons was involved. He could take no part in it. It seemed that life had taught Aldo a lesson in domestic diplomacy that no amount of pleading would shake.

When Paolo's marriage to Yvonne finally crumpled, his father would not be moved by what others in the family, notably his sister Grimalda, might perceive as harsh treatment of the wife and their daughters. "Patricia, his daughter, worked in the factory here in Florence. He didn't look after them."

Paolo denies this. "It was nonsense. The truth was that I did all I could in the circumstances and more. She had the house, worth nearly a half million dollars. I provided for them all financially. No, my aunt's version of events was rubbish."

He points out he had never wanted to marry Yvonne. He had only done so out of a chivalrous sense of duty. "When we first met, after I'd seen her in the cinema and followed her home, I thought I was in love with her. But it did not last, and I was about to break off the affair when she told me she was pregnant."

Marrying her, then fathering their second daughter, added up in Paolo's eyes to an argument in his favor. He subsequently married again. Aldo made no comment on either occasion.

Paolo's second wife, Jenny, must have had one of the strangest courtships and marriages on record. She met him when she and her sister were on holiday in Italy. Jenny Puddefoot Garwood, as blonde and Anglo-Saxon as Paolo is dark and Latin, apparently raised the English half of his blood to a new pitch of excitement. But not, it seemed, at first.

"We'd been introduced on a blind date and he said he'd get in touch but never did," she says. Jenny went back to England, where her father was a prosperous commission agent, and tried to forget about him.

On a second visit, however, he did call her. They met and discovered that they both had recently emerged from traumatic first marriages. The break-up of Jenny's marriage to a press-photographer in England had wounded her deeply. When Paolo told her that he was in much the same frame of mind over his own broken marriage, a sympathy formed between them.

The problem, when they decided to marry, was how they could manage to do so. Paolo was forbidden by canon law to marry again in his church, his marriage to Yvonne being sacramentally eternal in the eyes of Rome. So to wed Jenny he became a citizen of "Papa Doc's" Haiti. At the ceremony on the voodoo-practicing island she could not understand a single word of the service. "Afterward she had to take my word for it that we were really married," Paolo says. "I'm not sure that she was quite certain about it for a long time afterward."

Aldo at first was, it seemed, even less certain. But Jenny's charm, the birth of their children and the ease with which the new English Gucci fitted herself into their family life quickly overcame his reservations.

14

WAYWARD SHEEP

Paolo and Jenny married in 1978, the year when Aldo's American dream, his Gucci Shops Incorporated, recorded a record turnover of forty-eight million dollars and zero profit. Rodolfo blamed the failure on his adventurous brother's passion for expansion. The cost of launching the perfume company in 1975 and of opening and equipping branches across America had soaked up nearly all of the very considerable profit margins.

Back home in Milan the failure of the company to go into the black apparently spurred Rodolfo's anger at Aldo's refusal, as he saw it, to adequately discipline his son Paolo. Rodolfo was coming to his office every morning to find an ever-increasing number of complaints and requests about company management on his desk, all from his nephew.

One day Rodolfo's secretary told him that Paolo had taken it on himself to order the removal of his uncle's favorite new products from the window of the flagship store in Florence because, as he had written in a memorandum to his uncle, "I had not been consulted about its design."

In a sharp exchange Rodolfo told Paolo that he was, in effect, washing his hands of him and his career and if his brother Aldo wished to tolerate Paolo's behavior then he had better go and work for Aldo in America.

Paolo's response was to request a look at the firm's books. "Though I was an executive and shareholder, I had not been allowed to see any of the figures, or to know what was being spent of all the millions I knew were being made around the world. I claimed an absolute right to see what was going on."

His uncle refused. Paolo could do what he liked, but in Italy he was running things and no junior member of the family was going to tell him what he should or should not do with the business. He called Paolo to his office and told him that he would stand no more of the younger man's interference, which was how he perceived it.

Paolo felt he had no alternative. He went to his father and made a serious charge against his uncle. Rodolfo, he claimed, was infringing his rights, making it impossible for him to carry out his duties as the firm's design director, imposing his own ideas on the staff without consulting him. "What am I to do? I cannot work with my uncle," he said.

Aldo took the role of peacemaker. "Come and work for me in New York," he offered. "You need a break. You can take charge of accessories and design here, which will allow plenty of scope to put your ideas into practice."

Paolo says he went home that evening happier than he had been for a long time. The sense of freedom he felt as a result of his father's offer was to him proof of the frustration and tension he had been under for months. In America he would at least be able to create and design not only new lines and products but the marketing concept Rodolfo ignored.

His new bride had been fearful of the outcome of the meeting. "Don't worry," Paolo told her. "We're going to America. It's a new life for us. Aren't you pleased?"

More than pleased, Jenny was delighted. She had taken singing lessons and was keen to enter the world of professional opera. In New York there would be teachers who could help her realize her cherished ambition. And if Paolo's differences with his relatives were about to be resolved by the kind patronage of his at times rather scary father, then that too was marvelous.

Neither of them could foresee that Aldo was not in a strong enough position to shield his son indefinitely from his uncle's anger. Rodolfo was exercising increasing power in the Italian company and Aldo was pestered by accountants and advisers to cut costs, to see more return for the effort going into the business.

Even so, the days passed with no real hint of the troubles to come. Aldo enjoyed great adulation and respect in the city where, more than anywhere in the world, success opened every door. Paolo and Maurizio, soon to be in collision, explored a Manhattan that seemed at their feet.

They were wealthy young men married to beautiful women, with the glamorous name of Gucci to insure their entrée and acceptability. Maurizio already knew New York from his university days, when he had flown over to watch and study his uncle's management techniques. His work in the American operation was fitting him for a major power role in the company.

Until his rift with his uncle and his father's acceptance of his need to escape from Florence to a job in the American company, Paolo had paid only one brief visit to the States. But now, with the apartment his father provided less than two minutes from the Fifth Avenue store, and with a more than comfortable salary arrangement, he was well equipped to sweep aside the frustrations of Florence.

His father understood that a man of forty-seven with a young bride needed more than a career under a dominant uncle. He welcomed Paolo and Jenny to his homes—to the magnificent Manhattan apartment, his Palm Beach mansion and California retreat—all shared with Bruna and his daughter Patricia whenever harmony prevailed.

Aldo had already provided the same luxurious way of life for Maurizio and Patrizia. It was ironic that Paolo, Aldo's son, had left Rodolfo in rebellion while Maurizio, partly through his wife Patrizia, had at least partially made things up with his father at that time.

Maurizio, now thirty-five, was twelve years his cousin Paolo's junior, with none of his experience or amount of shares in the company. So he had no direct say in its management other than through his father. Paolo, on the other hand, was a stockholder and could use his position to get across his ideas with the board of directors. Aldo might see it differently, but Paolo's rebellion, his demands for a different approach to marketing had put a powerful weapon in the hands of Aldo's jealous brother, Rodolfo.

Rodolfo took every possible occasion to visit America to confer with his family while both Paolo and Maurizio were there. He was determined to see that his son, now that they had made up their differences, should attain the power and position that he, while devoting himself to his film career, had failed to get for himself. If Aldo's sons stood in the way, he would fight them. His anger with Paolo went beyond a flare of temperament. Behind it, one concludes, lay a deep-seated hunger for control of the company.

Aldo made Paolo vice-president and managing director of the U.S. corporation, in full charge of marketing and production. In this capacity he was able to become identified with Gucci far more than had been possible while running the factory in Italy. America was brimming over with unlimited possibilities. He wanted to seize those possibilities, using the modern ideas he saw on all sides, employing his own creative talents in new and different ways.

As always his father and the Gucci board were more cautious. In Paolo's view they were failing to exploit more than a minimal amount of potential. He wanted to move into areas he believed promised dazzling opportunities for increased profitability.

He had underestimated his uncle's ambition, though, as

well as the rancor left by his abrupt departure from Florence. Rodolfo now moved to gain board backing to punish Paolo. Hindsight suggests that he let pride overcome cautious judgment in making what could only seem, since his brother was still the president, a declaration of civil war.

He sent a handwritten letter to Paolo, delivering it to his nephew without informing Aldo. In it he fired Paolo from Guccio Gucci in Italy, the parent company, for failing to carry out his duties while in Florence in charge of the factory. With the weight of Rodolfo's 50-percent shareholding, it appeared an open challenge to Aldo, the president of all worldwide operations for Gucci.

Rodolfo was a stubborn man. He had, he believed, been driven beyond the point where Paolo's rebellious interference was tolerable. If he seriously meant to provoke a division by firing Paolo, it can only have been because he felt ready to challenge Aldo's envied position at the head of the company, to seize control for himself and in due course for his son.

"He wanted power," says his daughter-in-law, Patrizia. "Power can be like a sickness with the Guccis." She could see it in the rise of Maurizio and the fall of Paolo resulting from the rivalry of their parents. The havoc it brought, she believes, was typical of Florentine vendettas. "It could produce nothing good. If there was to be a winner, there had also to be losers."

Rodolfo's letter reached Paolo in the early morning, as he was leaving for the store. That same evening he repeated to Jenny what he told Bruna, his father's mistress. "If they are going to kill me, I shall kill them." His intention, he says, was to take the battle to the enemy, to attack and destroy his Uncle Rodolfo through his father's greater position in the company. It was inconceivable to him that Rodolfo, the ex-actor, could exercise anything like the same strength.

He had, however, played into his uncle's hands. Paolo

was on the payroll of the Italian company and therefore on its staff. Before he left Italy he was advised to write to the company, saying he was going to the States to work there for the company but leaving open his position in case of his return. "I suppose after three months or more away, it did rather provoke things."

Certainly, after that length of time, and when news of his appointment as vice-president of Gucci Shops, Incorporated, reached Italy, Rodolfo could not be blamed for questioning his unexplained absence. But the handwritten letter was more abrupt and decisive than Paolo could have imagined. "I was shocked," he says. "But my father was paying my salary, a hundred and twenty thousand dollars a year, which was twice what Maurizio was getting. It was good, but not exceptional compared to what Gucci managers now get. The real problem was that I was not finding it easy working with my father."

Aldo, in his son Paolo's eyes, was behaving like a domineering autocrat. "I wasn't allowed to do anything. I had no authority." Whenever he tried to use his initiative, he says, the design flair Aldo had once talked about, his father objected.

"Maybe I'd try something different, like stuffing the handbags with colored paper in place of white. He'd grab hold of them and say, 'Don't you know colors fade?' He'd do this in front of the staff."

Aldo was furious, too, when Paolo sent back goods that had been ordered and arrived late. "We've dealt with those suppliers for years. You can't treat them like that." Paolo ignored him and canceled the orders. "Then he blew up, but if I hadn't done it the stuff would have had to be sold off cheaply, at a loss, on the seventh floor, which we called 'Gucci Seven.'"

The one thing that went smoothly for Paolo was his decoration of the Fifth Avenue windows. His designs for these won him a prize. At first Aldo seemed quite happy with them. But then Paolo hired a young window dresser. "He was considered the best in the world, and I felt lucky to get him. But the day he came in I had to go to Italy, so I left him a theme—the 'Face of the Month'—to carry out. When I called New York and asked how it had gone, the manager told me, 'Your man left. Dr. Gucci came in and asked 'Who did this window? Fire him.' My father did that without a word to me!"

Another source of conflict was the catalog. "We had a real fight over that. He didn't like my budget for advertising, which I also handled. I proposed we put 1 percent of our turnover into a special account to meet promotion costs, and he said okay, but it was never done. The catalog was all wrong, he said. So I told him, 'Why do I stay in this company? I'm not allowed to do anything. I'd be better off in Florence.' "

If Paolo had any serious thought of going back to his old job in Florence, his uncle's letter of dismissal made it impossible. "I started then, when things were so difficult with my father, to approach people to see what the possibility was to do a few lines of my own, under my own name, Paolo Gucci. There were some people making jeans who liked the idea."

He was developing these ideas when his uncle's dismissal notice arrived. The letter offered no compensation. "I'd been twenty-six years with the company and was entitled to one month's redundancy money [severance pay] for each year, almost one hundred thousand pounds [then $240,000]. They weren't prepared to pay it, so I had to go to court in Florence against the company."

The action was a blow not to be ignored. Rodolfo demanded that his brother, now the sole employer of Paolo, should take action. While the row had been contained within the family, he had seen satisfied to deal with Paolo himself as a personal matter between him and his, as he saw it, rebellious nephew. But this was a public action, a threat, as he saw it, to the business.

Paolo appealed to his executive union to back his claim. Rodolfo made offers to pay the severance pay but never did so. "It was never there. He wanted me to give up all competitive enterprises—for the rest of my life, as I remember. No millions to compensate. Nothing. I couldn't even have any contact with my own small factory, where my daughters Patrizia and Elisabetta were working."

Finally the company offered the money, but on its own terms. Paolo agreed to take it. A month later he changed his mind. "It was so obviously not right. But they said, 'No, no, you signed.' So I had to take them to court. And then my father blew up. He had a registered letter sent to me from the New York office stating that the board of directors, with no reason given, dismissed me from my job."

News of Paolo's plans to market his own lines under his own name and trademark, and the official stamp the lawsuit put on the disagreement, angered Aldo almost as much as Rodolfo. Paolo, with the letter in his hand, found him in his office, a sumptuous annex to the store's new galleria that Aldo had created for expensive jewelry and filled with original works of art, including Picasso sketches and a beautiful Modigliani canvas.

As he saw his father's face, Paolo knew what to expect. Aldo was in a temper. "Yes, I fire you! You are an idiot to try to compete with us. A fantastic idiot! I cannot protect you any more!"

Paolo, disarmingly quiet as a rule, shouted back at him. "Why do you let them try to kill me? I only wanted to make the company into something better than it is, not to destroy it. All right, if you fire me I shall make my own company. Then we will see."

He was now out of both the Italian company and the American Gucci Shops, Incorporated, without status in the Gucci organization as a whole. Aside from his three-and-a-third shares in the company and 20 percent of Gucci Parfums, an 11 percent stake in Gucci shops and 16 percent of Gucci Boutiques, he was on his own. His remaining leverage was his name. If he used it, it could cause massive confusion in marketing circles. "I was very, very angry and upset. I walked out, leaving my personal papers and so on in my office."

Paolo had warned them. God had given him the name of Gucci and it would be used to full advantage. The product line he had designed and licensed must, he decided, be offered for sale. If its similarity to the main Gucci products diverted business from the family, too bad. He had his own family to think about, his own career. Such were his self-justifying thoughts in this super-heated condition.

At the first hint that Paolo was setting up in direct competition, threatening in effect as they saw it a trade war against the family, Rodolfo and Aldo took action. Lawyers were retained, and restraining suits taken out. In every market where Paolo Gucci goods appeared, Gucci's agents worked to prevent their sale. Paolo's suppliers and distributors were cajoled, persuaded and obliged to face the prospect of cancellation of long-standing trade agreements if they handled "PG" goods. The long, bitter, enormously expensive Gucci trade war began in earnest.

But Rodolfo was sick and aging. He had cancer and was receiving radiation therapy for it. To his son he confided, "You must fight Paolo with everything you have got. He must be defeated, utterly and quickly. He is threatening everything we have, and I will not be here forever." He was over seventy.

He was still refusing to let Maurizio know that he secretly intended to sign over to him his half-share in the company even before his death. Since his son's runaway wedding he had managed to overcome any barrier between them, but his possessive love for his one child did not seem to include great trust. Maurizio, too, found it hard to see his father in anything but an ambiguous light. His wife had the difficult task of keeping a tenuous peace between them.

"Aldo once asked us," Patrizia said, "when we were on our way south through Italy, to stop in Rome for a meeting in which he tried to convince us that we were both Guccis, that

Rodolfo would not live forever, and that we should forgive and forget—all the rages, depressions, everything. Maurizio, he said, should realize that what mattered most was his real work, his career with Gucci."

That was when Aldo told Maurizio, "Look, I know that just for the moment it will be very difficult for you to work for your father. Why not come to New York and work for me?"

It was the start of Maurizio's split life and experience between Milan and New York. It was also a major influence in creating a far deeper conflict between the two branches of the family than probably would otherwise have occurred. Looking back, it seems somewhat ironic that Aldo, the war's first casualty, proposed it.

He apparently did not sense that his nephew was following in his father's footsteps, that Rodolfo was and always had been envious of his elder brother's position in the business. Aldo, it seems, did not recognize the threat to his power in the company that Rodolfo perceived in Paolo's insurrection.

A proud as well as possessive man, Rodolfo made a dangerous foe, as others in the family were learning. Paolo believes that if his father had paid more attention to the depth of jealousy and ambition behind Rodolfo's behavior towards Maurizio, he might have been able to predict the path of his own future difficulties. "Instead, he made the mistake of believing that he was sheltered from my uncle's hostility by his own strength in the company. Perhaps, too, he equated his brother with himself. But my father is very different from my uncle. He does not notice details. He thinks only of grand plans, of sailing before the wind. It never occurs to him that barnacles can stick to his hull and drag him down."

Some might say that Paolo himself was one of the barnacles. But the full effects of his behavior were still to show themselves.

15

O ABSOLOM

For years Paolo had been quietly reviewing all Gucci accounts he could lay hands on. He wanted to see for himself what was going on in the inner workings of the Gucci offices, to confirm or deny his suspicions that the company was not making the progress and profits he thought it should.

Reading the balance sheets and other figures, Paolo noticed what he considered a number of irregularities. He knew that Aldo rarely concerned himself with such details, but these operations were being carried out in his father's name and under his chairmanship. Paolo located documents involving millions of dollars in taxable revenues that were being removed to offshore accounts in return for seemingly fictitious services. Did they not add up to a massive tax-evasion?

They were also weapons to use, indictments of the way the company that had rejected him was being run. They could be used, he told his attorney, Stuart Speiser, as ammunition in his trademark action, his campaign for the right to trade under his own name.

A lawsuit against the company was necessarily also against his father, Aldo, as head of the company. By introducing the papers as evidence of illegal goings-on, Paolo would incriminate his father, whether or not he was personally responsible. They would also, he believed, support his claim that he was being ignored and denied permission to offer his guidance on how things should be.

He had the documents copied and filed in support of his suit. They seemed to bespeak tax dodges and worse that had been carried out over the years. His explanation for submitting them to the court, and thereby bringing them under public gaze, was that such things would never have been committed if he had been allowed a say in the running of the company. Privately he let his father know that he would withdraw them before any damage was done, provided Aldo withdrew opposition to Paolo's trademark demands and settled with him.

If his father and the company did not agree, Aldo would face criminal charges. Whether Paolo considered or fully understood the possible consequences, he did know the bargaining power of what he was doing. What he did not know was that his father believed, incorrectly as it turned out, that even if convicted he would probably suffer no more than a stiff fine.

They were, then, set on a collision course that could only end in disaster for at least one of them. If Aldo did not give in it was Paolo's intention to reveal the evidence, though he says he never expected to have to do so. "Of course not. I only meant to make him see that I had a right to make a living. If he had talked to me it would have never happened. It seems Aldo did not believe he would ever go to jail. In fact, nobody believed it would come to that. I heard that Aldo understood that a deal had actually been made under which, if he paid several millions, my father would only be fined or given a suspended sentence."

According to Paolo, only one thing stopped the deal from going through. "When the case was reported in the press and on television the judge in New York received hundreds of letters from Americans all demanding Aldo Gucci's imprisonment. My father was a foreigner, an Italian selling luxury goods, his handbags cost eight thousand dollars. And so on. Why should money get him off?"

To some observers the action of a son, however wronged, in deliberately revealing damaging evidence against his aged if perhaps not entirely innocent father looked more like Old Testament wrath and vengeance than just retribution.

Paolo did not see it like that. It was not his fault, he maintained. If anyone had made an error of judgment, it was Aldo. "The papers were only intended to force his hand. I introduced them as a lever, to make him see that if he didn't let me have at least the use of my name, I would let some very nasty cats out of the bag. He was stupid not to realize what would happen."

It would seem Aldo should have known that if the case was not withdrawn and the apparently incriminating papers with it, they could hardly escape the attention of the Internal Revenue Service. Even if, as Paolo believes, Aldo chose to ignore the possible consequences, his refusal to offer some form of compromise to his sons does seem rather foolhardy. Given his position now, it would be difficult to claim principle as a reason.

Paolo's view is that his father believed too much in his own power, the weight of his wealth and importance. "Maybe he really thought he could beat the rap. He was spending a fortune on lawyers. It was his mistake not to offer me a deal, not mine."

No doubt the stubborn pride of the Guccis had much to do with it. Aldo said he was generally aware of what the documents contained and the extent of the danger he was in, even if he did not feel responsible. His lawyers tried to have them sealed and withdrawn from the court at the conclusion of Paolo's case. They were refused. "In the ordinary way," the judge told them, "I would accept a wish to avoid publicity of this sort, but when did the Guccis ever want to avoid publicity? That's something new."

The papers contained details of secret off-loading of Gucci profits. Panamanian companies, based in Hong Kong, were trading as creative-design suppliers to Gucci Shops, Incorporated. But what designs were forthcoming, if any, were to be regarded by the authorities as mere window-dressing. As soon as the United States authorities got wind of this, they began detailed investigations.

Perhaps the most damning document was a copy of a letter from Edward H. Stern, Gucci's chief accountant in New York. On October 20, 1975, he had written to Aldo: "In accordance with your instructions, I had several meetings in Hong Kong with Mr. Kerry Obonai and Mr. Anthony K. P. Yung . . . both of these gentlemen have been informed of the purposes for which the corporation was organized."

Stern set it out in detail. "Four invoices were made out to Gucci Shops, Inc. . . . In order to have substantiation for the services for which such invoices were rendered, and to document the underlying need for the company, it will be necessary to send a variety of fashion designs and sketches to Gucci Shops for approval or rejection. This is only to build up some sort of record."

There would be no bona fide supply of "fashion designs and sketches."

Stern went on: "The more numerous and varied such sketches and designs are, the better will be the possibility for substantiation of this as an expense by Gucci Shops, Inc. It is my wish and desire to build an overwhelming set of facts, with adequate supporting documentation, to explain the expense . . . There is [thereby] a good possibility that all profits generated in Hong Kong would be completely exempt from all income taxes."

And Gucci Shops, Incorporated, would be able to avoid paying millions of dollars in taxes to the United States Treasury on profits legitimately made there.

Once in possession of this evidence, and following a visit to Hong Kong where they unearthed the operations of the companies in which the money had been secreted, the tax men had their case. It opened and shut more firmly than a Gucci handbag.

It proved there had been siphoning off of large slices of the American Gucci profits for work not done. In the accounts of Gucci Shops, Incorporated, for the year ending August 31, 1979, the sum of $136,275.75 listed as "designer fees," and further items amounting in all to more than a million and a half dollars attributed to these far-flung "operations," were as false as the symbol on a Japanese fake Gucci.

But before the IRS completed their work, Edward Stern died. His removal from the case allowed Aldo to add a claim of total ignorance to his plea of guilty. Paolo's view was "Both my father and my mother must have known. When I looked into the Hong Kong side of it, I found that a commission was being paid to them both for all those fake transactions— through their Panamanian companies, Vanguard, which was my father's, and Rodolfo's Anglo-American—as if they were real."

Paolo insists that he had never disguised the fact that he meant to use his evidence if pressed. His father now had to face the fact that here was family war to the death. At least it would have saved money to have made peace before his own freedom was sacrificed.

Paolo's position was stated by Speiser in his submission to the court: "Paolo Gucci was fired from his position as vice-president of Gucci Shops, Inc., because of his persistence in attempting to bring to the attention of the Board of Directors irregularities in the business dealings of Gucci Shops, Inc., and because of his continuous refusal to participate in said irregular business dealings."

In other words, Paolo was saying he was innocent of any part of the illegal manipulations uncovered in the IRS investigation.

But in his Uncle Rodolfo's eyes, Paolo was being treacherous in trying to set up his own lines. His use, or misuse as it was regarded, of the Gucci name he had the luck to be born with was to Rodolfo an act that threatened unfair competition to the family business that had provided him with his upbringing and living.

One million eight hundred thousand dollars was authorized by the Gucci board in its first year to fight Paolo's venture. Rodolfo personally wrote cautionary letters to each of Paolo's suppliers and agents. Paolo's Manhattan lawyer, Stuart Speiser, was up to his shirtsleeves in writs, affidavits, pleas and counterpleas.

"The company's line was that Gucci could not continue to do business with suppliers while they handled a competing line. Our submission was that 'PG' was entirely separate. It could not be confused in people's minds with 'GG.' We countersued."

Judge Lee P. Cagliardi dismissed Paolo's case for "lack of justifiable controversy," legalese for arguable and tangible evidence. "We had been unable to prove actual interference," Speiser says, "with his marketing. Gucci had simply told him not to use his name, which did not constitute a threat."

Speiser tried another route, meanwhile collecting evidence. The trademark war entered its second phase, with legal fees spiraling upward on both sides.

How long could Paolo, now without salary, keep it up? Rodolfo believed he would soon be brought to his knees. Paolo's perhaps predictable reply was that he had no other course. He had been forced to do what he did. Being rejected by his father when Rodolfo was clearly out to block him had left him with no other weapon. He maintained that his determination to meet force with force was purely in reaction to the dismissive and contemptuous treatment he was receiving. It was at this time that Jenny began to accept that she had married into a very un-English family. "The situation was really appalling. What shocked me most was how self-destructive the Guccis could be. I had to suffer all their terrible spite, all the greed and conceit they show to each other. Because I was a Gucci I was expected to put up with it. But this wasn't at all how English people behave, it really was more as I imagine life with the Borgias must have been."

Sometimes, Jenny Gucci says, "I get to the point where I just scream 'Let me out!' If it was only legal, one could fight that, but it's not. It's all spite, one out to get the other. They double-cross and behave like spoiled children. 'I'm going to get Aldo!,' 'I'm going to get Giorgio!'—just like children at their worst. All they are doing is destroying everything they've got, their entire empire, and they can't see it. They see themselves as on a par with the Republic of Italy, or the Queen of England."

Nor was the war confined to her husband. Paolo's rebellion had apparently sharpened Rodolfo's interest in the acquisition of power for power's sake. Where before he had been more or less content to let his charismatic brother earn and wear the laurels, wield the power and enjoy maximum privileges, now he was acquiring a taste for being in total control.

Rodolfo's private and expensive hobby, which it seems had grown since his acting days into a near-addiction, was the making of his autobiographical film. It filled his life. A rather egocentric study of his family history, he intended to leave it to his son as a reminder of Gucci pride and destiny. Using professional studios and equipment in Hollywood, he spent a small fortune on the document intended to guide his son through life.

Nowhere in it did Rodolfo express his own keen appetite for the reins of power. But while paying scant but respectful tribute to Aldo, the script suggested that he, rather than his brother, had played the major part in building up the family business. In a montage of shots he played the last, perhaps greatest, role of his career, emerging as wise, philosophical leader of the family. Gucci's greatness, he seemed to be saying, was richly deserved. It was a revealing performance, yet it only hinted at the apparently growing appetite Rodolfo was developing late in his life for being in the driver's seat, leading to increasing differences between himself and Aldo. During one difference of opinion over the company's subsidiary perfume company, he probably showed Aldo too much of his hand.

The perfume company, Gucci Parfums, had by now become more profitable than the parent company. Its original purpose, to be a distribution channel for the new perfume and other related accessories, had been altered by the sale of the Gucci perfume license to the American company that made it. It then began marketing a number of items similar to those sold by Gucci itself.

What had begun almost as a sideline was now doing brisker business than the main company, including its small boutique offshoot that Giorgio had created and brought into the business. It was also in direction competition with them, selling identical lines.

This upset Rodolfo's plans. When the perfume company had been no more than a minor enterprise he had let himself agree to 80 percent of its stock being distributed among others in the family, including Paolo. Now, with the growing importance of the company and its healthy sales volume outdoing the parent company, his relatively meager 20 percent in it seemed to him, unfair, and it in effect diminished his fifty-fifty partnership in the main company.

Aldo therefore held the controlling interest and Rodolfo could be out-voted. Indulging Aldo's wish to give an incentive participation to his sons while providing a balm to Paolo's nagging complaints had threatened his power base.

"We should rationalize the situation," he told Aldo in New York. "It is quite inequitable for me, with half the main shareholding, to have only a fifth of the perfume company."

Aldo might have wondered if there was not more to his brother's request than a desire to straighten things out. Rodolfo's son Maurizio was left out of the original perfume company share-split because he was outside the company at the time, working with his father-in-law and at odds with his father. But if Aldo gave in, his own sons would have their shareholding reduced. "I can't see any reason now for making my sons part with their shares so that you can have more," he told his brother. "You and I hold equal amounts. Isn't that enough?"

By 1981 the conflict had reached the point where Rodolfo apparently felt he had to show who was the master. He ordered Roberto, responsible as president of the perfume company in Italy for its day-to-day running, to cease immediately using the Gucci trademark "in competition with the parent company." The new enterprise, Rodolfo commented, must conform to the same standards and disciplines as Guccio Gucci itself: there could be no show of maverick independence.

On October 19 Roberto telexed his uncle in Milan: "In the name of my father and brothers, I must warn of the serious consequences that these propositions could have for the solidity and structure of our company." In the same message he as much as told his uncle to cease all attempts to control the perfume offshoot: "I am absolutely surprised and shocked," he wired. "I firmly contest, as administrator of Gucci Parfums, your insinuations of failure to cooperate, and of causing market confusion between the two companies. I remind you that Gucci Parfums has the same rights as every company belonging to our Guccio Gucci group, was created by the same shareholders as Guccio Gucci, with you included, and that it distributes exclusively Gucci products for the improvement of our firm and the commercial well-being of our factory, in the full knowledge and adherence of its bylaws."

Behind this, it would seem, was the feeling already seen growing within the family that Rodolfo was making a bid for control of the company. "Without fully understanding what personal interests lie behind this," Roberto continued, "it seems very strange and absurd to all of us for you to want to overturn our [perfume company] undertaking at this time, in clear contrast to the interests of the Group." He wound up by requesting his uncle to "abstain from any further damaging interventions." He would, he said, reserve for himself the right to take any action necessary to protect his company and the Group "if you fail to do so."

Rodolfo did not yield easily. As for Aldo, he knew that his son Paolo's rebellion had made Rodolfo anxious for power, but he was not going to have his brother challenging his position.

This first major clash between the brothers, over the allocation of the perfume company's shares, left a bitter taste. Paolo remembers a scene between them: "My uncle began by threatening my father. He demanded more shares in the perfume company or else. This, I believe, infuriated my father, who could never stand anyone trying to browbeat him. He told me later he was going to have his brother thrown off the board of the American perfume company, Gucci Perfumes of America."

If Rodolfo's death had not intervened, the Gucci family war might have extended to other frontiers. By now Aldo was alerted to his brother's ambitions and began to move to protect his position.

He called a board meeting at which Rodolfo's situation presumably would be hammered out. Aldo saw it as a means of gathering the support of others in the family who owed much to him. He believed that it was only his enterprise and success that had built their business. Now he wanted their voting power, and he expected Paolo to help him get it.

Paolo, however, no longer saw his loyalty in terms of subjection to his father, or the firm. The long association he had had with Gucci had been compromised by what he saw as the unwarranted treatment he had received. "I told my father, 'Fine, but what about the use of my name? I have no objection to your using the stockholders to defeat Uncle Rodolfo. But, if I agree to that, will you give me the right to use my name on my products?'"

If the answer had been yes, most of Paolo's problems

would have been solved. It was becoming crucially important for him to honor agreements made on his own behalf since leaving Gucci. The licenses Rodolfo had refused to let him sell during his time with the company had been snapped up by suppliers when he left. They recognized the value of his name, even if the trademark had to be changed from "GG" to "PG." Both were Gucci, which was what mattered.

Timing was therefore vital. His licensees around the world were now ready to release the "PG" lines internationally. But the threat of legal action by Gucci, of cease-and-desist orders, impounding and confiscation, was a serious deterrent. They wanted further assurance from Paolo, which he could only give if his father agreed to his counterproposal.

Aldo's reaction, according to Paolo: "He went mad. I was making conditions, trying to force his hand. Nobody did that to Aldo Gucci! Nobody, in his opinion, had the right to challenge a Gucci—not even his own son."

Meetings between Paolo and his father were often emotionally charged, but his one in Aldo's office went beyond the usual limit. Aldo's charisma could thaw any official stiffness in most people. But he could make it hard, if not impossible, for younger members of the family to disagree with him. Paolo, however, was a different proposition.

"How can you expect me to help you fight Rodolfo from usurping your power when you won't even let me breathe?" Paolo said. "I must have some rights. If not in the company, then surely I can use my abilities outside. You fired me, remember? I didn't ask to be fired."

What happened next is described by Paolo as "typical of my father in his worst moods. He went crazy. The fact that we were in his office made no difference, this to him was a rebellion by one of his sons daring to challenge his authority. The business nature of our meeting was forgotten. It became a purely personal encounter."

Aldo's version of events may well be different, but he refuses to discuss the matter. Perhaps, wounded by what he views as his son's betrayal, and having suffered humiliation and a prison sentence in his eighties, he considers the less said the better. Paolo remembers a crimson flush of anger spreading across his father's handsome face. Aldo's voice, he says, rose in a soaring arpeggio. "You . . . you . . . you dare to threaten me? Get out, get away from here, you crazy idiot."

Aldo had seized an ashtray. It was made of lead crystal, a Gucci item that Paolo had designed and had made near Florence. In a gesture of fury and despair his father, he says, smashed it, accompanying this with a stream of invective, including, "You're crazy, why don't you do as I tell you?"

The ashtray shattered, showering Paolo with splinters of crystal. Paolo says he realized that the argument had got out of hand. Controlling himself with an effort, he said, "Well, if you think I am here only to do your bidding at the point of a gun, you are the one who is crazy." He then went out, slamming the door.

That night Paolo went to his father's house. Bruna was alone, Aldo had not come home yet. When Paolo told her what had happened, feeling the comfort of a woman who knew his father's ferocious temper as well as he did, he felt better. "I tell you," he said, "if they really mean to ruin me, I will do everything, everything in my power, to destroy them."

He apparently had no idea how this was to be accomplished, but it was no empty threat. "Of course. If they wanted my extinction, why should I not have theirs? They were the ones who had chucked me out, forbidding me even to use my own name to make a living. Why should I spare any of them?"

He knew that he already had made potent enemies within his family. They and their millions were not to be crushed by mere threats. They believed they had infinite resources with which to fight off any attempt Paolo could make to bring them down.

Well, they would soon see what he could do. Paolo had

other means. During this time in New York working for the firm, he had found ideal manufacturing conditions in Haiti. These promised considerable profits, the cost of labor amounting to less than a tenth of what American labor had to be paid. And he had obtained local permission to develop products there.

"So though I had to stop all that production for the company once I was fired, that didn't stop me setting the same machinery to work on my own 'PG' lines. I could and did use some of the processes I had set up for my own products. The machinery was still there, and I knew where to get hold of the best Italian craftsmen to operate them. They trained local workers. While Rodolfo was taking out more and more lawsuits to prevent my marketing my goods, I was working to establish my name."

It did, of course, put him in direct competition with the family business. His skills, and the contacts he had made both in the manufacturing side of the business in Italy and the commercial world in New York, were valuable assets. The moment he showed that his determination to market his own products was no empty boast, the family trade war settled into a costly, bitter battle.

Paolo's licenses, the marketing of his "PG" lines, was fought wherever they appeared. Rodolfo seemed to make it his personal crusade. Lawyers in every country where they showed up were retained and instructed to sue to suppress the distribution of the products.

Paolo's brother Roberto, on Rodolfo's orders, handled the campaign for Gucci. The lawyers were to claim that the lines were "counterfeit Gucci products," which would serve to obtain sequestration orders.

And, of course, the costs mounted daily. Roberto, the only one in the family assigned the tedious task of administration, said that they were incurring extravagant legal fees. Rodolfo secured a grudging agreement at board level to meet the entire budget, but Aldo wanted it to end, and Paolo was showing no signs of giving in.

He was in the better position. Though he was earning nothing, and fighting another lawsuit against the company for nearly $175,000 in severance pay due on his discharge from the Italian company, the sale of licenses was bringing in some forty or fifty thousand dollars each. Every supplier or manufacturer who signed a contract with Paolo was in effect subsidizing his expenses in the campaign. The battle might have lasted for years if Aldo had not persuaded his irate relations to call a halt.

Suddenly the board of directors of Gucci Perfumes of America, under Roberto's presidency and Aldo's chairmanship, proposed an armistice. From Paolo's viewpoint the terms were too good to be ignored.

First, if he dropped all charges he would be paid his severance pay, plus interest and additional sums for the extra months involved. Then a fundamental change would be made in the whole Gucci empire. The scattered and separately owned Guccio Gucci main company, and the various operations such as Gucci Parfums and Gucci Perfumes of America (as well as the British and French Gucci Ltd. firms and Gucci Shops, Inc., of America) would be welded together to form Guccio Gucci, S.p.A., a new company for which stock would be offered on the Milan stock exchange. The names of the different companies would remain but their ownership would be equalized. Thus Aldo's three sons would receive 11 percent of the whole. Paolo would have to give up his trademark. And to counteract his dismissals from all previous posts, a new division of Gucci Perfume, Gucci Plus, would be set up under this directorship with licensing capability. It seemed his dream would come true!

This reorganization was conceived as a means of ending the fighting. A freshly created line of merchandise, to include the items Paolo was producing or licensing under his "PG" logo, would give him scope to design and expand his ideas around the world. More, his contract would be guaranteed for six years and be renewable thereafter. The black sheep, as some viewed him, could return to the fold.

It was too good to be true, Paolo thought. He knew and distrusted his uncle. "I was suspicious, so I tried to build in as many safeguards as possible. I felt it was obvious that they would try and do me in if I didn't watch every word in the contract."

The inducement was that he and his brothers were each to receive 5 percent of the gross profits of the new Gucci corporation, drawn from all areas of the company. In return they would give up their shares in the Gucci Perfume companies. Paolo's advisers pointed out that he would be left with approximately 8 percent of the whole, while Rodolfo would at least achieve his goal, an overall 50-percent share.

Was it a fair deal? "Absolutely not! These shares in the profits could be voted away at any time. It was crazy! Stupid, legal madness!" says Paolo.

Yet Paolo signed an agreement on February 17, 1982, establishing the formation of the new company. And when the statutory one month's period for registration has passed in March 1982, he attended its first official board meeting. A meeting that was to change the whole nature of the war of the Guccis.

16

THICKER THAN BLOOD

As Paolo tells it, the meeting had been going on for more than an hour when he decided that it was time to make one last attempt to get things straight. Until then he had had the feeling that he was talking only to the four paneled walls of the boardroom. "One thing still bothers me," he said. He thought he saw a flicker of impatience cross his father's face.

"Well, what is it?" Aldo said, tapping a notebook with a pencil, controlling himself with obvious difficulty. What was his son wanting now? Weren't they bending almost double to give him what he wanted? His pale blue eyes fixed on Paolo with cloudy intensity.

His son glared back. "As a company, don't you think that we are now mature enough to extend our range to include a younger, less affluent public? Hasn't Gucci reached a position in marketing, manufacturing, fashion and so on that we can now also come down-market and sell our lower-priced lines in a wider field?"

His uncle looked across at Aldo, who was chairing the meeting. "Will you please remind Paolo that we are not going to prostitute our business to accommodate his fantastic notions?" He winced. The cancer in his body, which he believed was being arrested by the deep radiation treatment, still bothered him under stress.

"Paolo knows what our policy is," Aldo said. "He can't expect the new position we are offering, the entire restructuring of the company and his position in it, to change our fundamental direction. That is quite impossible."

One thing was not impossible. By now Paolo was owed three to four times the 100,000 pounds ($140,000) he had at first claimed as severance pay. Once he signed the agreement, which would not be binding until officially ratified, this would be paid to him. His unsalaried life would be over. At the least he could get what he felt was rightfully his out of the deal.

But, it seems, suspicion still haunted him. On the face of it the deal he was being offered looked fair and attractive. If he accepted, he would be back in the firm with an executive role, a director of the new company and with a considerable share both in equity and profits. In addition, and this was a most important matter for him, the licensing contracts he had made for his "PG" wares would be taken into the company.

Fine, but would that allow him to develop as he wished? Or would the concepts he wanted to put into effect in expanding through licensing be delayed and suppressed as in the past?

Could he trust the fine print in this contract? Did he read the meaning correctly? Would he, as the offer seemed to allow, be able to incorporate his own ideas in the restructured company, along with the lines he had been developing independently, which he called now "Gucci Plus"?

"Absolutely," Rodolfo, who was to be the new president, told him.

"Yes, but will my signature *on its own* be sufficient to make such commitments?" Paolo asked.

Paolo remembers there was an awkward pause. "Naturally, you will require board consent to any decision requiring a contract with the company." Rodolfo was smiling, but Paolo thought he saw a small vein under the skin of his forehead pulse into life.

So that was it—he was to be allowed scope, but not, by his lights, to be fully trusted. Their fear of changing their image of Gucci as a tight family business would only let them go so far. And knowing that he would balk at anything less than total authority, they had, in his view, fudged this issue.

"Rodolfo's jealousy wouldn't let him agree to anyone but himself placing orders. He wanted to control them all, through the wholesalers he dealt with," Paolo says.

As director of design in the factory, Paolo remembered how he had once upset his uncle by buying direct from a Spanish tie manufacturer who supplied top-quality goods at prices that could not be matched anywhere else. The offer had seemed a profitable chance to use the same methods worldwide, to override the wasteful use of middlemen. But Rodolfo had removed the chance of that.

"Once again I saw that I was to be given power in name only, the merest shadow of authority. Not by any means enough to alter their narrow thinking or to persuade them to go into licensing, which they were still totally against." Nevertheless, he felt he could not afford to turn the offer down without a full-scale tryout.

"Very well, I agree," he said. "But what you are asking me to do under this contract"—he waved the document at them—"is to give up entirely my own business, the marketing of my lines under my 'PG' trademark. It takes away all my shares in the perfume company in exchange for a percentage of profits. And it does not even allow me to make my own decisions without the full consent of the board, even though I am to be an executive director."

They let him have his say. It was Paolo, after all, the rebellious one. If he signed, who would worry about what was going on in that head of his? One by one they took out

their Gucci pens and added their ornate Florentine signatures, more like oriental calligraphy than Roman letter-
ing.

"Time for lunch." Aldo, dapper as always in a Gucci
blazer and dark steam-pressed flannels, led the way. Rodolfo
followed, as he had always followed his elder brother. Paolo
was left alone in the empty room.

He knew they had left the boardroom believing that the
worst of their problems were over. But his signature meant
nothing, he decided, unless he allowed it to stand unchallenged. Until he and his lawyers had gone over every
point, sifting and dissecting the whys and wherefores, he
believed that signature of his was worthless.

Then, unexpectedly, Aldo telexed Paolo not to sign anything to do with the new company, Gucci Plus. He had heard
that Paolo was still in touch with suppliers. "I was contacting—only contacting—but he wanted to know what I
was doing. He took away the only power I had."

Eventually a form of agreement was reached under
which Paolo withdrew all but one of his lawsuits against the
company. Then to his surprise—it is considered unusual
practice for a lawyer to make a direct approach to a principal on the other side in litigation without the authority of
his opponent's lawyer without the express authority of his
opponent lawyer, which is *not* to say such authority was not
granted in this instance—he received a call from an American lawyer representing the company.

"He asked me to give up my claim, now amounting to
eight million dollars, for unfair dismissal. I called Speiser in
New York and said, "They want me to drop the case. Should I
do it?" Speiser's reply was a blunt no. And a question about
who was going to guarantee that the Gucci Plus–lines deal
would go through.

The answer to that, as Paolo well knew, was nobody. He
called the company's lawyer back and told him, "Okay, I'll

agree to do that. But only in six months' time, when I see what is happening." There was also something else on his mind that needed thought and discussion. It concerned the almost-forgotten family matter of how his father and uncle, between them, had secured the whole of his Uncle Vasco's shares after his death.

"After my Aunt Maria, Uncle Vasco's widow, died—soon after him and leaving everything to a brother, sister and niece, Josanna—I'd seen from papers that she had signed away all his shares in Guccio Gucci. The whole lot went to my father and Rodolfo in exchange for the million pounds in cash which they paid her."

But Paolo believed that there were other shares his aunt was unaware of. So far as he knows, his late Uncle Vasco had held shares in all Gucci's foreign empire. "These were, as I knew, exactly the same as my father's and uncle's. They had been divided equally between the three brothers when each of the overseas companies was formed."

Had his Aunt Maria signed those away too? Or had they otherwise become the properties of his father and Uncle Rodolfo?

There seemed only one way to find out, since he could not rely on any of those who could have told him, such as his father's lawyers. "I went to my aunt's successors and put it to them. They had no idea what I was talking about. 'What shares?' they asked. I knew if I told them what I believed they might have lost they would never get over it. Instead I said, 'I am not sure about that. But there is a possibility that some of the shares owned by your late sister and aunt should rightly belong to you.'"

Paolo told them, "I am prepared to help you track them down if you will form a company with me in which I have a half-share." His interest was in the voting power the shares would give him. But the relatives behaved, in Paolo's view, in an obtuse fashion. "They refused to listen to me! I believe I could have made them millions, but they didn't want to know."

The relations may well have suspected that he wanted to entangle them in the family feud. They had had more than enough of it while Vasco was alive. The problems dividing the Guccis were apparently not something they wanted to take sides in for the sake of a few shares.

But due to a clause in the original deeds of the company set up by Guccio, "any son who dies leaving no sons to inherit his share in the company must sell to the others." Paolo's Aunt Maria had obeyed this without question. "She had never traveled abroad, never been in England in her life," Paolo explained. "How could she know the value of those shares in the English, French and American companies? And how could she have given her approval to part with them if she thought she was only selling the Italian company shares?"

His failure to obtain the shares was not Paolo's last card. Diligent investigation by the IRS in America, on Aldo's trail following Paolo's exposures, had revealed a further mysterious absence of large sums of money. No less than eighteen million dollars had, as they put it, been subtracted from the revenues of Gucci Shops, Inc.

Paolo seized on this. "At least half must have gone into Rodolfo's pocket, but what happened to the other half I couldn't say. My father said nothing about it when admitting to the Hong Kong tax situation."

To the rest of the family, Paolo's seeming vendetta appeared pointlessly destructive. What was the sense in crippling or even wounding those running the company? He himself held shares in it worth at the very least many millions? Why diminish them?

Maurizio, watching his father's angry embroilment in the feud, saw little to evoke his sympathy for either side. "I had to ask myself why we didn't build for the future. Why were we living in the past? For all those years we had been giving space to our competitors, letting them build up on our

success. We were the first to go overseas, the first in everything. My uncle had created the image, and my father was a
fantastic creator of beautiful things, but you have to put in
seed to get the crops, and they just weren't doing that."

He found himself standing outside the emotional atmosphere of the battle. "Only one-half of my blood was
Florentine. I had my mother's German, too, and in that I was
very different from my father, who trusted nobody. Maybe
after three years he might take someone at his word, but not
before. And my uncle's temperament was wholly Italian.
That was why I was not always of their opinions."

His lawyer's training had taught him that litigation was
very often unnecessary and always expensive. "Paolo started
going his own way with no knowledge of other things, no
board of directors [Maurizio was a firm believer in surrounding himself with a body of legal advisers]. He thought he
could do as he pleased because, in his own opinion, he was a
genius."

Maurizio on his cousin's behavior in the business: "There
were always problems with Paolo, dating back to the early
sixties. Not that I had anything against him personally but
he was a strange guy. Maybe he was overshadowed by the
figure of his father, I don't know. But I remember when I
went into the factory as a very young man he would always
be moving around, going from one job to another. First he
was a designer, then he was not a designer. Then he left the
factory and went to America. Then from America, back to
Italy. Then from Italy . . . always trying to conquer something he could not conquer."

While in America Maurizio had had his first glimpse of
the Paolo who had taken it upon himself to go against the
rest of the family. "I was there with Aldo when he came over
from Italy. He started right away refusing to accept the way
his father was doing things in the shop. I tried to tell him he
was maddening my uncle but it didn't work."

Maurizio says he once saw Paolo storm into his father's
office demanding an explanation of why one of his designs

had not been approved. Aldo pointed out that a similar line already existed, that Paolo's design ran counter to company policy. "There was the usual emotional, excitable scene. Paolo left in a fury. Later, when all the evidence had been collected and taken to him, he said, 'You're right, you're great,' as if nothing had happened."

Roberto Gucci also was a critic of his elder brother. "I have an affection for him. He had a place inside the company, like I had, but he wanted to go his own way. Nothing in the company pleased him, everything was no good in his eyes. We were 'living in the past,' ancient people with out-of-date mentalities."

He laughed. "Yes, Paolo insisted we must license—here, there and everywhere. And if you said, 'Listen, Paolo, when you license an exclusive name it means you're finished, it means you are selling out, like squeezing the juice out of an orange,' he refused to listen."

The one of the family whom Paolo referred to sarcastically as "my darling brother," Roberto, gazes across at the blown-up photographs of Guccio and Aida, his grandparents, and at the array of framed shots of his many obedient children decorating his modern office in Florence. As the company's administrative director he enjoys what his brother had scorned, a safe position.

But he shares Maurizio's concern for the costs of the family conflict. "We told Paolo, 'Look, you must respect the rules of the game if you want to stay keeping your shares. You can't fight the company and remain inside it. If you want to go your own way, outside, then sell your shares. You can't be part of us and a competitor at the same time.'"

Roberto confesses that he personally "didn't follow all that went on in the company outside Italy." He only knew that in his view competition of the kind Paolo was threatening could be fatal. "It was like this. A close friend gets a tumor. You come home from seeing him, throw open the window, breathe deeply, and say 'thank God I'm healthy!' But the next morning you wake up and find you too have a cancerous tumor. Who knows which of us was going to be in danger at any moment?"

For Roberto, their achievements, the fact that by 1986 there were seventeen Guccis working in the business, outweighed all other problems for him. His paternalistic view of the empire built by his grandfather and father was that nobody, certainly not anyone with Gucci blood, should be given the chance to damage it. "And if all of us started using our Gucci name for a competitive business, then it would be good-bye to everything."

Roberto widened his pale blue Gucci eyes. "Can you imagine how he ever reached the point where he confronted his own father that way? Wasn't that fantastic?"

Strong words, but it is a view apparently shared by his cousin, Maurizio. "To do these things to your own blood relations, your own father . . . how did you explain it? I had no words." He added quickly in bewilderment, "Yet they love each other! Six months ago they met in Rome and it was 'Oh, Paolo!' and 'Oh, Father!' "

Their Aunt Grimalda and Uncle Giovanni take, if possible, an even stronger view. Giovanni was angry as he spoke. He had seen a good deal of Paolo during the six months it took him to complete the building of the Scandicci factory. He says he sensed then that one day Paolo's nature would make trouble for them all. "He didn't know what he was doing, he was attacking his own family business . . ."

Opinions of similar heat and anger flow freely between the Guccis. Patrizia, Maurizio's estranged wife, does not underestimate the danger the family was in. "They didn't know what harm they were doing to themselves. To their own company!"

Paolo Gucci remained unmoved. After that informal preliminary meeting with his father and uncle to discuss the new company in February 1982, he felt very sure of his ground. Once he had received the severance pay and interest due to him, he would take stock very carefully before parting with his shares or any other leverage he still possessed. They had promised much, now let them convince him that they could deliver.

Aldo's and Rodolfo's proposed armistice was an olive branch offered to Paolo. Apparently they had as yet no idea that he was still evaluating the whole deal, knew nothing of his suspicions or that he was debating whether or not to trade the foundations of his "PG" business for their offer.

Thirty days were required to elapse before the Articles of Association of the new company could be ratified by the Florence *Tribunale,* allowing time to collect the money due to him and still being able to back out. Fortunately, from Paolo's viewpoint, there had been a delay in obtaining the transfers for his shares in the perfume company, so they were still in his possession.

"Meanwhile my Uncle Rodolfo telexed me to bring a list of my proposals to the first meeting of the full board in March. He wanted a detailed rundown of the contracts I had made and any other marketing ideas I had. As I understood it, my 'Paolo Gucci' lines would be approved without question so that my suppliers—the ones I had contracted to make my 'PG' products—would have their contracts altered and incorporated in the new company."

His "Gucci Plus" lines were highly competitive merchandise. He covered four pages with a detailed projection of them, and of the marketing factors that made the lines attractive. He summarized in detail why he proposed to introduce them to the new company. Then he took the list of his proposals and his licensing contracts to the meeting in Florence in the hope at last his ideas would be considered.

He would be disappointed once again. "Instead of accepting my proposals, and without even letting me show them the contracts, they voted against them. Every one. They said the whole concept was 'contrary to the interests of the company,' when those very interests were what I had been appointed to promote. What else had they expected but my ideas, my designs?"

His Uncle Rodolfo had, he said, promised, "You are to be
the director of this whole project, to handle its production
and sell its goods." Paolo had believed him. As he said, "The
licensing was to be in my hands, so I was given to understand. Then when it came right down to it I was nothing—
they had put in the contract 'with the approval of the board
of directors.'"

In his Cousin Maurizio's view the opposition to Paolo
was an essential protection against his "radicalism."
Maurizio still had no shares to vote but he watched critically
as Paolo kept up his determined campaign. "He wanted to
sign contracts when and wherever he chose. Without reference to any of us. Of course, that was completely unaccepta-
ble. And there was another side to it, too. Every time he dealt
with something of ours, he invented another one of his own,
which he claimed to have the right to use under his own
name. Those lines of his really belonged to us."

But Paolo has only scorn for such objections. "Until that
meeting I had had no idea I needed board approval to do as I
wanted with the licenses. I was elected. I believed I had the
right of signature, independently of any of them. My job was
to run the show, and that clause about the approval of the
board was not really valid in my case."

Valid or not, the new board's refusal to listen to or accept
Paolo's ideas and commitments seriously widened the
breach in the family. Rodolfo, a sick man but still continuing
his full duties in the belief that his radiotherapy treatment
would hold the cancer in check, conceded to Aldo that the
device to bring Paolo back into the fold had failed to clear
the first hurdle. "At least we tried," he said wearily.

About a month later, while Paolo remained in the
powerless position of director, another meeting of the new
company recommended an entirely different set of
guidelines. Franchises were to be negotiated with leading
stores and outlets of distinction in places where no Gucci
shops existed, and goods would be supplied wholesale to
these franchises.

It was in direct contradiction to Paolo's licensing

scheme. He wanted to sell the right to make and market Gucci goods to approved manufacturers around the world. He was certain that this strategy would solve the company's financial difficulties, but not one of the family or their fellow directors took his side.

In the opinion of at least one senior Gucci executive, to do so would have been self-destructive. "In the short term it would have made money," Franco Crudeli believes, "but in the medium to long term it would have spoiled the brand and ruined Gucci's image."

There are cases, Crudeli explains, mainly in high technological areas such as watches, where Gucci could accommodate licensed products. "But only with difficulty. And outside of those our structure, internally, is not equipped to monitor goods made in that way, outside our direct control. No, I don't think there is any incentive for Gucci to go into licensing, none whatsoever. We are being constantly offered everything, from tiles to furniture and airplanes, but it's not our policy."

The new proposals placed Paolo in what he viewed as an impossible situation. If accepted, the suppliers he had licensed to make and sell his "PG" lines would have no place in the new "GG" company. And Paolo would be forbidden under the terms of his contract to go ahead with the marketing or licensing of lines under his own name. "I felt a complete fool. All those assurances given me by my uncle were worthless. They had just been to obtain my agreement, to stop me from competing with the company."

He was also, he says, refused access to company funds in order to settle outstanding fees incurred on their behalf. "During the month leading up to all this, I had been commissioning suppliers to produce Gucci Plus lines. The company told me that the costs involved were entirely my responsibility. I had to find close to a hundred thousand pounds [$140,000] out of my own pocket."

On his lawyer's advice an appeal was immediately lodged asking for more time. It was refused. "We have already considered Paolo Gucci's proposals and rejected them on the grounds that they go against the interests of the company." Meanwhile the board approved the new proposals. As Paolo said, "I was dead even before I had been sentenced."

The following month his signature was formally declared invalid. Paolo was to remain on the board at least for the time being, but without the power to support his designs. His initial agreement still stood, but under it he could not continue with his own business, nor could he let the people he had licensed to make his own lines go ahead.

If the family thought that he would sit back and do nothing about all that, they were very, very wrong.

17

NAUGHTY CHILDREN

Pressures on Paolo to give up his "PG" venture, to come back into the family fold were steadily increasing. "There were terrible scenes. I was more hurt than anything else. I got Speiser to write to the company saying I had been a designer for many years and wanted to start marketing my own products. I sent the company ten designs, to show that I was using my name in such a way as not to be confused with Gucci. They ignored them. After that, I said, okay, I'll carry on on my own."

Suppliers and outlets were told not to have anything to do with the "PG" products. "I sued them for restrictive practices," says Paolo, "but there wasn't enough proof. We couldn't show that they were actually stopping my marketing, because I hadn't yet been able to put my lines on sale."

His family were fighting to stop the perceived threat of direct competition from Paolo's handbags, leather-wear and fashionable clothes. Suppliers assured Paolo that given their heads, his "PG" lines could soon be turning over four to five hundred million dollars a year. Much of this volume, of course, would have come from sales lost by the boutiques, the perfume companies and Gucci itself. "Manufacturers were paying me twenty to thirty thousand dollars to make and sell my lines under license, so I could see plenty of prospects in licensing if Gucci could not!"

Furthermore Paolo was now seen as likely to cost them more in legal fees and lost markets than the expense of bringing him back. The way things were going it seemed probable that victory—and vengeance—might be his even without his threat of competition.

So Paolo was not at all surprised when they made a new approach suggesting a settlement. "After the smoke cleared they wanted to make peace. My uncle's condition, of course, was that I should give up my right to use my name, and sell my shares in Gucci Perfumes back to them. So long as I did that I could choose what I liked to do—go back into the company or go into interior decorating, if that was what I wanted. Anything but run a rival Gucci trademark."

But what of the licensing contracts he had already signed on behalf of Gucci Plus, the new division he was supposed to be in charge of? He had, as he puts it, made those agreements in good faith, believing himself to be empowered as a director to license lines where appropriate. How could these fit in? After discussion Paolo was assured that they would be honored.

At the February meeting Rodolfo had asked Paolo to reconsider. In front of the entire board he gave him his personal assurance that if he dropped the case against them and accepted their proposals he would have nothing to worry about. "Believe me," his uncle said, "I am handling this and you will be fully protected."

Paolo told him, "No, I'm sorry." He was not prepared to trust anyone, least of all those in his family who had been making life difficult for him.

The following day he received his severance money in full and three months later his dismissal. "I was fired again, first from the new Guccio Gucci, S.p.A., which included the Gucci Plus division, and later from Gucci Shops Incorporated." The armistice, it seemed, had brought nothing but more bad feeling between the two generations of the family. Paolo was as far as ever from a satisfactory reentry into the firm, and his own business was poised to take off.

"I immediately moved into production with the lines Gucci had rejected. My licensees were ready to flood the market with designs bearing a symbol scarcely distinguishable from Gucci's. I flew to America, took advertising space in the New York *Times* and appointed an agency to handle the launch of the first Paolo Gucci line, a handbag."

The agency, Safran, was promptly ordered by Aldo's Gucci Shops, Inc., to stop having anything to do with the so-called rebel son. Unwilling to upset such an influential concern, they did so. Paolo sued his family again.

He was now attacking the combined forces of his father and uncle and determined to fight them with everything he had. "Their lawyers tried to get this case dismissed on the same grounds as before, namely that my goods were not on sale. But they were and I proved it. They had to switch their case and countersued me for using their copyright, unfair competition, passing off, I don't know what else. Some of those actions have still to be settled."

The Guccis must have begun to feel that there had never been a peaceful moment among them. Aldo tried to appear unconcerned, but at heart he was deeply worried. His friend Alexandra Murkoska saw behind the debonair facade. "He hated it. Aldo was a generous father who had shown his children great love, affection and kindness. When Paolo had no place to go, when he had been voted out of Italy and lost his job as head of production in the factory, his father took him in. All he got in return were problems."

In her eyes, Aldo's belief that the war was forcing the family to suffer a tragedy akin to "the last days of Pompeii" was no exaggeration. "This is exactly what it was. He had worked so hard to make the company great, one of the wealthiest and most powerful commercial businesses in Italy. Gucci was now a very important force, not only because they were the best but because they believed in what they were doing."

With Paolo's open rebellion, according to Alexandra, Aldo could see it all being swept away. His usual sense of humor was muted. Not only his son's behavior but the power struggle being waged by his brother Rodolfo upset him.

Alexandra watched his relationship with Bruna growing increasingly strained. "Their daughter Patricia was grown up, and working in the company. She'd been educated in expensive Swiss and English schools and could see what was going on. Incredibly, it didn't seem to upset her, I suppose because she's made of the same stuff as her father. But, I mean, by the time she was eight she had attended a board meeting!"

And Patricia was showing little sympathy for her mother's distress at Aldo's long absences. Alexandra heard her tell Bruna, "Mummy, you're silly. But it's your life." As her father's friend noticed, "She talked down to her mother all the time, as if *she* was the older woman."

In the main, the Gucci women were keeping their distance from one another. Too much was at stake for drawing-room parliaments and conferences, and the wives and mistresses knew their traditional places—in the shadow of the men. "We were pushed into the background," says Alexandra. I liked Bruna, and I suppose I was as close to her as most of their friends. But there was no way I could help her problem. It was the same with the others."

Paolo's English wife, Jenny, had worked as a medical secretary in a London hospital, as well as in several other jobs, before her marriage. Now, in the heat of the family war, she was pregnant, distressed by what was going on and disappointed at having to leave New York as a result of her husband's dismissals. "I'm fairly tough, but I must say the never-ending battles in the family did damage my health. I was very tense, suffering from what later became an acute thyroid condition brought on by stress. It wasn't a normal life we were living."

Her hopes of launching an operatic career had also, she says, been dashed. "My singing was just taking off, and I was building up a lot of contacts, but when we had to come away all that went by the board. I can't blame everything on the Guccis, that's for certain, because I'm a lazy student. But having to give up when I did virtually destroyed any chance I had."

They had gone back to live in Florence, and also bought and renovated an historic country house in England. It was hard at first to get accustomed to being outside the business and the family. Paolo continued to attend shareholders' and other meetings, to plan strategies, legal actions and designs.

Jenny was obliged to put up with things as best she could. "I was sad about Aldo. Whatever he had done or said to Paolo, I still had an affection and admiration for him. And he is Paolo's father, after all. I was personally very grateful to him." And she tried to keep in touch with the other wives. She telephoned Patrizia, Maurizio's wife, knowing that her young cousin by marriage was as much against the war as she was. Patrizia was happily married and bringing up her two baby girls, Alessandra and Allegra, in Milan.

Maurizio was not yet fully involved in the struggle. But Rodolfo, sick and aging, had changed towards Patrizia. The anger and hurt pride he had once felt over her family's defiance, when he had forbidden Maurizio to marry her, had slowly faded. Though he still found it difficult to put complete trust in his only son, he confided to Patrizia, whose own father was no longer alive, that he was anxious about the way Gucci would be run when he was no longer able to wield the power of his 50-percent holding in the company.

Patrizia found it difficult to understand why her father-in-law seemed to be fighting so hard to gain more power, more authority in the business. She sensed that his illness was in some way behind it, but she did not realize how seriously sick he was. And feeling his life ending, Rodolfo was apparently developing powerful fixations. He had a deeply rooted objection to Paolo and his plans for expanding the business through licensing. And he no doubt felt a need to establish his position in the company so that Maurizio would be able to carry on what he had started, although he seemed to lack faith in his son's ability to handle such authority when the time came.

Patrizia, in whom he confided, tried to convince Rodolfo not to have radiation therapy, feeling that it was shortening his life. "He would not listen. He was so obstinate. And there was a gap growing between us, a generation gap. My father-in-law had very fixed ideas about how young people should behave. He was quite old, after all Maurizio was not born until November 1946, when his father was thirty-six. By the time I really got to know him he was in his fifties."

The privately made film of his life makes it clear that Rodolfo had little time for the young. Now he resented Maurizio's maturity, having idealized his infancy. As a result he bore an impossibly possessive love for his son—a love no human being could have lived up to.

In business matters, too, he could be both demanding and rather tricky. There was a memorable occasion toward the end of his life when Rodolfo infuriated Aldo by trying to persuade the law firm his brother had retained to change sides and represent him instead. The occasion was a board meeting in Lugano, and Aldo's son Paolo was on his way to it when he happened to catch sight of his father's lawyers sitting huddled round a café table with Rodolfo and Maurizio. Paolo reported what he had just seen to Aldo, who hit the roof. "Treachery, treachery," he shouted.

As soon as the meeting started one of the defecting lawyers announced that he was changing sides although his firm wished to continue to represent Aldo. Aldo's reaction was immediate. "What? One of you on each side? Ridiculous! You should both withdraw."

In Paolo's judgment, if his father had insisted on them doing so he would have spared himself many of his worst problems. "But in the end he agreed to let them stay, and so the same firm of lawyers was acting on both sides. The result was that my father lost everything."

It was not until the fateful July Gucci board-of-directors meeting when, by his account, Paolo was physically assaulted that the generation gap between Aldo and Rodolfo on the one hand and their sons and in-laws on the other became significant and, indeed, fateful. Paolo came to the Florence meeting determined to make trouble unless his questions regarding the board's behavior received satisfactory answers. In his view, as an executive and shareholder he had a clear duty to make these inquiries. The fact that they infuriated his older relations only increased his suspicion that they had something to hide.

His brothers, Giorgio and Roberto, should, he felt, have been as keen as he was to hear answers to the questions. "I at least expected support from them. All I got was a physical attack." Which to Paolo also seemed to indicate their need to bury things they did not want to see brought out in the open.

Although the incident was fully reported in the world press with details of Paolo's injuries, his claims, his lawsuits and doctor's reports making it clear, that, even by Gucci standards, this was no ordinary business disagreement but a thoroughgoing family clash, the others present did not volunteer their versions of what took place. Aldo, pressed by reporters on both sides of the Atlantic, said enough at least to suggest that his son had been attacked: "Who is the father who has never given a slap to a reckless son?" he asked. Except this was no slap.

As Paolo would tell Jenny afterward, the way events shaped was highly questionable. "From the start, when we all met in the offices above the main shop in the via Tornabuoni, I sensed hostility. Everyone was formal, exchanging the usual courtesies, but there were sinister undertones. Of course I greeted them all, my father and uncle, my brothers, Roberto and Giorgio, who had come from Rome. My cousin Maurizio was there from Milan, and the lawyers were gathered around him in force. I felt uneasy about what was going to happen."

Aldo was presiding at the head of the long boardroom table. He declared the meeting officially open, and asked the secretary to read the minutes of the previous meeting. As soon as these had been approved, Paolo asked if he could make a statement. "And immediately there were angry mutterings from my brother Roberto. I saw members of my family exchange glances that told me that they had already decided among themselves that I was not to be allowed to have my say. My father asked, 'Why? What do you want to say?' "

Now there were signs of exasperation, grumbling and gestures from the others. Paolo had expected resistance. "For that reason I had brought the tape recorder along, in my Gucci dispatch case. so as to have it handy if all else failed. Whatever they felt, said or did, I was determined to exercise what I believed were my just rights."

He began, "I want to say that as a director of this company I have been denied any opportunity to see or go through any of the company's books or documents. I want my position clarified before we go any further at all—"

Before he could say more, there were, as he tells it, loud shouts of disgust and denial. Paolo says he feared that the others had come armed with an agreement to fire him from this company as well. Which would have left him powerless. "I had to get all I could from them, or make them deny me what I wanted. And I had to do it now, at this meeting, or I might never have succeeded in doing it at all."

His main goal, as he puts it, was to get his questions put on record, including their embarrassing consequences. They dealt with the legal performance of the company, stressing his belief that he had been unlawfully dispossessed of his fundamental rights. They also spoke of glaring discrepancies, including details of the surreptitious Hong Kong companies and other alleged irregularities. Everything suspicious that he had been able to trace during his research and investigation was in his list of questions, all grist to his mill.

"I had had the list made out in Italian. And a translation in English sealed by the American consul in Florence, attesting to the fact that it was a fair and proper translation of the content. I held up both lists. 'These are my questions,' I tried to say. But already they were shouting and throwing their arms about."

When the Guccis are enraged they behave, says Maurizio's wife, Patrizia, "like *birichini*" (naughty children). Her husband's legal tussles later earned a rebuke from the London *Sunday Times:* "There has been little of the elegance of Gucci goods in the abuse that has flown, or in the legal battles that have embroiled the Gucci clan." There was no elegance now in the Florence boardroom.

Eventually, Paolo was able to make himself heard. "Who are the two mysterious shareholders in Hong Kong who are receiving money from the company?" he demanded. "Why is this going on when we know nothing of them, or what they have done to earn these huge sums?"

Pandemonium. Dominating it was the voice of one of the lawyers, telling him: "Ask your father if you want to know these things!" And another intoned: "That doesn't concern you."

It was at this point that Paolo noticed that the hands of the secretary appointed to take the minutes were idle over her shorthand notebook. Not a word of what he was saying, or had said, was being recorded. He thumped the table for silence.

"Are you refusing to answer, then? In that case, if all you can say is that I am talking rubbish and nonsense, I demand a record both of my questions and of your refusal to answer them. I want it put in the minutes."

Two of the directors were on their feet, waving papers at him. "No, no. These are not matters that concern the meeting."

Paolo threw his lists on the table between them. "Very well, then attach these documents to the minutes. Put them on record."

The two men on their feet fell back onto their chairs in mock exhaustion. "Can't you understand? We don't want your questions. They are nothing to do with the company."

Paolo was still standing. "Well, in that case"—he opened his briefcase and took out the tape recorder—"in that case you cannot object if I record what you refuse to record. I shall read my questions into this machine and note on it that you have refused even to listen to them.

Paolo's version of what happened in the next few seconds was revealed in his thirteen-million-dollar lawsuit alleging unprovoked assault. In the heat of those moments, it seems some of the details were not entirely clear to him at the time, and he was unable to identify his attackers.

Paolo said, "I didn't know what it was that scratched my face, I only discovered it was bleeding profusely when I put my free hand—my other was pinned behind my back—up to it because it was stinging. I believe it was Giorgio, my elder brother, who had grabbed my tape recorder and wrestled with me for it. Someone else had jerked my head back with my arm round my neck."

The blood, he says, had an immediate sobering effect on the others. "They must have seen it, because all of a sudden a hush fell on the room. I hardly knew what I was doing but I had the sense to grab my briefcase and run out, leaving the tape recorder in Giorgio's hands."

Paolo ran through the building, shouting at the astonished office staff, "Call the police, call the police!" Typists and clerks had no idea what to do. They had never before seen a director, one of the family, explode out of the boardroom with blood on his face, shouting for police help.

The woman operating the telephone switchboard was

too horrified to move. Paolo took over her instrument and called both his doctor and lawyer. The main showroom of the shop was filled with Americans. Some were longtime Gucci customers. Paolo says, "I made sure they were not spared the sight of my face, which was still running with blood. I called out to them as I ran past, "See? This is what happens in a Gucci shop when the board of directors has a meeting."

Only one of those present will go so far as to admit that Paolo's injuries occurred at all. Roberto ridicules his elder brother's dramatic version of the fracas. "It's not true that we refused him the right to speak. Of course he was entitled to do so. But to tape-record what was being said at a private meeting, that did not seem ethical. What happened was simply that my brother Giorgio was waving his arm—I don't remember whether it was his right or left arm—in the air, in the way we Italians have when we get excited. In some way it must have come in contact with Paolo's tape recorder, and I think Giorgio's fingernail scratched Paolo's face. Not an assault at all. No, Giorgio shouted something like, 'Come on, Paolo, don't be so crazy!' and that was when it happened. Of course we all joined in then to restrain Paolo, who was screaming and carrying on."

Whatever, and whichever version one accepts, in the extreme heat of those highly charged moments, and taking into account that Paolo may, understandably, not be entirely clear about some of the details, there unquestionably was a violent episode. Paolo has a photograph of his cut face and medical reports of his injuries, which took more than a week to heal.

At the time, he says, his uppermost thought was to get as much publicity as he could from the situation. But the dramatic finale did not come until Dr. Nepi, Paolo's doctor, arrived and insisted that he take his patient off to his clinic for a full examination and report.

Not until that evening did he realize that he was in a state of shock. When his wife, Jenny, saw his white and bandaged face, she too was horrified. "I couldn't believe it!

All of them, grown men, fighting like silly hooligans! It didn't make sense." An English friend who was with her when Paolo returned, journalist Vicki Mackenzie, was equally astonished. "Imagine members of a family business worth millions behaving like that?" She was to learn that with the Guccis behavior is often eccentric or, as Paolo would say, "bizarre."

His brother Roberto was appalled by the media coverage that followed. "To see all this mud thrown, and in public. Sensationalized stories in newspapers and so on. Disgusting!" He says it with obvious distaste. But the others keep quiet about it; they all privately regret Paolo's attempts to bring the dispute among them into the public arena. Aldo, it is reported, refuses even to read what has been written. Those outside the family who were present, mostly lawyers, keep their mouths shut.

In New York Paolo's lawyer, Stuart Speiser, advised that, whatever else, his client had provided himself with a strong cause for another, more expensive, action against his director-relatives, and filed claims against his assailants for "assault, with emotional and physical injury and with breach of contract, it being his right as a director to investigate company affairs."

The case was dismissed in the New York State court. They declined to take jurisdiction, holding that, as the incidents involved occurred in Italy, it was not the proper court to hear the case. Which hardly addressed the right or wrong of it.

Paolo, seething, seemed now more than ever determined to get even with his family. As his wife, Jenny, puts it, "He felt he was being pushed to his knees. It was destroying him, which pained me terribly. Fortunately we're very close, but it was a very difficult time."

Paolo believed that the most stubborn obstacle in his path was still his Uncle Rodolfo—Rodolfo, who had frustrated his early plans to introduce new concepts, to broaden the marketing base of the company with his own designs and licensed products. It was also Rodolfo whom he saw as the less able of his two senior relatives, his father having at least earned his respect for his energetic and successful handling of the firm's expansion. For the others, his two brothers and his cousin, Maurizio, Paolo felt only scorn.

In the spring of 1983, on May 16, Rodolfo died. His daughter-in-law Patrizia believes his death was hastened by the destruction of tissues in his body by the therapy. "It killed him. He had lost too much."

Medical opinion might disagree. Just before the end he told her how he feared what would follow his death. "He urged me to expect a great change in Maurizio. He said, 'Once he gets the money and the power, my son will change. You will find you are married to another man.' I didn't believe him because I had no reason to." She did not have long to wait for fulfillment of this prediction. Two years almost to the day after her father's death, Maurizio left her and their two children in quest of what he asked her to believe was freedom. "I recalled Rodolfo's words then. He had been completely right," she says bitterly. "Since his death I have come to think that he was not such a bad man after all."

Her father-in-law had indulged her, though never at any cost to himself or the company. His way, reminiscent of Guccio's pretense of wanting nothing to do with his sons' expansion plans, was to refuse everything she asked, accusing her of gross extravagance, and then to grant it. "You are trying to ruin us all," he would shout at her.

Patrizia adds: "But I learned that with him you had to push, push, push, then he would give in." When she and Maurizio were first married and went to live and work in New York, he had let them stay in a small hotel and kept Maurizio on a modest salary. At that time Patrizia thought her father-in-law "terribly stingy." But, as Paolo points out, Maurizio was earning sixty thousand dollars a year, not precisely beggarly.

Patrizia pushed Rodolfo, she says, into moving them first into "one of the most beautiful suites" in the St. Regis Hotel. For a twenty-three-year-old girl fresh from Milan, it was a fantastic taste of how the Guccis could live when they chose to. "I felt absolutely on top of the world!"

Then she was shown the Olympic Tower building being erected by Aristotle Onassis. "The moment I went inside the penthouse, which is one of the finest in New York, I fell in love with it. I told Maurizio, 'I'd love to have this place!' He said, 'You're crazy! Can you imagine me going to my father and saying I want a penthouse like this?' I said, 'Okay, then I will go.'"

So she went, and Rodolfo hit high-C. "You want all my money! I told you before, you won't be happy until you ruin us all!" Patrizia told him, "But this is an investment." And Rodolfo's voice lowered. "Let me think about it," he said. Three months later she had the apartment.

In the Gucci family, what one does not ask for one does not get. There was one snag, however, that applied to more or less everything she owned: her penthouse; the magnificent duplex apartment in Milan, which Rodolfo also provided; even the hill in Acapulco, which she says she "fell in love with and persuaded him to buy for me." None of it was in her name. Rodolfo signed for everything he gave her on the company's behalf. Thus on his death it only remained hers and Maurizio's to use in their lifetimes, and at the discretion of the board of directors. At the time this did not bother her. "I didn't want to sign anything, why should I? I had a marvelous husband to look after things for me and to provide for us all. It wasn't my business to own things. And do you know why I never had diamonds? Because I would never ask my father-in-law for jewelry. For houses, apartments and land, yes. Those were for us, as a family. But I would not ask him for things for myself."

She thought she understood what seemed Rodolfo's tightfistedness, even though it kept her husband on what she considered a short rein. "He had a power complex. A great, deep envy of his brother, Aldo. That is the reason for this silly war dividing the family now. A psychologist would recognize that and explain it."

When she saw Rodolfo's prophecy about his son come true, the realization came too that she had virtually nothing of her own in the marriage. This was worrying, but worse to her was the change in her husband. "Maurizio, the man I loved, was almost a stranger. All of a sudden I saw him become taken with power."

She says she tried her best to understand, to share the burden with him. "But the heritage was too much." At the same time Patrizia felt he was surrounded by people who might take advantage of him.

Maurizio had a carefully worked-out plan, a clear idea of what he would like to do with the company. His father had been bedridden for six months before he died, and Maurizio had had time to decide what he would do once he inherited his father's share of the company. But all this time he had no idea that he already had his father's half-share in his possession. "He [Rodolfo] had kept that a very close secret. So it came as a complete surprise to me when the lawyers told me. I now had fifty percent of the company and Aldo and his three sons held the other fifty percent."

But with only a bare 50 percent he would not be able to insure support for his plans, his proposals to build Gucci into a multinational corporation that they could be proud of. "I lacked sufficient voting power to carry out my concept. So I had to go about things another way."

The past had not been easy, knuckling under to his father's dominant personality, being allowed to share little of his uncle's charismatic, center-stage position in the great Gucci drama. Now, the "other way" seemed both natural and just. He had to take it, he told himself, in order to realize his dreams.

18

THE END OF THE PARTY

It took Maurizio several months to realize that he was free of his father's possessive, dominating love, that now, at age thirty-five, he could at last do as he liked, make and act on his own decisions. He would arrive at his office in Milan every morning and find the important decisions Rodolfo had always handled personally set out neatly for his attention. "In his father's time he'd been so frustrated," Patrizia says. "Nobody was allowed to say no to Rodolfo. I think in a way Maurizio was relieved that his father was dead, and he wanted to make up for lost time."

He was also impatient to get his plans for the company rolling, to establish the multinational control and organization that, in his opinion, had been lacking under his father's and uncle's, in his view, somewhat haphazard management. He took to working twelve hours a day in the office, spending weekends in conferences and discussions, seldom finding time for the sports he loved or the company of his family.

His father's wealth, in properties, possessions and money, was far greater than he had imagined. Apart from the magnificent string of residences—the St. Moritz mansion, the Olympic Tower penthouse, the duplex suite in Milan presided over by a butler (and soon to be filled with Art Deco treasures collected by Patrizia)—there was also a yacht previously owned by Stavros Niarchos.

Maurizio had studied law, but to cope with all this and the business as well he needed help. His first task was to find reliable, qualified assistants. The company was heavily involved in lawsuits fighting the cheap imitation Gucci products, his Cousin Paolo and others. He had to have people with sound commercial and legal experience to handle what he had inherited. Above all, he had to straighten out the family problems, the "Gucci War," as the press was calling it.

Fortunately for him, though Italian he held Swiss residential status and his right to work in the United States was unchallenged. His doctorate, his university training, made it possible for him to take an international view of the situation, which was the crux of his plan for what Gucci should become: no longer just an Italian luxury-goods firm operating all over the world but a multinational corporation offering its investors, staff and clientele sophisticated global advantages. His father's and uncle's anti-expansionist strategy was a policy he intended to abandon as quickly as time would allow. After which, he would deal with his Cousin Paolo's rebellion. He had ideas for that, too.

The problem was fitting all this into a life that until then had revolved pleasantly enough around family and friends. For almost a year after his father's funeral he managed to push the problem aside, but in the spring when the business was stretching him to the fullest extent he recognized the impossibility of his position. He had learned to make decisions and this was to be the hardest decision of his life. To carry the burden his father had left him, he felt he could no longer afford the luxury of full-time family and social life.

On Wednesday, May 22, 1985, Maurizio packed a small suitcase, told Patrizia he was going to Florence the following day, kissed her and the children, and left. His wife called him the day after. "He said nothing about staying away," she says.

"But on Saturday he sent his doctor to tell me he was not coming back."

For five days Patrizia had no idea where her husband was. He had come back to his office, handed everything over to an assistant, giving the man full authority to handle all his affairs, personal and otherwise, and left. Patrizia received assurances. Her financial position was unaffected. There would be no immediate divorce or attempted annulment. But he was not coming back.

In July Maurizio telephoned and arranged to see the children on weekends. For a few weeks he kept distantly in touch. Then, in late September, he returned home. "He wanted me to go with him to the inauguration of the polo matches Gucci was sponsoring, In fact, I presented the cup. He was here at home for five days, and he kept asking me for freedom, freedom. I haven't a great experience of life, but what is this freedom? To me it is having a good life, children a family and a good job. But he was asking for freedom to go down the Grand Canyon in a boat. And to buy a red Ferrari. That was his freedom?"

She says she tried to make him understand that he could no longer behave like a boy wanting to show off to his friends. "In his position? Of course I didn't agree. I would like a white Rolls-Royce, but it's only if you're a nobody and want to make a splash that you buy things like that. If you're really somebody, then you have to lead a normal, quiet life. That is my personal opinion, and that is why I was too strict for him, apparently."

Maurizio, she says, accused her of imprisoning him. "He told me, 'First I had my father, now I have you. I have never been free in all my life. I didn't enjoy my youth, and now I want to be free. If I want to, I'll come home at three in the morning!' Imagine, a man who falls asleep at eleven o'clock in the evening, wanting to stay out all night!"

She was planning to take the children to St. Moritz for Christmas. "He said he would come too. We talked it over and agreed that we should only let the children know what was happening little by little so that they could learn to understand. I was telling myself, 'Give it time, this cannot last.' I had been madly in love with my husband ever since I'd met him fourteen years before and I still loved him. I deeply, deeply hoped that Christmas together would solve everything, because to me Christmas is . . . well, I'm like a child about it. For me, it is Santa Claus, miracles, everything."

It Italy, the day of celebration is December 24. "Christmas Eve, I was up to my elbows in silver, making incredible decorations and a beautiful tree. I'd really created a wonderful Christmas atmosphere. And that night he'd promised to go to midnight Mass with me, which we'd never been to together. I prayed that with God's guidance, which we needed, all would be well."

But at ten o'clock that night Maurizio went to bed. "He just said, 'Goodnight.' Not even 'Have a nice Christmas.' Nothing! I told myself, well, let's hope Santa Claus will come in the night and tomorrow everything will be all right."

Next morning Maurizio woke Patrizia up very early. "We have to give the children their presents," he said. She was still hurt and angry. "I'm not coming," she told him. "Why did we come here, then, for Christmas, if you're not going to take part in it?" She told him, "Okay, you're right." And they got ready.

She says she was expecting only a small present from him. "Not an expensive one, just something to show that he cared and had thought of me. You know what I got? A keyholder, made for the yacht *Italia!* And a watch, an antique gold watch—he knows I detest antique watches!"

Some might find this shaky grounds for indignation. Her present to him was a set of cufflinks and studs in diamonds and sapphires. She says, "That was our usual standard. And all the others were given presents that showed that he had thought about them, an ashtray for one of the staff who smoked, that sort of thing."

That evening they were invited to a party, and Maurizio refused to go. "Since he'd taken over the business, he hadn't liked to meet people, to go anywhere or socialize. But now I was sure he was just doing it to upset me again. I told him, 'Okay, well I am going alone.' And I did."

At the party one of their closest friends came over to Patrizia and said, "You know Maurizio is leaving tomorrow?" She was shocked. "Leaving? What do you mean?" "Oh yes," the friend said, "he called me and told me he is, quite definitely."

Patrizia was sure there was some mistake. He had told her, she says, that he would stay over the Christmas holiday. But next morning he was up early and she saw him packing his case. "I asked, 'What are you doing?' He told me, 'I have to go to Geneva.' I was absolutely stunned. So this was our Christmas! And before he left he took our elder daughter aside and told her we didn't love each other anymore so he was leaving. 'And daddy has a nice new house where you can come and stay with him, one night with him and one night with mummy.' Our agreement had been that we'd only let the children know by degrees."

After Maurizio left, she says, "The child became hysterical. And for the next three months that we didn't hear from him, all that time she was crying. At school it was terrible. I spoke with the doctor and he told me she was trying to take advantage of the situation. I said, 'Yes, it is a game with her. But inside the game there is pain and trauma.' "

Maurizio accused her, she says, of trying to keep the children from him. "I told him, 'You can't do this. Meeting them for a brief twenty minutes is upsetting them too much. I can't let you have them.' If he'd behaved more like a normal father I'd have let him have them."

Patrizia says that when she next tried to take the children to stay in the St. Moritz house she found the doors barred to her. "The servants told me Dr. Gucci had ordered them not to let me in. I called the police. They asked if I was divorced and I explained that I was not and that the only difference was that my husband was not living under the same roof with me. They immediately came and obtained the keys and let me in."

The sad state of Maurizio's marriage also seemed to be affecting his business relationships. Patrizia says she received telephone calls from members of the staff who wondered, as she had, what had brought about such a change in a man who, as she says, "they had greatly loved." Some were resigning. "They asked me 'what is happening to your husband?' We used to be a big family but now everything is different. It's as if something has happened to him. I had to tell them I could do nothing about it, but more than once I was asked, 'Signora Gucci, why don't you try to take the situation in hand?'

"In a factory with a tradition such as Gucci has always had, we must be a family, otherwise we become like the others. While we keep that alive, we'll always be Gucci." Maurizio, she felt, seemed to be violating that tradition.

Maurizio, on the other hand, claimed that he was learning to relax, to be "serene in myself," though Patrizia saw few outward signs of it. He loved sports and had always enjoyed exhausting himself at games of squash, fighting for victory on a tennis court or skiing down the most hazardous pistes of his favorite slopes. Now, there was little time for such pleasures.

His new authority, she felt, seemed obsessive. He told her: "If you want to carry big responsibilities, the first need is to create a foundation of professionalism." He used autoracing analogies to describe his grand plan. "I couldn't enter Formula One unless I had the right car, driver, mechanics and spares. A lot had to be done, and none of it would be accomplished in a panic." His overriding need, he says, was to obtain the total control of the company that his father, who had only the same number of shares as Aldo and his sons, had failed to achieve.

As a first step he proposed a restructuring of the small Gucci Boutiques company that Giorgio had set up in the late sixties. It had been brought back into the portfolio on his return to the family business. Maurizio proposed that Guccio Gucci, S.p.A., the new restructured company set up by Rodolfo (though with Paolo's shaky agreement), should buy out all shares in it held by the family and bring them into the main firm.

Aldo agreed to this quite happily, and two of his sons, Giorgio and Roberto, followed suit. Maurizio could buy them out, and settle the equity of the boutiques in the company he owned 50 percent of. But Paolo argued that the move unfairly altered the balance of power. Rodolfo in his lifetime had held only 15 percent of Gucci Boutiques, so why should his son now have half of the entire business? Previously, it had always been possible for Paolo and his brothers to vote against a decision of that particular board. Now they could never be sure of a majority.

Ultimately, Paolo gave in. There was much he did not approve of about his cousin's handling of events since his uncle's death, but there seemed no point in forcing a stalemate while his father and brothers were happy with Maurizio's proposal. Also he had come to hope that the changes Maurizio was engineering would be to his advantage.

For one thing the reshuffling going on, the introduction of new directors and the alterations Maurizio was making in Milan strongly suggested that now would be an excellent moment to resolve all his differences with the company on his own terms. He was growing tired of the war and the idea of freeing himself from the whole imbroglio was appealing.

But before abandoning his position, which depended largely on the equity given him under Rodolfo's reorganization of the company, he would have to be sure of getting what was owed to him. He was still without salary, though the contract he had signed was for six years, and he had held his post under it until suspended. As he paced the floor at night worrying about his future his wife began to question the purpose of it all.

"He just wanted his freedom, I could see that. But it was

so sad, because he knew they would stop him whatever he tried to do. It turned my life upside down because I was having to bear his problems as well as my own and there seemed to be no end to it."

At last Paolo decided to seize the opportunity while it existed, while his cousin was waving a flag of truce over his new domain. In a call from New York to his cousin's chief financial adviser, Gian-Vittorio Pilone, Paolo proposed a deal by which he believed the whole difficulty could be resolved. For his shares he would take only their value, and "the right to market my own goods under my own trademark, Paolo Gucci."

How much was "only their value"? At a rough guess the company was now worth something on the order of eight or nine hundred million dollars. He was, he said, prepared to take twenty million for his shares, provided he could go ahead without interference in his own business. And two days later, Maurizio called him. "I've got a better idea that takes care of everything," he told Paolo. "Let's talk."

He and Paolo, he suggested, should form a company together to license Gucci products. Paolo's lines would be taken into the new company. "That way," he said, "we don't have to worry about competition with one another, we can join forces."

Paolo agreed, and in June 1984 a meeting was planned at which they would decide how it should be done. Maurizio came with the draft of a formidable agreement (which would become known to Paolo's lawyers as "the bible"). In it he named the new company Gucci Licensing Services since that would be its main and most profitable function. He explained to Paolo that it would be necessary for him to have 51 percent of the shares, leaving 49 percent for Paolo, on account of suspicion from the other Gucci shareholders that he might be giving away too much.

"He told me," says Paolo, " 'If I don't have control I won't be able to get it past the rest of the family. I won't be able to get things moving.' So I went along, assuming that regardless, I would have the same authority as he had in the operation of the company since I could sign on the company's behalf."

Indeed, at least on the face of it, Maurizio was being generous. Having had the company valued at something over eight hundred million dollars, he may have been offering Paolo less than half the realistic value of his 11-percent equity, but the rest of the terms, and the ending of the war with its restoration of Paolo to the family business, certainly made an attractive package.

Paolo was to receive the whole twenty million in cash for the shares, as well as a contract guaranteeing his appointment as president of the new licensing company at a salary of half a million dollars a year, a joint signature, and 6 percent of the profits over the next seventy years.

Paolo decided to accept, but he would stay vigilant. If it turned out to be a sour proposition or less advantageous than it seemed, he would withdraw while he still held his shares. He had no intention of surrendering those until everything was signed, sealed and ratified.

"On top of which, I had to be sure that I could do as I liked with the licenses I had already sold in different countries. The people I had sold them to had been prevented from making and selling products under my trademark. I had to clear that up. And when I talked to Maurizio about it, he agreed that we should set up a committee to consider each one on its merits. Those approved would simply have to alter their contracts to Guccio Gucci in place of Paolo Gucci, which I knew would suit them very well."

Maurizio then asked for a proxy for Paolo's shares in the perfume company in order, as he explained, to be able to exercise majority voting power at a coming meeting. "Since the formation of Guccio Gucci, S.p.A. in March 1982, there had been eight directors, four appointed by Rodolfo (and now Maurizio) on account of his half-share, and four by my father. One of my father's directors was his daughter Patricia, and she was to be replaced, I thought, by me."

Paolo says he only agreed to sign the proxy, and to be represented at the meeting by a delegate appointed by Maurizio, because he fully believed that this was all that his cousin intended. "I could not see how he could possibly expect me to take on the responsibility of the new position without giving me a position on the board itself."

If things had gone as Paolo expected, the balance of votes cast with Maurizio and his group would merely have outweighed any resistance from Aldo's side. "I agreed to support him because I thought that was all he had in mind, but in fact he sacked the whole board—using my votes to give him the power to do it."

Maurizio therefore held 61 percent of the voting power in shares and could do very much as he liked.

Aldo was forced to step down as president, since he no longer had a controlling interest. Three weeks later, apparently as a face-saving gesture, Maurizio offered his uncle the title of honorary chairman. Aldo's reign was over. "When my father went to his office in New York," Paolo says, "his desk had been cleared, all his papers were in boxes and the locks had been changed." For a long while afterward Aldo was forced to carry on his business from his string of luxury homes, working out of his Gucci dispatch case.

At the same time Maurizio showed that he was not going to be bound by the old rules of the company, made during his father's time. Paolo was furious when he heard that he had appointed nine new directors in place of the eight that were supposed to balance the power evenly. "He had got my delegate to vote in favor of it, without my knowing about it."

But in one way Paolo had benefited. Before parting with the vital proxy, he had shrewdly insisted on being paid a deposit of 10 percent of the agreed purchase price for his shares in hard cash. "I knew Maurizio wanted that proxy very badly and I was sure he would pay."

The family grouping that had voted with Maurizio

against Aldo then parceled out the remaining entitlements among them. Giorgio was to be vice-president, operating from the Rome office, and his thirty-year-old son Alessandro would join the board as a director. Giorgio pledged allegiance to his father's successor. Roberto was out, not even a director. But he remained in Florence as administrator.

Maurizio was elected the new president by a unanimous show of hands. It gratified him to know that there was no opposition from the rest of the family. As for any suggestion that there might have been something improper about using Paolo's shares before he had concluded all aspects of the purchase deal, he says: "I had paid a deposit in good faith, and the proxy was completely legal. The fact that my election was unanimous should have satisfied people."

Did it?

"Well, no. Not entirely. It did not stop people saying I acted unfairly. They said I used Paolo's vote to get rid of his father, but that is not true. At the time he was approaching eighty and very happy to go. They've changed the story since, but that is the truth."

"Look, I was accused of wanting to control the company. It was said that I wanted to dominate, to force my will on people. How could I? What we proposed had been authorized by the board of directors two years before my time."

He said his plans were no more than a tightening of the rules laid down by his grandfather. "We were a multinational company, but for the past seven years we had been running things like a cottage industry. Those who were in charge did not want to recognize that times were changing. Giorgio and the others, for them it was 'we'd always done it that way.' I tried to make them see that there was no wish on my part to seek power for power's sake, but they still clung to the view that things should go on as before."

Allegations of rather too clever dealing reached a peak when news began to leak out that Maurizio's deal with Paolo was not firm, that the votes he had used so effectively— Paolo's proxies—might not end up to be his after all. The dilemma *that* posed could only be resolved if Paolo completed the deal.

Negotiations to this end dragged on. But at almost the
same time Maurizio had to deal with far graver and more
personal accusations. Aldo did not seem "very happy" at
being forced to step down from the position he had occupied
since the founder's death, and, it was reported in the press,
gave information to Italian magistrates with Roberto that
accused Maurizio of having received his father's shares and
fortune by fraud. The signature on the transfer of the shares,
which could escape inheritance taxes only if they were given
to Maurizio in Rodolfo's lifetime, was alleged to be that of
someone in his office. According to the Italian press, calligraphy experts were able to confirm that it was not Rodolfo's,
and that the shares should have formed part of the estate
inherited by Maurizio *after* his father's death.

Once again, it seemed a Gucci had turned against a
member of his own family. Yet, Maurizio continued to speak
well of his uncle. "My uncle was always like that. One minute
a kiss, the next a sword, that was it exactly. It was his
Florentine blood, I suppose, which I only share fifty percent,
that was responsible."

Maurizio refused to believe that Aldo's accusations could
damage him seriously or affect his position at the head of the
company. His estranged wife, Patrizia, was told nothing of
such problems, though as they developed she became involved in them herself. "He thought he would get out of
everything with everyone feeling sorry for him for what he
had been through."

Shoring up Maurizio's confidence was his belief that
Paolo would complete the deal. They had both signed a
contract. The terms, he thought, were agreed on.
Switzerland's premier bank, Crédit Suisse, was acting as
broker, and he and Paolo had arranged to complete the
agreement in their Geneva offices.

Paolo's shares were being held by the bank in escrow.
They were only to be released to Maurizio and his advisers

on delivery of the money. It seemed that nothing was holding up the deal other than insignificant details, such as where the new company should most advantageously be registered.

Paolo says he genuinely wanted to go ahead. "But I was becoming more and more suspicious. Maurizio first wanted to have the company set up in Denmark, then Holland. When neither of these offered what we needed—freedom from massive taxation—we moved to Guernsey and Jersey in the Channel Islands. Supposedly, these were ideal tax havens. I asked to be told what advantages Jersey could offer. He sent me a brochure from the bank that was nothing more than a guide to the island's prosperity, something put out by their publicity people. Useless."

And Maurizio too was acting with considerable caution. His contract specified that, once its terms had been fulfilled, it could under no circumstances be rescinded. He signed on his own and the company's behalf, Paolo's signature beside his. He had, he felt, reason to believe that, after his payment of the balance of the twenty million dollars, which still had to be realized from the company's funds, the war would be over.

In November a final meeting between them was arranged. Maurizio says he came in high spirits, wearing his position as company president like a wreath of laurels. Paolo, much the smaller of the two in stature, seemed dwarfed by his cousin. Maurizio now asked, "Just one small point, What happens if we can't agree? If one of us wants to sign a licensing contract and the other objects? How do we resolve such a deadlock?"

Paolo did not think this could happen. "We have joint signatures, don't we? Surely either one of us has the right to authorize on the company's behalf, without reference to the other? But if there is a deadlock we'll go to arbitration." Maurizio shook his head. "Oh no. That can't be. I have to have the final say, of course, because I am to hold fifty-one per cent of the shares. If a decision is deadlocked, then the shareholders must decide."

It was not what Paolo had wanted, but he says he still believed that Maurizio would honor his undertaking in regard to the licensing contracts already signed by Paolo on his own behalf. So he raised no immediate objection. "But I took independent advice, and when we went to Switzerland to complete the deal I took my lawyer and an official appointed by the court with me. I was not going to have my shares handed over without everything being strictly in order."

The staid offices of Crédit Suisse seemed an unlikely setting for what followed. Paolo was welcomed and shown into an air-conditioned, quiet office. This could be the biggest day of his life if it came off. By the end of it he expected to be a multimillionaire not only on paper but in hard currency cash.

The bank executive was reassuringly professional. A few millions changing hands was hardly something to raise his Swiss blood's temperature. "Everything seems to be in order," he said. "We have the envelope containing your share certificates, Mr. Gucci. It is registered as a valuable security. Document No. 132, in the bank's safekeeping, and will not be delivered to the other parties until we have received the funds due to you."

There was no more to be said. Paolo waited. And the minutes passed. "I didn't know what was going to happen, but something told me there was a snag. Then a girl came out of the legal department. 'There seems to be a problem with some of the money,' she said. 'Mr. Piloni is in the other room and would like to talk to you.' My lawyer said, 'Don't go!' I told the girl it was impossible and she went back inside."

There was another pause, this time more worring. What could have held up Maurizio's, or rather the company's money? It was nearly eleven o'clock when the bank's legal director joined them, looking grave. He had the deeds of the proposed company with him, documents which to Paolo seemed different from those he had agreed to.

"And it was clear that these were not what I had told the bank to accept on my behalf. There was no mention at all of my appointment as president. Maurizio and I were to hold only proxy voting rights as directors, which could be withdrawn at any moment. I asked the bank lawyer, 'What is all this? Does it meet with your approval?' He said it did not. And I said, 'Well, then I deny any part of it.' "

Maurizio prefers not to comment too closely on what followed, since arbitration to settle the dispute is continuing in Geneva. "But I'm confident it will be settled soon," he says, "then we will see who is right." Meanwhile, he does not deny that Paolo had apparently arrived at the bank with every intention of completing the deal. And Maurizio's version of events in general seems to correspond with Paolo's.

The document did not offer the joint authority Paolo had expected. To his apprehensive mind it was yet another extension of Maurizio's overall control. He was in no mood to put up with what he saw as no more than a piece of legal jargon. He had no intention of being maneuvered, as he saw it, out of his position for anything less than the terms previously, as he thought, agreed upon. The final convincer for him was Maurizio's failure to come up with the money.

To Paolo, as he put it, he was once more in danger of "being screwed." He demanded back his envelope containing his shares from the bank. "They gave it to me and we left. The truce was over."

And the war resumed.

19

SAUSAGE MEAT

The collapse of Paolo's deal doomed the last hope of settlement. Maurizio's inability to heal the breach put the situation back where it had been, with Paolo planning his next move. In New York his father's tax problems were under intense investigation. The IRS investigators were turning up more troublesome developments. The Gucci war had become, to those engaged in it, a high-stake poker game.

Paolo could do nothing about the apparently incriminating papers. He sympathized with Aldo, deposed from the presidency and possibly facing criminal charges, but he also blamed his father for refusing to compromise with him. "I knew the risk he was running, but I couldn't believe he would be so misguided as to let the whole thing blow up. I was sure he was going to cut the fuse in time before it exploded. I still thought he would have to come to a deal with me." As for Maurizio, he had both hands full. His marriage's drift toward the rocks was only one of his problems. Gucci, he found, was like a car that had been left standing too long. It was hard work getting the engine to turn over, let alone to start. "Imagine, America was taking in forty-five million dollars a year with a profit of only point three percent! I brought that up to ninety million and thirteen percent. But it needed great management to do it. I couldn't do it alone. We had to find, select and win over the best team in the world. And we had to do it in six or eight months."

The man he hired as his assistant, Franco Crudeli, came by chance. A business associate of his father's, he happened to be out of a job. Maurizio asked what he thought of the Gucci concern, and Crudeli risked being tactless. "I called Gucci some strong names. I said, 'your potential is a thousand and you are only doing ten.' Maurizio asked me, 'How dare you say a thing like that?' I said, 'Dr. Gucci, if you want me to please you, I'll tell you Gucci is the Number One. The blah, blah, blah . . . But I'm telling you the truth.' Maurizio fell back in his chair and said, 'That's why I need people like you.' "

Crudeli was experienced in the silk trade. "I knew people in the market dealing with Gucci, and what they thought about Maurizio taking over the business. As I'd told my wife, 'The day his father dies, they're going to eat Maurizio alive!' I didn't see myself in St. George against the dragon, but I saw the man was needing help. And I liked his courage. If I think people have guts I'll do anything I can to give them a hand. So I took the job when he offered it without even asking what the money involved was."

He found himself working with what he considered a dedicated crusader, a man who determined even at the cost of his own family happiness to cure what he saw as the company's sickness. Maurizio's concept of a multinational status apparently inspired Crudeli. They shared a desire, he says, to set the business on an unrivaled global course. "I'll tell you something. The Gucci image in Japan was big, big, big, but our turnover was zilch. Because they'd hired inferior agents on the spot long before Maurizio took over. America was their only aim in those days."

He refers to "lack of professionalism before the coming of Maurizio Gucci," and praised the efforts they made together to overcome what he considers early mistakes. "We were just applying the rules of the game, not inventing anything. The company should have grown up and been aware that protection against them in various markets was maturing faster than they were. They should have expanded while there was no opposition, instead of which we were now having to build from the bottom up."

In his opinion Aldo had not recognized such a danger. "In Australia things were going on that the company knew nothing about. Nothing had been done in Germany, can you believe? One of the biggest European markets. In England, what had we done? Almost nothing. They were selling millions in America, and were very good in Europe, and a little bit somewhere else, but that was it. They could have tripled the business."

Crudeli believed Maurizio would correct the slide, as he saw it, if anybody could. "Yes, thank God, he got things going the right way. We achieved what we set out to do. There were still problems, of course. But in terms of marketing we became more aggressive. And we hit most of our targets, almost doubling turnover worldwide."

He had joined Maurizio soon after Aldo's removal from the presidency, when forces in the family were more divided than ever before. Holding Paolo's proxy voting power had given Maurizio control of the board, and his promotion of Giorgio to vice-president insured the support of his most likely rival, Aldo's favored eldest son. But he says it was some time before he sensed the deep, underlying tensions in the family.

Crudeli speaks of the consequences of the Gucci friction. "There are problems in all families of entrepreneurs, but to come to such a point . . . well! I know this, Maurizio was absolutely shocked by what Paolo did to his father. Nobody was more upset than he was. He told me, 'Whatever Aldo has done, he did not deserve this.' "

In Crudeli's opinion Aldo Gucci had been victimized by

his blood relations. "I think the jury in America took advantage of a situation that allowed them to alert people to what Italian importers in the fashion business could get up to. Unfortunately Aldo had to pay for that. It was terrible, because he was the pioneer, the one who made Gucci what it is. His only error, it I may say so, was that he did too much toward America, forgetting a little bit about the rest of the world. I mean, Japan could have been very close in volume to the U.S. . . . . absolutely. Other brands had done it."

He saw Maurizio's seeming indifference to Paolo's persistent claims as a mark of strength. Paolo, in his view, was holding onto stock in companies he no longer worked for. "A suicidal course." Maurizio, far from being eaten alive, was "winning the battle." Crudeli used his boss' metaphor to describe it all. "Gucci is like a fine motor-racing stable. There has only been one Nicky Lauder. In my opinion Maurizio Gucci is the Nicky Lauder of this buiness."

As related by Crudeli, Paolo had missed his chance. "Maurizio Gucci told me that Paolo blew the deal in Switzerland. Paolo did not like the agreement. He'd had four lawyers on it, but he still claimed that it was not what he'd understood it to be. What kind of a man is that?"

Paolo was equally unprepared to accept what had happened. He apparently saw the deal as having been arranged to prevent his trading under his own name. His loss of earnings due to its failure, he claimed, amounted to several million dollars. And his cousin, in blocking his right to trade, had broken America's antitrust laws.

So arbitration to settle these matters had to be started in Geneva. "It will decide who is right and wrong, then we will see," Maurizio said. "But, in any case, he caused the dispute. Not me."

By then Maurizio himself was facing an ugly situation. Aldo's presentation contested Maurizio's assertion that the "gift" from his father was made without his knowledge during Rodolfo's lifetime. The statements before a magistrate alleged that the signatures and dates of the transference of the shares and estate had been forged in order to backdate the documents and thus avoid death-duties.

Maurizio was also, subsequently, charged with exporting capital contrary to Italy's exchange-control laws, since the shares had been put into his private company in Switzerland, Gucci Finanziaria. Though he made light of this, his luxury apartment in Galleria Passarella, the heart of fashionable Milan, was raided and documents were confiscated. However he came out of it, the situation was being taken seriously by the authorities.

Also by family.On the day of the raid his estranged wife, Patrizia, was spending a weekend away with friends. She was telephoned the news by a woman friend who was looking after the children—Alessandra, ten, and Allegra, five. They were about to leave for school. "My friend rang at seven in the morning to tell me that five men from the prosecutor's office had burst in with a search warrant demanding to look at everything. Apparently they had ransacked the entire apartment, even breaking open locked cases, in search of whatever it was they were after. It shocked and scared me because I'd no idea what it was they were looking for, or what I could do about it. I called a lawyer friend who asked, 'Is there anything incriminating in the house?' I had absolutely no idea!"

Then she remembered that there were some drawings in her bedroom that she had promised Allegra she could take to school with her. "I asked my friend to put them in the child's satchel. I spoke to one of the men and begged him to be gentle with the children. I knew they were only doing their job, whatever it was."

What Patrizia did not know was that wiretappers were listening in on her telephone conversation in another building, including her request for the drawings.

"They came rushing to the house after the children had left. It was pandemonium. They wanted to arrest everyone, my friend, the chauffeur, even the servants. My car was searched."

Though they apparently found nothing the investigators were still suspicious. "They went to the school that's run by Sisters of Mercy and demanded to see Allegra's satchel—a terrible shock for Mother Superior! When I returned, which I did right away, my lawyers advised me, 'Don't go home immediately.' I felt like a criminal!"

Maurizio was in Australia as part of the official sponsorship by Gucci of the yacht *Italia*, one of Italy's two unsuccessful challengers for the America's Cup. To her surprise he stayed there several weeks, despite these difficulties at home. To Patrizia he seemed to be seriously underestimating the gravity of what was happening.

"In my opinion somebody was hiding the truth from him. Because he said, 'Oh, everything will be okay.' What kind of man was it who spent all that time in Australia with this hanging over him?"

In addition to charges relating to the alleged forgery of his father's signature,and thereby the evasion of death-duties estimated to be no less than one hundred million pounds ($125,000,000), Maurizio was being sued by his cousin Paolo for substantial damages following their abortive deal. Paolo wanted millions in compensation and interest.

Maurizio scoffed at the action. "He [Paolo] tried to make a case out of the fact that Gucci had a monopoly of leather goods. It was absurd, and the judge dismissed it. After that, all we had to fight over was his right to use the Gucci name." Maurizio believed he would have no difficulty in preventing that use despite Paolo's persistence.

He had instructed lawyers to challenge every attempt by Paolo, or his licensees, to market products under his trademark. "We were confiscating his goods whenever and wherever they appeared. We'd already done so in Italy, Hong Kong and Switzerland. It was only in Japan and a few other countries that we'd failed to stop him. Of course, it was costing a lot. We were spending more than four million dollars a year to defend our rights, not only against him but against fakes and trademark invaders everywhere."

And not always successfully. In New York, around the

corner of Fifth Avenue from the Gucci store, a twenty-yard
section of roadway was cordoned off, covered with fake
Gucci watches and jewelry then crushed by a steamroller.
Still the fakes, mainly from the Far East, continued to pro-
liferate. Spotting them had become something of a Gucci
family game.

On at least one occasion their sleuths impounded a con-
signment of suspected fakes that turned out to be the genuine article. "It was a continuing battle," Paolo says. "Visitors to Hong Kong could buy 'Gucci watches' for a tenth of
the price."

Maurizio was signing, on the average, ten proxies a day
for the local lawyers in the countries where the fakes were
made, authorizing them to sue on Gucci's behalf. "I had to do
it as a protection for our shareholders and cutomers." Legal
costs were great, but in his view both these and Paolo's lines
had to stamped out. The roots of the trouble, in his judgment, lay back in his father's time when he had had no
shares, no say in the running of the company. He was determined to make up for what he considered the laxity that had
let this situation come about.

But in his estranged wife Patrizia's eyes Maurizio had
become a victim of ambition, a man who saw himself as a
titan dragged down by the power struggles of his grasping
family. "Sometimes I asked myself, why did a young man of
thirty-six, with his position and money, make war? I believed
Maurizio could have put together the whole family and
found a solution to all the problems. So why didn't he do it?"

"I trust people," Maurizio told her. "Sometimes it is not
good to trust so much. The more you trust the more you
suffer. If you trust less you get less, but you also suffer less.
When you find your trust has been given to someone who
does not deserve it, that is very painful. I like to be as open as
possible. But on the other hand, once somebody betrays me
that is the finish."

He was mistaken if he believed that his uncle Aldo had
accepted his defeat with good grace. Aldo could not hide his

feelings from his son, Roberto. "Poor man, of course he was very unhappy. He was thrown out. He had lost everything he had built up with his own hands." Paolo's comment was somewhat less sympathetic: "If he had made peace with me all this would never have happened. He was wrong—not only in letting Maurizio take over but also in believing that he would never go to jail over the tax swindles."

In September 1986, United States Federal Judge Vincent L. Broderick looked across a Manhattan courtroom at the tearstained face of eighty-two-year-old Aldo Gucci, the man who had built one of the world's most revered status symbols, and told him: "I am persuaded that you, Mr. Gucci, will not commit another crime. You will go to prison for a year and a day."

As the New York *Times* commented, such a relatively light sentence was far less severe than would customarily have been given. Eleven million dollars of profits had been "diverted" out of the country. Taxes of over seven million had been evaded. The punishment was mitigated, the judge implied, both by Aldo's age and his obvious repentence. An additional fine of thirty thousand dollars seemed almost trivial alongside the repayment plus interest of the entire sum, which Aldo, admitting his culpability, promised. Reportedly one million had already been repaid to the U.S. Treasury.

Some clemency was also known in the selection of his prison. Aldo was sent (for what would be little more than four months, with time off for good behavior) to a jail known during the Watergate trials as America's "country club clink"—Eglin, a former air-base penitentiary in Florida. His own Florida mansion in Palm Beach was not too far away to prohibit occasional visits. As the prison superintendent, Mike Cooksey, was reported to have said, it was not anyone's intention to "strain an old man of eighty-one."

From the dock Aldo allowed himself the ambiguous reflection that "some have done their duty and others have the satisfaction of revenge. God will be their judge." But

Maurizio believes that his uncle told the judge that he forgave his son Paolo for having brought him to this plight. He
said nothing of his late brother, Rodolfo, who had clashed
with Paolo, after which came the superheated family war in
which Aldo was the first major casualty. Nor did he say
anything about his nephew Maurizio, who had used Paolo's
proxy shares in the vote that deposed him.

Compassion seems an emotion the Guccis seldom show
in their dealings with one another. This was Maurizio's comment on his incarcerated uncle: "He should not have done it
in the first place. I am always careful to see that every penny
due in tax is paid. I never allow a single item to be bought in
my name without a check on it. I list every little thing, even
telephone calls."

What he could not list, or add up in the figures of his
daily accounting, was what the family war would cost him if
Aldo's and Roberto's accusations of forgery of his father's
signature were upheld in court. All he did know was that
such a decision could destroy him.

20

POMPEII'S LAST HOURS

Gucci was still a highly successful and valuable corporation, regardless of whether, as Patrizia believed, the divisions within the family were driving staff members to leave the firm and thirty-six people had been recently fired. Despite the splits, frictions, squabbles and lawsuits in the family that may have superficially hurt its reputation and weakened its financial resources, the excellence of Gucci goods and the integrity of its trademark had firmly established the company in a strong enough position to guarantee its survival.

In Italy alone Gucci was turning over two hundred million dollars a year, with a 1985 profit figure of 8 percent after a most scrupulous observance of taxes.

In America, Gucci Shops, Inc., recorded a further turnover of sixty-two million dollars with net profit of more than five-and-a-half million. Not a bad performance by any standard. Aldo may have been under considerable pressures during that year with his company under investigation and his personal liberty threatened, but he had kept the customers crowding into his shops to buy his goods.

London had managed a further turnover of more than ten million pounds ($12,500,000) in that same year, with an operating profit of 10 percent. Nearly two hundred employees in the Bond Street shop saw no drop in their sales charts.

By late 1986 Maurizio could claim that the one hundred and fifty-three stores around the world (fourteen of them wholly owned) were grossing nearly half-a-billion dollars a year. As mentioned, his personal estimate of the companies' combined worth was about eight hundred million dollars.

None of the personal crises seemed to affect the elegant image created and enhanced imaginatively by three generations of Guccis.

But what if the shares had to be sold? The power structure laid open to invasion by outsiders? That—in the opinion of financial experts—would be another matter entirely. And in the spring of 1987 the official receiver appointed by Milan's Attorney General Dr. Felice Paolo Isnardi to deal with Maurizio's alleged forgery called a shareholder's meeting in Milan to appoint new directors. Maurizio's confiscated stock, held in his private company, Gucci Finanziaria, and the charges against him removed any possibility of his appointment to the board until a settlement of the actions against him had been reached. His appeal to be released from these charges had been refused, and so a new president had to be elected.

Maurizio himself had not been seen in Italy since the raid on his home following the confiscation of his stock and his temporary expulsion from the presidency the previous September. His chief adviser, Gian-Vittorio Pilone, was under similar charges involving Maurizio's claimed gift from Rodolfo.

Giorgio and his son Alessandro were the only other

Gucci directors on the board that consisted largely of hired lawyers and accountants, among whom were signors Pilone, Consoli, Corbo and Jacovacci.

What the official custodian, Francesco Cangiano, had to ascertain was how many, if any, of the Gucci family could retain their directorships. None of the senior members seemed a likely candidate. Aldo was still in jail. His evasion of U.S. taxes over a number of years left little chance of his being considered eligible, despite his record of success in the business.

Allegations by the company that some years previously his son Roberto had improperly favored his wife Drusilla's brother, the son of the Duc de Caffarelli, and a prominent Rome businessman and property developer, by granting his brother-in-law the exclusive rights to operate all duty-free concessions for Gucci goods in Rome's airport and shops and airports throughout the world, were still gathering dust in Italian courts.

In other ways, too, Roberto's behavior did not go unnoticed by the family. In 1984 he had marketed a whisky under his personal endorsement, and displayed it in the windows of the via Tornabuoni shop in Florence as if it were a Gucci product. "Glorious Twelfth Fine Old Blended Scotch Whisky—Selected by Roberto Gucci" was advertised widely as a drink "for glorious harmony." Gucci's agents and distributors throughout the world were offering it for sale.

Roberto, as managing director of Guccio Gucci, S.p.A., filed suit against his brother Paolo's trademark application in Tokyo, under which Paolo would be entitled to market "alcoholic beverages" (Italian wines) under the family name. The official objection was backed by an affidavit in which Roberto stated that this application threatened the whisky he was already selling under Gucci's trademark. And he backed up his legal attack with copies of his "Glorious Twelfth," although it seemed nobody had approved its sale.

Robert had perhaps not given due consideration to his cousin Maurizio, the newly appointed president. He was not like his older relatives, who tended to do what they liked without consulting one another. Since Maurizio, and the company, had had no previous knowledge of the Scotch being sold under Gucci's trademark or given approval for its sale, he had Roberto's stock of two million bottles of whisky confiscated.

Later Roberto tried to patch things up with his cousin, offering to sell the whisky for between two and three million dollars. But by then the family war was at its height, Roberto and his father were challenging Maurizio's right to shares and no deal was possible. Somewhere in the world there are probably still cases of the Gucci liquor in bonded warehouses with no likelihood of their release. The whisky is no doubt maturing nicely, but so far as Roberto is concerned, it seems there will be no profits from them.

His oldest brother, Giorgio, had also at one time been accused of acting against the interests of the company and dismissed from the board. His reinstatement followed the crucial meeting when Maurizio secured a "unanimous" vote in favor of his presidency and Aldo's resignation.

The custodian Cangiano clearly faced a difficult task. According to Paolo, the last days of this conflict were rapidly approaching. "The banks were saying there was no more credit available, that there had been too many mysterious disappearances of millions into too many unknown pockets. And all these charges and indictments were not helping to establish confidence."

On balance, uncertainty about Maurizio's right to his father's shares free of inheritance taxes was perhaps the most disrupting factor in the Gucci web of problems. A criminal conviction could cost the suspended president not only inheritance taxes of several hundred million dollars but possible imprisonment or heavy fines. In raising funds to meet such a contingency Maurizio would presumably have to part with some if not all of his stock. If this happened, his voting authority would go, and with it the management concept he had struggled to apply to the company. Gucci would, at least temporarily, be back where it was. But under new management.

Paolo believed that if that happened "we would see the licensing program I had been trying to persuade my family to embark on put into full operation. I would welcome that, because I'm sure it would greatly improve the financial health of the company."

Others in the business world shared his view. So far the conflict had remained inside the family and had not damaged Gucci's value in the open market (which Aldo at one point put at two billion and Paolo, more cautiously, at eight hundred million dollars), but the dangers of that war becoming a public matter still threatened the company.

Paolo's interest was not academic. If he failed in his court cases against his family and the company, and lost the right to trade under his own name, he could end up the least advantaged of the present shareholding Guccis. Still, there was always his potential inheritance. "I don't know what will happen. But I know this. If father should die and leave me nothing—if his will, that is, does not include me—then I promise I'll keep the lawyers busy for the next fifty years."

His determination to secure a place in his father's succession raised a parallel question: how much, whoever Aldo should leave his fortune to, will anyone inherit?

Aldo's difficulties with Olwen had not stopped him from female companionship during his time in America. His friendship with Alexandra Murkoska had been followed by other relationships. His generosity to his lady friend astonished his son Paolo and his wife, Jenny, who had been with them in Palm Beach when, in his seventies, Aldo had enjoyed bathing with a topless girlfriend. "He must have spent millions of dollars on her. She had diamonds the size of bullets," Paolo says.

Nevertheless, Bruna Palumbo was the only one to have borne his child. His long if intermittent years with her place her (and their daughter Patricia) high in the list of those likely to benefit from Aldo's estate. Bruna was well looked after, and if Aldo's efforts to free himself from his marriage succeeded, she had reason to hope that one day she might be even more favored.

In December 1984 Aldo moved to divorce his English wife Olwen. By now she had partially recovered from an attack of thrombosis in 1978, which had left her unable to walk without some difficulty. Olwen was living quietly in Rome behind electrically locked and barred gates. Aldo petitioned for an English divorce on the grounds that the marriage had "irretrievably broken down."

By some mischance a copy of the petition was mailed to Olwen's cottage in Oswestry. She read its contents with astonishment. Her husband had stated that "we had been quarreling frequently for a considerable time, and finally decided in the summer of 1956 that the marriage would never work and we would live apart."

She claimed, as mentioned, to know nothing of any such decision. She and Aldo had ceased to live together as man and wife, but whenever he was in Rome he visited her. They spent time together and he seemed to treat the place as his own home. But, she said, there had never been any mention of divorce, let alone an agreement to seek one.

Attached to the petition was a copy of a questionnaire. In what could be taken to have been Olwen's handwriting, it declared that she "would not defend the case," that she "consented to a decree of divorce being granted" and that she would make no financial claim. It did at least state that she objected to paying the costs of the divorce action, but gave no grounds for this.

Under this extraordinarily generous statement was a signature, written in what seemed a shaky hand that it appeared bore a somewhat crude resemblance to her own. The address beside it—"Wellsbridge House, London Road, Sunninghill, Berks"—was, as Olwen would learn, the house her husband shared with Bruna.

Through her brother Ewart in England, Olwen immediately protested. Paolo and Roberto then took up their
mother's case and spent thousands of dollars preventing the
divorce taking place. Paolo hired one of England's most expensive and influential solicitors, Sir David Napley. Napley
sent Pamela Collins, one of his partners, to Italy to hear
Olwen's side of the story in person. She returned with a
sworn affidavit by the seventy-year-old lady.

By this time legal actions had begun, and Aldo, who
swore that Olwen *had* signed the petition and that the signature in the shaky hand was hers, was granted a temporary,
interim Decree *Nisi*. As Paolo and his advisers knew, this
would be made final if no successful opposition to it was
raised.

With little time to spare, Napley used Olwen's deposition to quash Aldo's claim. In it she had stated that she had
seen Aldo, that he had told her there would be no divorce,
"that it was all nonsense. We were too old for such things."
He had apparently not explained about the incorrect address, her alleged agreement to a divorce and her signature.

About the last, though, Olwen acknowledged that very
often "my husband asks me to sign documents relating to the
house or taxes. I regret that I have signed such documents
without reading them." She agreed that for this reason the
signature might well be hers. She was unable to say with
certainty.

But the address of the petition, Bruna's Sunninghill
home, was "not familiar to me, although it may be an address known to my husband." An oblique way, perhaps, of
intimating that she preferred not to know, officially, of the
love nest in Berkshire bought by Aldo for Bruna when she
was bearing his child. (Bruna lives there much of the time
now, having become devoutly steeped in spiritual life and the
teachings of Buddha.)

Finally his wife insisted: "I do *not* accept that the marriage has irretrievably broken down, nor do I consent to a
decree of divorce. My husband and I never discussed separa-

tion, nor divorce—save as previously stated, when he said it was all 'nonsense.' "

Sir David Napley had no hesitation in declaring to Paolo that, armed with this sworn statement, "an application to set aside the Decree *Nisi* of divorce and obtain dismissal of the Petition" was then only a matter of form and would be urgently set in motion.

During her visit to Olwen, Pamela Collins felt she had established something important: "She does not appear to accept that she and her husband have truly separated. Although she had long been aware of the existence of Bruna Palumbo." According to Paolo, his mother had also been aware of other companions in her husband's life. In refusing to give Aldo a divorce she was clinging to her legal rights. She was also, relevantly or not, insuring that she stood the best chance of being her husband's chief benefactor if she survived him.

As Paolo explained, "Under Italian law the children must inherit equally. But a widow may get a third of the estate and part of her inheritance in *usufruit*—that is, for her lifetime. Unless, of course, the contract of marriage included a list of possessions."

So far as Paolo knew, Aldo's marriage to Olwen did not include such a list. He was therefore hopeful that he and his brothers would one day inherit. But Aldo, remarkably vital in his early eighties, seemed likely to keep the family waiting a long time.

With his way of dealing with things that stood in his way, Aldo apparently had never concerned himself with detail. The situation, therefore, was fluid. Paolo discovered that, following Rodolfo's example, his father had made over his 40 percent share in the Italian company to his sons Roberto and Giorgio, who, in his opinion at the time, merited the gift, excluding Paolo. "He did this in 1984 when he was trying to get his divorce, and perhaps that too was in his mind. But mainly, I think, he wanted to avoid death duties."

Aldo, despite his tax penalty, was still an exceedingly wealthy man. His close friends had seen him acquire a portfolio of great value in real estate alone. "He bought property wherever he went," Alessandra says. His art collection, some of it displayed in the Fifth Avenue galleria, was also worth a fortune. If his holdings in Gucci's various companies retained only their then value, Aldo's worth could hardly have been much less than a billion dollars.

It raised an interesting question, which affected not only Aldo but all Gucci-family stockholders. How much were the certificates attesting to their equity holdings worth? What price would Gucci bring as a result of the family war, and in the still unpredictable future?

Whatever, there seemed more enemies within than dangers without. But the value of the company divided against itself was beginning to reflect a reluctance to take it over, to inherit its problems.

The situation therefore had to be seen through many differently placed eyes. From a trading point of view, Gucci was a formidable giant. It had first-class sites, a sophisticated network of prime dealers, an enviable image and record and a close, glamorous connection with the world of high fashion and celebrity. As Aldo so often said, there were very very few in the marketplace with the cachet of Gucci.

It seemed unlikely that anything, other than adverse trading conditions, could threaten that position of strength. Paolo was still determined to force a showdown to induce his relatives to sell. On the other hand, if his deal with Maurizio was subsequently upheld he could find himself reinstated to a high executive position with the power to change the company's fortunes.

If things went on as they were, with nobody profiting but the lawyers, then it appeared Paolo intended to fight on for as long as he had the money to do so, which could be for a very long time. "Well, what should I do? I'm only fighting in self-defense. They are destroying Gucci Parfums, in which I have the biggest holding. So I could be left with only my three-and-a-third percent of Guccio Gucci. That's what they want."

And his price had risen. The twenty million dollars

Maurizio had agreed to pay for Paolo's shares in the perfume and other companies now seemed too little to Paolo. "It should be double. Say the company is worth only eight hundred million, then with my eleven percent of Gucci Shops Incorporated, my twenty percent of the perfume company, et cetera—say ten percent of the lot—that has to be worth eighty, not twenty, million dollars."

He also knew that the company would have to put its house in order if it ever did have to sell. And that they would then, he believed, be obliged to pay his price. "I'll tell you, I'm going to put Maurizio and the others in the position of having to sell out. They won't be able to afford to keep it."

But how long would that take? "A couple of years, at most." After which he was convinced that his campaign would have persuaded the family to sell, though they never in over half a century parted with a single share other than to blood relations. "Yes, but due to all this mess, nobody—no purchaser—wants to come near. Financially they are losing income and the debts are growing."

The company vehemently denied this, despite the shadows of suspicion surrounding Maurizio and his key advisers. "Gucci today is a reality as it has never been before," Franco Crudeli argued. "Its value has never been higher. If I had to put a figure on it worldwide, I would say perhaps, with its potential, close to a billion American dollars, maybe more. We have requests daily from the biggest banking corporations offering deals with suppliers, seeking licensing agreements and whatever. I am constantly saying no to them. Because Dr. Gucci has no intention of selling."

Maurizio asserted that he had created a highly qualified and specialized team of top and middle management. His 1986 reorganization, he said, had swept out many of the old hands and hired in their place "a team of successful and aggressive professionals graduated from excellent multinational companies [General Electric, Proctor and Gamble, Unilever, Playtex, et cetera]."

Paolo ramained critical. "I have just discovered that the

company owns a jet. Why? Maurizio has no business in capital cities like Paris and Geneva, only in Milan and Florence, which you can reach more easily by road. Tell me how you can fly to Florence in winter? It's often impossible. But it's only one hundred sixty miles from Milan, and a train will take you there in two hours."

The cost of Maurizio's "aggressive professionals" also seemed to Paolo to involve undue extravagance: "The managers are on fat salaries, and all of them have company Mercedeses. Maurizio's salary from the perfume company alone is three hundred and seventy-five thousand dollars a year—yet they need money! I hear that Pilone [Maurizio's chief advisor], is setting up financial companies to raise loans. One of these days the banks are going to want their monies back. The banks will get the company."

With Gucci's capital assets showing on their last (1985) published balance sheet at over six hundred million dollars, the likelihood of such a catastrophe occurring seemed highly unlikely. "This is a highly profitable company," Crudeli said. "Why should we sell? On the contrary, we are enhancing our worldwide presence. So it would be contradictory, the antithesis of logic, even to think of selling."

In an acrimonious legal battle in the summer of 1986, Maurizio canceled the distribution contract between Gucci Perfumes and the American Manetti-Farrow company, which, according to *Women's Wear Daily*, was "estimated by market sources" to be worth a turnover of one hundred million dollars, thereby executing a part of his global strategy. In the future Gucci would handle as much of its own distribution as possible. The accessories—mostly scarves, small leather goods and key chains—would be relayed to and sold exclusively in their own and thirty franchised stores throughout the United States, Canada and American possessions.

Crudeli saw this as a further instance of Maurizio's sound commercial logic. "Because outside our outlets these are our only products. And the distribution of them is an important part of our strategy." Then how could these views, Maurizio and his team's bullish assessments, and Paolo's dismal predictions, be reconciled? A closer understanding of the entire intricate Gucci company structure—present and future—becomes necessary to make some sense of it all.

21

DIVIDED WE FALL

The tangle of complex, bitter and often destructive actions of the Gucci family persists into 1987. It would be comforting to say that the worst is now behind them, that the feuds and fisticuffs that have disturbed this wealthy and successful family are unlikely to be seen again in the fine paneled boardroom of the via Tornabuoni. Comforting, but probably untrue.

Spring sunshine may be sparkling now on the polished silver and glass of their elegant storefronts, but the imbroglio goes on. Indeed, rumors of attempts at coercion are surfacing, threatening to unfold another dramatic episode in the "Dallas-on-the-Arno" scenario of this dissension-wracked family.

Paolo heard of these new developments firsthand during a visit to Milan in March 1987. He had flown in from New York, where he had hoped to visit his imprisoned father and perhaps arrange some sort of détente. His wife Jenny was working at her singing lessons and planning a career that

243

would also free her at least temporarily from the turmoil of the family conflict.

The news he brought back to Italy was that Aldo was being moved from his Elgin Air Force Base prison to Miami, where the remainder of his year-and-a-day sentence would be spent doing "public service" with the Salvation Army. Paolo also heard that his father's phone calls had been restricted because he tended to spend so long on the phone and ran up a huge bill. Through Aldo's secretary in New York, he finally managed to call his father for one brief chat.

It was in the usual Gucci style. When they talk business, the Guccis almost invariably use, to put it mildly, unflattering expressions about each other. "What is that crazy idiot doing now?" would be a rather mild example. The words "mad" and "crazy" tend to be almost terms of endearment. And Aldo was in fine spirits. "Don't worry, I'll be out any day now," he told his son cheerfully. "They'd be crazy to keep me here any longer than they have to, I'm costing them too much."

When he landed in Italy, Paolo heard less hopeful news from a woman who had worked for Gucci in Rodolfo's lifetime. She is no longer with the company, but her knowledge of what went on could make hers important testimony in the matter of Maurizio's transferred shares. *If* there was a forgery, and aware that Rodolfo's son then faces the possibility of a ruinous decision against him, the ex-employee is in an unhappy position. According to Maurizio's estranged wife, Patrizia, she said she felt obliged to testify after all those years with the company on account of what she owes to the name of Gucci.

Since then, Paolo says she told him, she has come under pressure to withdraw from the case. She says her telephone is tapped. In Italy this is unlawful unless under official sanction, and she has reported it. Paolo says, "It introduces a very worrying element in the case."

So the file marked "Gucci" in the Milan prosecutor's office grows steadily thicker. Maurizio's personal position is extraordinary, his control of the company taken over by the official Custodian. His personal affairs—including supervision of Patrizia and his family's domestic expenses, estimated to vary between eighty and one hundred twelve thousand dollars monthly—are in the hands of his legally empowered deputy, signor Pilone. In Maurizio's absence the business is being run by him and the lawyers and executives Maurizio recruited.

How long this situation can last is anybody's guess. The tragedy is that if some form of accommodation could still be patched up between Paolo and the problem-laden company (Aldo convicted, Maurizio suspended and charged with criminal offenses, Roberto involved in civil actions with the company, and Paolo still working for his right to trade under his own name), the straying sheep could be brought back into the fold and the costly war settled. Indeed, if Paolo's cousin Maurizio can manage to acquit himself of the charges against him, perhaps the most likely solution of the family struggle would still seem to be for the company to pay the price necessary to end Paolo's action. Surely Paolo would think so. His competing trademark is an aggravating issue— others might point out that Gucci has faced stiff competition before and survived—and not coming to terms with it now could prove far more costly in the end. The company is spending money on lawyers around the world and there is a fourth generation of Guccis on their heels who will doubtless ask awkward questions if their elders allow internecine rivalries to destroy the company.

Giorgio's son Alessandro, whose 1986 marriage was attended by all Guccis who could get to it, is already a director, and member of what Maurizio calls "our executive committee, a kind of strategy planning group." Guccio, his twenty-five-year-old younger brother, named after the founder, works in Florence in the company's sales division. Of Roberto's six children, three of the four boys—Cosimo, Phillipo and Umberto—are grown up and in the company. Paolo's daughter by his first marriage, Patrizia, is on the staff of the factory in Florence. And unless a firm basis of agreement and settlement is reached among their contentious elders, these younger Guccis, as their involvement in the company increases, are just likely to take matters in their own hands.

If Maurizio has his way, however, any gains and laurels they hope to win in the company will be hard-earned. Late last year, before his suspension, he rejected criticism that he preferred outsiders—such as most of the top managers—to his own family members. "It is not true that I don't believe in the family, but to me a name is immaterial. I believe in the individual. If tomorrow I have to select whoever is going to run the company in the future, I must pick the best there is, not only for me but for the shareholders. It would give me enormous pleasure if the Number One happened to be named Gucci, but if it was someone else I had to select, then it would have to be so. I want my family to succeed in spite of their name, not because of it. And I see it as my duty to see that that happens."

So the question of who in the family is to succeed and who is to fail depends on several unpredictable factors. Aldo is one of them. He could still be a potent factor in the next phase of the battle. According to Roberto, who has kept in touch almost nightly by telephone calls from Florence during Aldo's prison term, his father is in great shape, full of fight and anxious to get back in the fray. Indeed, with a new president to be appointed by the official Custodian, and little hope of Maurizio regaining the post while his trial is pending, the Gucci board may almost be ready to reverse their earlier decision and welcome Aldo's return.

On the other hand his sons Giorgio or Roberto—or perhaps even Paolo—could be elevated to the presidency. Certainly Maurizio's fate will bring about a massive change in company strategy. If convicted he will have to serve either a long jail sentence or pay a huge fine. In addition he will be required to settle more than two hundred million dollars in inheritance taxes, and it seems highly improbable that

Maurizio can meet such a cost without selling at least some of his shares. What that would result in no one can say. Disposal of Maurizio's stock at anything like its true value might prove difficult. But even allowing for a loss in value due to the troubled state of the company, the stock would probably sell for half a billion dollars on the open market.

If Paolo's trademark case should eventually meet with success, there would be not one Gucci on the market but two. The divided house would then be permanently split and in direct competition with itself. Paolo's skills and contacts, gained from his years in the parent company, make him a formidable consideration however much his family might scorn his plans.

The question, then, would seem to be why is it so difficult to bring the conflict to an end? The answer seems to defy business logic: the tangle of lawsuits, for example, has grown so that nobody can see a way to unravel all the knots. In New York at this writing a judge has postponed Paolo's further action over the so-called broken agreement with the company on which all of these hinge, and in which, if he is successful, he will claim damages of a hundred million dollars for each of the years since 1984 that he has been prevented from trading. Pressing for this would seem to work against hope of settlement. "But why should I have this chain around my neck?" Paolo asks. "Why should I be tied to this stupid agreement?"

At the same time Paolo is suing for dividends on his shareholdings in the companies. He claims that these have been declared but never paid to him. "I haven't seen anything yet, though in June 1986 five million dollars was voted by the board of the perfume company to be paid out in dividends. I'm told that the money is back in the company as a loan. It seems to me that what they've done is a sort of juggling act to stop me from getting any money."

Paolo is also suing for his quarter share of the 15 percent of pre-tax profits of all Gucci companies worldwide, amounting to several million dollars plus expenses. The alleged grounds for his action are that if the agreement of the February 1982 meeting is valid in forbidding him the use of his trademark, as they claim, then it must also remain valid in regard to the other parts of it that guarantee him this cut.

In yet another action he claims that a licensing agreement made by Guccio Gucci in Italy, under which the perfume company granted a license to a firm called Scannon to make and distribute Gucci perfume, was improperly made to prevent him from benefiting financially. "I have only three point three percent of Guccio Gucci, while in Gucci Parfums, which should have made the deal, I own twenty percent—a whole fifth share of the entire company. Guccio Gucci has nothing whatever to do with the perfume company."

And that is not all. Paolo alleges that five million dollars were paid by the Scannon corporation to Gucci Shops in America, but nothing to Italy, where the perfume company was registered. "Because my father needed the money to pay for the new building in America. So I am putting all this in the case to let the judge decide if what was done was proper, or if it was a fraud. If he thinks it was a fraud, then it will have to be prosecuted and tried as a fraud under criminal law."

In Switzerland, too, an arbitration decision is pending over Paolo's aborted deal with Maurizio. A decision in his favor there could mean that he has to be reinstated and paid for his shares, though at considerably more than the original price agreed upon. And in New York yet another of his actions is due to be heard. This one charges illegal alteration of the company by-laws and failure to abide by the shareholders agreement made at the meeting of February 1982 (under which four directors on each side were to have been appointed instead of the nine actually sanctioned).

Paolo's several actions are not all of Gucci's problems. To them add Maurizio's. If the energy with which the present investigations are being pursued is an omen, the case will be brought against him and anyone else allegedly implicated with considerable intensity. Americans are not alone in demanding that a prominent person must be given no special concession or privilege.

In February of 1987 Maurizio made a vain attempt to have the Attorney General's appointment of an official Custodian set aside. He and lawyer-colleagues and associates are working hard to shift the burden from their backs. Nobody can say how it will go, or what will be the verdict. Time can be an important element. With motions, the case is unlikely to be heard until well into 1988. Meanwhile Maurizio's shares must remain withheld and his presidency suspended subject to the Custodian's appointment.

Roberto and Aldo are also in hot water. They face an American Gucci Shops, Inc., company action over the Manetti-Farrow cancellation, charging fraud, conspiracy, neglect, directorial misconduct, breach of trust and misappropriation of commercial opportunity. The case against them involves claims of damages of ten million dollars. And Roberto is also being sued by the company for having allegedly appointed a company called Sidital to sell Gucci lighters and pens in duty-free shops around the world without the consent and knowledge of the board.

Any possible comic-opera aspect of these charges and countercharges is misleading; they are both serious and threatening as well as immensely costly. In yet one more suit, which still awaits settlement, Aldo's American company, Gucci Shops, Inc., is alleged to have been responsible for an unexplained disappearance of more than a million dollars. The plaintiffs are the American company itself suing Aldo, his son Roberto and the companies in which they held directorships in London.

Aldo and Roberto firmly deny the charge that they somehow misappropriated the money, as claimed in the suit brought by the U.S. company in October 1985. As yet the company's legal action has failed to explain what did happen to it, where it went or how it could be entered in the New York books of Gucci Shops as repayment of a loan to the British company. This loan, according to the London au-

ditors, was neither received by Gucci Ltd. nor is it on record
as having been made by them to the American corporation.
So until the action is settled, the million joins the other
alleged skeletons in the Gucci closet.

Almost a century since Guccio Gucci washed Lily
Langtry's dishes and served Dame Nellie Melba in London's
Savoy Hotel, the family business he founded on a shoestring
is entangled in more binding threads than Gulliver encountered on his travels. Whatever happens, the family members
know they are facing a period of great difficulty and disrup-
tion. A tightly held family concern, their successful business
may no longer be able to contain the power plays of individual members. In spite of all the money spent on lawyers, the
disputed contracts, and the well- or ill-intentioned efforts,
the Guccis are obliged to endure governance by outsiders.

They are no longer in control; no longer is it only a
family squabble. Whatever happens, even if there is no danger of them returning to the Florentine equivalent of rags, it
clearly is going to take far more than business as usual to
restore a healing and revivifing harmony among them.

Appendix A:

GUCCI EQUITY HOLDINGS

Information drawn from legal and other published sources

	ITALY [Guccio Gucci, S.p.A.]	U.S.A. [Gucci Shops, Inc.]	LONDON [Gucci Ltd.]
Aldo [Honorary Chairman]	Lifetime use ("usufruit") of voting rights, dividends, & benefits, of 40%	His company Vanguard Ltd controls 16.7%	Via Vanguard 40%
Maurizio [Suspended president]	Via his Gucci Finanziaria company 50%	Via his Anglo-American Manufacturing Researches Ltd. company 50%	Via Anglo-American 45%

251

Giorgio [Vice-president]	From Aldo 20% Via his company Gika Ltd. 3.3%	Via Gika 11%	Via Gika 3.3%
Roberto [Administrative director]	From Aldo 20% Via his company Anfars Ltd. 3.3%	Via Anfars 11%	Via Anfars 3.3%
Paolo	Via his company Retailing Wholesales Promotions Ltd. 3.3%	Via Retailing 11%	Via Retailing 3.3%

PARIS [Gucci et Cie]	HONG KONG	GUCCI PARFUMS		GUCCI BOUTIQUE [Rome]
		[S.p.A. Italy]	[International]	
Via Vanguard 40%	Nil	Direct 8% Indirect 19.2%	Partly via Gucci Shops Inc. 50%	Nil
Via Anglo-American 40%	Via Anglo-American 10%	50% of 80%	Partly via Gucci Shops Inc. 50%	50% of 85%
Via Gika	Via Gika	Nil	Nil	Nil

3.3%	10%			
Via Anfars	Via Anfars	Nil	Nil	Nil

3.3%	10%			
Via Retailing	Via Retailing	Via Retailing		Nil

3.3%	10%	20%		

Appendix B:

THE GUCCI EMPIRE

Gucci Companies—dates of incorporation

Guccio Gucci	1923
[became 1) Societa Anonima Guccio Gucci	1939
2) Guccio Gucci srl.	1945
3) Guccio Gucci spa.	1982]
Gucci Shops, Inc. (U.S.)	1953
Guccio Ltd. (UK)	1961
Gucci et cie (France)	1963
Gucci Boutique	1963
Gucci (Hong Kong) Ltd.	1974
Gucci Parfums (Italy)	1975
[became Gucci Parfums spa.	1982]

Gucci Stores—opening dates

Florence	1923
Rome	1938
Milan	1951
New York	1953
London	1961
Paris	1963
Palm Beach	N/A
Bal Harbour	N/A
Beverly Hills	N/A
Chicago	N/A
Hong Kong	1975
(Buy out of six I. Magnin	
Gucci Boutiques in U.S.	1985)

Appendix C:

DOCUMENTS

File Legale

688 FIFTH AVENUE

PHONE (212) 826-2600

NEW YORK
PALM BEACH
BEVERLY HILLS
CHICAGO
BAL HARBOUR
LONDON

GUCCI

NEW YORK

FLORENCE
ROME
MILAN
MONTECATINI
PARIS
HONG KONG

September 23, 1980

Mr. Paolo Gucci
NUOVA G S.R.L.
Via Della Massa, 8
50012 Bagno A Ripoli
Florence, Italy

Dear Mr. Gucci:

At a Board of Directors meeting of GUCCI SHOPS, INC., held in the
City of New York, pursuant to notice, on Monday, September 23, 1980,
the Board of Directors of GUCCI SHOPS, INC., by majority vote of
the Board of Directors, voted to remove you as an officer of
GUCCI SHOPS, INC., to wit, Vice President, and to terminate your
employment with GUCCI SHOPS, INC. as of the close of business on
September 23, 1980.

Very truly yours,

GUCCI SHOPS, INC.

Marie Savarine
President

MS/lmm

Registered Mail,
Return Receipt Requested

Translation attached

GUCCIO **GUCCI** SOC R L.

FIRENZE

73 • VIA TORNABUONI

TELEFONO 28 72 51 . 2 - 3

RACCOMANDATA R.R.

Firenze, 7 Aprile 1978

Egr. Sig.
Paolo Gucci
Piazza degli U nganelli, 3
FIRENZE

A seguito di recenti spiacevoli fatti avvenuti
in contrasto con gli interessi aziendali e dei quali
é già stato ampiamente discusso con i Soci, in accordo
con gli stessi, é stato deciso di sospenderti tempora-
neamente da ogni incarico ed attività da te svolta nel
seno della ns/ Società, in attesa di ulteriori accer-
tamenti.

In una assemblea della Società, che mi premurerò
di indire quanto prima, saranno messi in discussione
gli atti inerenti al danno subito dalla Società.

Ti invito a rimanere a disposizione per i chiari-
menti.

Saluti.

GUCCIO GUCCI S.R.L.   REGISTERED R.R.

FLORENCE, APRIL 7, 1978

Mr. Paolo Gucci

Piazza degli Ungarelli, 3

Florence

Following the recent occurrence of unpleasant actions in conflict with the company's interests and which have already been extensively discussed with the Shareholders, in agreement with said Shareholders, it has been decided to temporarily suspend you from every duty and activity undertaken by you within our company, awaiting further verification.

In a Company Meeting, which I will hasten to call as soon as possible, the acts inherent to the damage sustained by the Company shall be discussed.

I invite you to remain available for clarifications.

Best regards.

(Signature of Rodolfo Gucci)

Firenze,13 Ottobre 1981

I Sigg. Aldo Gucci, Giorgio Gucci e Roberto Gucci, in proprio e quali titolari
di azioni nelle rispettivi Società, si impegnano ad acconsentire nelle apposite
sedi assembleari, mediante il loro voto favorevole,acché il Sig. Paolo Gucci
possa svolgere in futuro la sua attività di designer in proprio o tramite una
Società ~~professionale~~ senza limiti di promozione e pubblicità.

Questo impegno da parte dei Sigg.Aldo, Giorgio e Roberto Gucci si annullerà au-
tomaticamente ove sarà creata la linea "Gucci più" tramite la Società Gucci Parfums, nei tempi tecnici necessari per l'attuazione e nelle dimensioni e secondo
i programmi a suo tempo delineati tra i Sigg. Aldo,Giorgio,Roberto e Paolo Gucci.

Contemporaneamente, e senza alcuna riserva, con la firma della presente da parte
sua, il Sig. Paolo Gucci si impegna ad abbandonare le cause da lui promosse nei *in America*
confronti della Gucci Shops e di tutti i vari convenuti, dando instruzioni immedia
te ai propri legali. Alle formalità necessarie per l'immediato abbandono di queste cause, saranno incaricati i rispettivi legali del Sig.Paolo Gucci in America
e del Sig. Aldo Gucci.

Il Sig.Paolo Gucci si impegna naturalmente a non riproporre in futuro le dette
domande giudiziali presso qualsiasi corte.

TRANSLATION

Florence October 13, 1981

Misters Aldo Gucci, Giorgio Gucci and Roberto Gucci, personally
and as shareholders of the respective companies, pledge themselves
to consent to, at the appropriate meeting headquarters, through
their favorable vote, that Mr. Paolo Gucci can develop, in the
future, his activity as a designer, personally or through a
company, without limits of promotion and publicity.

This pledge, on the part of Misters Aldo, Giorgio and Roberto
Gucci shall be automatically annulled when the "Gucci Plus"
line shall be created, through the Gucci Parfums Co., within the
period necessary for its actualization and within the dimensions
and according to the programs outlined at that time by Misters
Aldo, Giorgio, Roberto and Paolo Gucci.

Contemporaneously, and without any reserve, Mr. Paolo Gucci,
with his signature of the present agreement, pledges to abandon
the cases initiated by him in America, with regard to Gucci
Shops, and to abandon all the various agreements, giving immediate
instructions to his own lawyers.
The respective lawyers of Mr. Paolo Gucci in America and Mr. Aldo
Gucci, shall be charged with the necessary formalities for the
abandonment of these cases.
Naturally, Mr. Paolo Gucci pledges not to re-propose, in the
future, the said legal petitions with any court whatsoever.

(Signature Aldo Gucci)
(Signature Paolo Gucci)
(Signature Roberto Gucci)
(Signature Giorgio Gucci)

(Signature of witness)

TLX 1245
19 OTTOBRE 1981

ATTENZIONE AMMINISTRATORE SOC.GUCCIO GUCCI S.R.L.
SIG.RODOLFO GUCCI

RISPONDO TO TELEX DATA 16 OTTOBRE 1981 ASSOLUTAMENTE SORPRESO
ED ALLIBITO SUO CONTENUTO.
CONTESTO DECISAMENTE QUELE AMMINISTRATORE DELLA GUCCI PARFUMS
TUE INIZIATIVE ATTE A INSINUARE SITUAZIONE INESISTENTE CON-
CORRENZA E CONFUSIONE MERCATO PRODOTTI GUCCI PARFUMS ET GUCCIO
GUCCI.
TI RICORDO CHE SOCIETA' GUCCI PARFUMS EST OPERANTE DAL 1975 ED
HA UNA SUA STRUTTURA COMMERCIALE DI UFFICI ED DIPENDENTI COME
L'ALTRA NOSTRA SOCIETA' GUCCIO GUCCI SRL E SOPRATTUTTO GLI
STESSI DIRITTI DI OGNI SOCIETA'APPARTENENTE AL NOSTRO GRUPPO GUCCI.
LA GUCCI PARFUMS EST STATA CREATA DAGLI STESSI SOCI DELLA GUCCIO
GUCCI, TE COMPRESO E DISTRIBUISCE ESCLUSIVAMENTE PRODOTTI GUCCI.
PER IL PROGRESSO COMMERCIALE DELLA NOSTRA AZIENDA E ANCHE PER IL
BENESSERE COMMERCIALE DELLA NOSTRA FABBRICA NEL PIENO RISPETTO
DEL SUO STATUTO SOCIALE.
IL MARCHIO GUCCI A CUI TI RIFERISCI EST DI ASSOLUTA E·FINORA·
INCONTESTATA·PROPRIETA' DI TUTTE LE NOSTRE SOCIETA' GUCCI I.CUI
STATUTI CONFERMANO DI FATTO, CON LE LORO ATTIVITA' DI MOLTI ANNI
DI PROFICUO LAVORO QUESTA INEQUIVOCABILE REALTA'.

A TUTTI NOI SEMBRA MOLTO STRANO ED ASSURDO VOLERE OGGI RIBALTARE,
SENZA ALCUN MOTIVO,QUESTO ASSUNTO, NON COMPRENDENDO BENE QUALI
INTERESSI PERSONALI SI VOGLIA, IN PIENO CONTRASTO CON QUELLO PIU'
ALTO DELLE SOCIETA' DEL GRUPPO GUCCI, PROTEGGERE.
NON NASCONDO COMUNQUE MIA VIVA PREOCCUPAZIONE, ANCHE A NOME DI
MIO PADRE E MIEI FRATELLI PER I GRAVISSIMI RIFLESSI CHE TALI
PROPOSIZIONI POTRANNO AVERE PER LA COMPATEZZA DELLE STRUTTURE
DELLE NOSTRE SOCIETA'
COMUNQUE, TI PREGO, IN NOME DEL BUON SENSO CHE TUTTI NOI DEVE
ANIMARE IN QUESTO MOMENTO, DI NON PRENDERE DECISIONI O METTERE IN
ATTO ·PROPOSIZIONI CHE VADANO AL DI LA' DEI POTERI DI AMMINISTRATORE
CONFERITI DALL'ASSEMBLEA DEI SOCI DELLA GUCCIO GUCCI SRL.
TALI GRAVISSIME DECISIONI CHE COINVOLGONO IL FUTURO DELLA NOSTRA
AZIENDA, E IN TAL SENSO TI CONFERMO LA VOLONTA' DI MIO PADRE ET
DEI MIEI FRATELLI, SONO COMUNQUE DI ESCLUSIVA COMPETENZA DELLA
ASSEMBLEA DEI SOCI DELLA GUCCIO GUCCI SRL.
COMUNQUE IN ATTESA DI TALE URGENTE ET IMPROROGABILE ASSEMBLEA,
CHE CONTERRA' MI AUGURO AMPIE SPIEGAZIONI DEGLI ULTIMI AVVENI-
MENTI, CREDO DI INTERPRETARE LA VOLONTA' DEI SOCI E DIPEN-
DENTI DEL GRUPPO GUCCI PER UN INVITO A TUTTI AD UNA MAGGIORE
CONSIDERAZIONE DEI PIU' ALTI INTERESSI DEL NOSTRO GRUPPO GUCCI,
OFFESI NEGATIVAMENTE DA QUESTA ULTIMA CIRCOSTANZA.
TI PREGO INFINE DI ASTENERTI DA ULTERIORI DANNOSI INTERVENTI
IN ATTESA DELLE DECISIONI DELLA PROSSIMA ASSEMBLEA NOSTRA
SOCIETA' GUCCIO GUCCI SRL E GUCCI PARFUMS SRL RISERVANDOMI,
IN CASO CONTRARIO L'IMMEDIATA TUTELA DELLE NOSTRE SOCIETA'
AFFETTUOSAMENTE COME SEMPRE.
ROBERTO GUCCI.

TRANSLATION

Telex 1245
OCTOBER 19, 1981

To the attention of the Administrator of the Guccio Gucci S.r.l. Co.
Mr. Rodolfo Gucci.

I respond to your telex dated October 16, 1981, being absolutely
surprised and shocked at its contents. I firmly contest, as
administrator of Gucci Parfums, your initiatives taken to insinu-
ate a situation of nonexistent concurrence and market confusion
with the products of Gucci Parfums and Guccio Gucci.
I remind you that the Gucci Parfums Co. has been operating since
1975 and has its own business structure of offices and staff,
as does our other Guccio Gucci S.r.l. company and above all,
has the same rights of every company belonging to our Guccio Gucci
group. Gucci Parfums was created by the same shareholders of
Guccio Gucci , with you included, and it distributes exclusively
Gucci products for the business progress of our firm and even for
the commercial well being of our factory, in the full knowledge
and adherence of its By-laws.
The Gucci trademark to which you refer to is the absolute and,
to date, incontestable property of all of our Gucci companies,
whose By-laws confirm this, in fact, with their long-standing
profitable business activity, which is an unequivocal reality.

It seems very strange and absurd to all of us to want to, at
this time, overturn, without any motive, this undertaking, not
fully understanding what personal interests one wishes to protect,
in clear contrast with the uppermost interests of the company of
the Gucci group. I do not hide, however, my real preoccupation,
even in the name of my father and my brothers, of the serious
consequences that these propositions could have for the solidity
of the structure of our company.
I ask you, however, in the name of good sense, something which we
must encourage at this time, not to make decisions or put into
action any propositions which surpass the authority of an administrator, authority which is conferred by the Assembly of the
shareholders of Guccio Gucci S.r.l. Such grave decisions, and
in this aspect I confirm to you the willingness of my father and my

-2-

TRANSLATION

brothers, are, however, part of the exclusive competence of the
Assembly of the shareholders of Guccio Gucci S.r.l.
Therefore, awaiting this urgent and most important assembly,
one which can no longer be put off, which will contain, I hope,
ample explanations of the most recent happenings, I think I am
interpreting the desire of the shareholders and staff of the Gucci
group for an invitation to all to arrive at a higher consideration
of the most important interests of our Gucci group, whom have
been most offended by this last circumstance.

Finally, I ask you to abstain from any further damaging interventions, and await the decisions of our next Assembly of Guccio
Gucci S.r.l. and Gucci Parfums S.r.l., reserving for myself
any immediate tutelage (protection) of our companies if you fail
to do so.

Affectionately as always·
Roberto Gucci ·

②

Dott. MARIO M. NEPI
Medicina Interna
FIRENZE

Studio: _____
Abit.: S. Margh. Montici, 5 - Tel. 681785
Riceve per appuntamento

Il Sig. Gucci mi comunica di
avere ancora disturbi visivi
e violenta cefalea.

Il suddetto mi comunica che
le soprascritte lesioni e le
condizioni qui descritte, gli
sono state causate in una
violenta colluttazione avve-
nuta fra due persone.

Giudico queste lesioni e questo
stato guaribili in 8 gg. (otto) s.c.

In caso contraro per gli un-
consentiti dalla Legge.

[firma]

Dott. MARIO M. NEPI
Medicina Interna
FIRENZE

Studio: _____
Abit.: S. Margh. Montici, 5 - Tel. 681785
Riceve per appuntamento.

16 Luglio 1982

Ad ore 12,30 si presentava al
mio Studio il Sig. Paolo GUCCI,
di a. 51, residente attualmente
in Via L. Masso #8 FIRENZE.
Il medesimo presenta una ferita
lacero contusa di circa 2 cm. alla
reg. Temporale sinistra, ed ac in
Reggia alla reg. Zigomatica risulta
un'altra piccola ferita di circa
Cm.1. Presenta inoltre lesioni in
ingiarmento alla reg. lesioni del
collo e della mandibola.
Il Sig. Gucci è in importante
stato di shock, il P.A. è 90/60
& la F.A. 90/60

Dott. Mario M. Nepi
 M.D. -
Via S. Margh. a Montici, 5
 Florence   July I6th I982

At I2.30 p.m. Mr. Paolo GUCCI, aged 5I, and now resident
in Via della Massa n. 8, Florence, appeared in my consulting room.
The above named presents an approx. 2 cm. lacerated-
contused wound at the left temporal region and a lower
one of approx. I cm. at the left zygomatic region.
He also shows scratching injuries at the right region
of his jaw and neck.
Mr. Gucci is in a serious state of sphock, his pulse is
I00' and the A.P. is 90/60.
Mr. Gucci is also informing me that he has sight disorders
and an acute head-ache.
The above named informs me that the aforesaid injuries and
above mentioned conditions have been occurred to him during
a violent fight that happened a little while before.
I consider that this state and injuries are curable in 8
(eight) days if no complications set in.
This certificate is made out in unstamped paper for the uses
permitted by law.

Dott. Mario M. Nepi
  M.D. –
Via S. Margh. a Montici, 5
     Florence   July 16th 1982

At 12.30 p.m. Mr. Paolo GUCCI, aged 51, and now resident
in Via della Massa n. 8, Florence, appeared in my consulting room.
The above named presents an approx. 2 cm. lacerated-
contused wound at the left temporal region and a lower
one of approx. 1 cm. at the left zygomatic region.
He also shows scratching injuries at the right region
of his jaw and neck.
Mr. Gucci is in a serious state of sphock, his pulse is
100' and the A.P. is 90/60.
Mr. Gucci is also informing me that he has sight disorders
and an acute head-ache.
The above named informs me that the aforesaid injuries and
above mentioned conditions have been occurred to him during
a violent fight that happened a little while before.
I consider that this state and injuries are curable in 8
(eight) days if no complications set in.
This certificate is made out in unstamped paper for the uses
permitted by law.

County of   ᴺEW YORK

Inᵤ)x No.

Plaintiff designates
NEW YORK

PAOLO GUCCI,

County as the place of trial

The basis of the venue is

plaintiff's reside

Plaintiff

against

ALDO GUCCI, GIORGIO GUCCI, ROBERTO GUCCI,
RODOLFO GUCCI and MAURIZIO GUCCI, individually
and as Officers and Directors of GUCCI
SHOPS, INC.,

Summons

Plaintiff resides at

25 W. 54th Str

Defendant

County of

New York

To the above named Defendant**S**

𝕲ou are hereby summoned to answer the complaint in this action and to
a copy of your answer, or, if the complaint is not served with this summons, to serve a not
appearance, on the Plaintiff's Attorney(s) within 20 days aftᵉ. the service of this summons, exc
of the day of service (or within 30 days after the service is complete if this summons is not pers
delivered to you within the State of New York); and in case of your failure to appear or answer,
ment will be taken against you by default for the relief demanded in the complaint.

Dated, New York, July 16, 1982

SPEISER & KRAUSE, P.C.

Defendant's address: ALDO GUCCI: 25 W. 54th St.NY
Giorgio Gucci: Cortina D'Ampezzo, RomaItaly
Roberto Gucci: 60 Costa San Georgio, Florence
Maurizio Gucci:641-5th AvenueNYC
Rodolfo Gucci: 641-5th AvenueNYC
Gucci Shops, Inc.: Two East 54th Street,
NYC

Attorney(s) for Plaintiff

Post Office Address

200 Park Avenue, Suit
New York, New York
212-661-0011

Inc)x No.
Plaintiff designates

1 SUPREME COURT OF THE STATE OF NEW YORK
   COUNTY OF NEW YORK
2 -x
3 PAOLO GUCCI,
4   Plaintiff,   VERIFIED COMP
5   -against-
6 ALDO GUCCI, GIORGIO GUCCI, ROFERTO
   GUCCI, RODOLFO GUCCI and MAURIZIO
7 GUCCI, individually and as Officers
   and Directors of GUCCI SHOPS, INC.,
8 and GUCCI SHOPS, INC.,
9   Defendants.
10 -x
11   Plaintiff, complaining of the defendants, by his
12 attorneys, SPEISER & KRAUSE, P.C., alleges upon information
13 belief that at all relevant times hereinafter mentioned:
14
15   1.   Defendant, GUCCI SHOPS, INC., is a domestic
16 corporation duly organized and existing under and by virtue
17 the laws of the State of New York, with its principal place
18 of business at Two East 54th Street, New York, New York.
19   2.   Defendants, ALDO GUCCI, GIORGIO GUCCI, ROBER'
20 GUCCI, RODOLFO GUCCI and MAURIZIO GUCCI, are officers and
21 directors of GUCCI SHOPS, INC.
22   3.   On or about February 17, 1982, the defendant
23 GUCCI SHOPS, INC., and the defendants ALDO GUCCI, GIORGIO G
24 ROBERTO GUCCI, RODOLFO GUCCI and MAURIZIO GUCCI, acting in
25

1 capacity as officers and directors of GUCCI SHOPS, INC.,

2 entered into an employmen: agreement with the plaintiff, th

3 terms of which provided that the plaintiff would serve as a

4 Vice-President of GUCCI SHOPS, INC., in New York, in return

5 monetary remuneration.

6   4.   Thereafter, plaintiff attempted to undertake

7 position as Vice-President of GUCCI SHOPS, Inc., in New Yor

8 but was prevented by defendants from doing so.

9   5.   Defendants have refused to pay plaintiff the

10 remuneration due him as Vice-President of GUCCI SHOPS, INC.

11 under the terms of the said contract.

12   6.   Defendants have refused to reimburse or unde

13 the reasonable and necessary expenses which plaintiff incur

14 in his attempt to perform his employment contract.

15   7.   As a result of the foregoing, the defendants

16 have breached the employment contract with the plaintiff,

17 thereby causing him to suffer damages in the sum of EIGHTY

18 THOUSAND ($80,000.00) DOLLARS.

19   AS AND FOR A SECOND CAUSE OF ACTION

20   8.   Plaintiff repeats and reiterates each and e

21 allegation contained in paragraphs 1 through 6 herein with

22 same force and effect as if more fully set forth at length

23 herein.

24

25

-2-

SER & KRAUSE, P.C.
100 PARK AVENUE
K FOR AM BUILDING
W YORK, N.Y. 10166

1   9. The defendants, acting in concert, conspired

2   intentionally mislead the plaintiff by hiring him as a Vice

3   President of GUCCI SHOPS, INC., even though they had no

4   intention of allowing him to perform any business activitie

5   10. The defendants, acting in concert, conspired

6   to thwart any attempts by the plaintiff to function in his

7   appointed position as Vice-President of GUCCI SHOPS, INC.

8   11. Said conduct by the defendants as aforesaid

9   was an intentional act calculated to cause the plaintiff to

10 suffer severe emotional distress, public ridicule and publi

11 humiliation.

12   12. Said conduct was extreme, outrageous and bey

13 the standards of human decency and did cause the plaintiff

14 suffer severe emotional distress, public ridicule and publi

15 humiliation.

16   13. As a result of this intentional infliction o

17 mental harm, the plaintiff has been caused to suffer damage

18 in the sum of TWO HUNDRED FIFTY THOUSAND ($250,000.00) DOLL

19 and the plaintiff is entitled to exemplary or punitive dama

20 as to each defendant in the sum of ONE MILLION ($1,000,000.

21 DOLLARS.

22   AS AND FOR A THIRD CAUSE OF ACTION

23   14. Plaintiff repeats and reiterates each and ev

24

25   -3-

S J motion

ER & KRAUSE, P.C.
PARK AVENUE
FOR AN BUILDING
W YORK, N.Y. 10100

allegation contained in paragraphs 1 through 6 and 9 throug

12 herein with the same force and effect as if more fully s

forth at length herein.

15. The intentional breach of the employment co

as set out above was a malicious act committed by the defe

with the intent to injure the plaintiff, without any econo

or social justification on the part of any of the defendan

either joirtly or severally.

16. As a result of the foregoing, plaintiff was

caused to ~uffer lost wages and incur business expenses al

his damage in the sum of EIGHTY THOUSAND ($80,000.00) DOLL

AS AND FOR A FOURTH CAUSE OF ACTION

17. Plaintiff repeats and reiterates each and e

allegation contained in paragraphs 1 through 6, 9 through

15 and 16 herein with the same force and effect as if more

fully set forth at length herein.

18. On July 16, 1982, pursuant to formal notice

GUCCI SHOPS, INC., held a meeting of its Board of Director

19. Said meeting was attended by all the indivi

defendants named herein, as well as the plaintiff.

20. During the course of said meeting, the plai

attempted to question the conspiratorial and malicious con

of the defendants, as heretofore set out.

-4-

Inu)x No.

21. The defendants, GIORGIO GUCCI, ROBERTO GUCCI and MAURIZIO GUCCI, at the behest and instigation of the defendants ALDO GUCCI and RODOLFO GUCCI, willfully and maliciously assaulted, battered and beat the plaintiff abou his person,using their hands,fists and various objects.

22. Due to the aforesaid actions of the defendant GIORGIO GUCCI, ROBERTO GUCCI, MAURIZIO GUCCI, ALDO GUCCI, RODOLFO GUCCI and GUCCI SHOPS, INC., the plaintiff was cause to suffer lacerations of the face along with other personal injuries, psychic injuries, shock and trauma all to his dama in the sum of ONE MILLION ($1,000,000.00) DOLLARS.

23. Moreover, said acts and course of conduct by the defendants was oppressive, -intentional, malicious, wantc and abusive, thus entitling plaintiff to punitive or exempla damages as to each defendant in the sum of ONE MILLION ($1,000,000.00) DOLLARS.

WHEREFORE, plaintiff demands judgment against the defendants on the First Cause of Action in the sum of $80,00 on the Second Cause of Action in the sum of $6,250,000.00; o the Third Cause of Action in the sum of $80,000.00; and on t Fourth Cause of Action in the sum of $7,000,000.00, together the costs and disbursements of this action.

SPEISER & KRAUSE, P.C.
Attorneys for Plaintiff
200 Park Avenue
New York, New York 10166

VERIFICATION

STATE OF NEW YORK   )
COUNTY OF NEW YORK)   ss.:

STUART M. SPEISER, being duly sworn, deposes and says

That he is a member of the firm of SPEISER & KRAUSE,

P.C., the attorneys for the plaintiff herein, maintaining

offices at 200 Park Avenue, New York, New York; that he ha:

read the foregoing complaint and knows the contents thereo:

and that the same is true of his own knowledge, except as 1

matters therein stated to be alleged on information and

belief, and that as to those matters, he believes it to be

true; that the reason why this verification is made by

deponent and not by plaintiff is because plaintiff is not

within the County of New York, which is the county where

deponent has his office.

_____
STUART M. SPEISER

Sworn to before me this /6 t-h

day of July, 1982.

_____

ELIZABETH MARTINEZ
Notary Public, State of New York
No. 41-4732160
Qualified in Queens County
Commission Expires March 30, 19 84

T.RANSLATION   CORRIERE DELLA SERA, Wednesday July 21, 1982, p. 5

A Suit in New York over a Business Discussion Which Occurred in Florenc

The Gucci Brothers Fight: The One Who Was Hit Asks for Two and a Half

Billion Lire in Damages.

Florence- Aldo Gucci, 77 years old, the patriarch of the most famous

leather goods family in the world, tends to re-formulate the event.

His son Paolo from New York, speaks,instead,of hard words, slaps and

punches which he sustained from his brothers Giorgio and Roberto and

his cousin Maurizio during the last Board of Directors Meeting. He

also states that his brothers and cousins were "instigated" by his

father and by his uncle Rodolfo, who was well known in the years of

white telephones as Maurizio D'Ancora, the handsome (actor) of that tim

He adds that he was also hit on the head with a tape recorder.

"The story is exaggerated", repeats the patriarch, the son of Guccio,

founder of the firm. But Paolo went to the Manhattan Supreme Court to

request a compensation of two million dollars, about two and a half-bil·

lion lire. And he adds that Paolo wants to start his own business usin(

the name Gucci, and it has been some time that he has tried to do so.

Now it has been agreed that he may, but using not only the surname but

even his full name, "Paolo Gucci", but, of course, not the trademark.

But Paolo speaks of slaps, punches and the tape recorder smashed on hi:

head. Aldo Gucci affirms that it regards a purely familial occurrence,

a father who gave his wild son a slap. But he denies the fact of the

tape recorder. Nobody would have hit him over the head with it. Paolo

as has been affirmed in Florence - came to the Board of Directors meet-

ing with a tape recorder, and wanted to tape everything, but this was

not tolerated. The fight started from this.

It happened on Friday, the 16th, on via Tornabuoni, in the offices

above the stores of the firm. The dragging out of an old story which

started five years ago when Paolo decided to start his own business

using the family name.   His relatives warned him.   A suit was
also initiated in America, where Paolo resides, and the "wild"
offspring realized that the warning was revoked.

                                        G.P.

TRANSLATION

IL MESSAGGERO Newspaper,   July 21, 1982

A CHARGE / VIOLENT SUIT IN THE GUCCI HOUSE

New York - The fashion designer, Paolo Gucci, has filed a complaint
with the State Supreme Court in Manhattan against five of his relatives,
accusing them of having hit him in the head with a tape recorder
during a family meeting called to discuss his employment situation.
Gucci, who claims to have suffered a possible concussion, has requested
a compensation of about 2 ½ billion lire.
The episode happened last Friday in Florence, where Paolo Gucci went
for a meeting with five members of his family who manage the New York
stores.   According to Gucci's attorney, he attended the meeting with
a tape recorder.
At that point, sustains Paolo Gucci, his brothers Giorgio and Roberto
and his cousin Maurizio, "assaulted him knowingly and maliciously,
hitting him with their hands, their fists and finally, with the tape
recorder".   According to Gucci, the attack was instigated by his
father Aldo and by his uncle Rodolfo.
Paolo Gucci stated in his charges   to have left the Gucci store in
1980 in order to become an independent designer, but he was persuaded
by the family to return.

Anche il «pensiero religioso» dopo molte polemiche fra le materie

La Camera ha ripreso dibattito e votazioni sui 33 articoli della legge che riforma la scuola secondaria superiore. L'articolo 3, codificando l'insegnamento religioso come «una finalità» del corso scolastico, sembrava avesse chiuso la questione. Semmai questo era ormai un problema di dibattito fuori aula (come è avvenuto nel Pci) da riprendere magari al Senato. L'art. 4 ha riaperto il problema. Tutto è riemerso per un inciso di due parole: «pensiero religioso», riferito ad una delle indicazioni sulle future materie da insegnare che il Parlamento dà al governo per stabilire i futuri corsi scolastici. «E' un doppione che cela una enorme ambiguità oppure è una ripetizione vuota?, si è chiesto Massimo Teodori, radicale, ritenendo valida la prima interpretazione. La polemica è stata ripresa anche dai comunisti, con un loro emendamento soppressivo votato con quello analogo dei radicali. E' prevalsa, a scrutinio segreto, la maggioranza con 241 voti.

Il nodo della questione. L'art. 4 è un elenco dettagliato degli insegnamenti in comune all'intero quinquennio, a parte gli studi particolari, «di indirizzo», previsti poi nell'art. 5. Gli studenti saranno chia-

scenze e le capacità critiche su una serie di settori. Tra questi «il pensiero scientifico, filosofico e religioso».

La tesi del Pci. Risulta dal discorso in aula di Amabile Morena Pagliai. «Siamo contrari a questo riferimento al pensiero religioso perché se rientra nell'ambito dell'insegnamento della filosofia è inevitabile che ci sia ma se rappresenta un doppio canale (accanto all'ora di religione, come previsto dall'art. 3, n.d.r.) lo riteniamo negativo. Sull'intero articolo 4 il Pci si è astenuto, soddisfatto del chiarimento nella legge che le parole «pensiero religioso» non corrispondono ad una futura «distinta disciplina».

La tesi radicale. Massimo Teodori ha insistito sulla «pericolosità» a svantaggio dei laici.

La tesi della maggioranza. Per primo ha parlato Aldo Gandolfi del Pri, premettendo: «Io sono un ateo. Il mio partito non ha proprio nulla da rimproverarsi in fatto di laicismo. Tutti i laici si sono battuti, sempre, per l'insegnamento del pensiero religioso in senso critico e storicistico. Ci sembra perciò illogico l'atteggiamento del Pci e dei radica-

Marco Polo a di Verdi sulle nuove mil Ma è proprio l

Le mille lire con l'effige di Giuseppe Verdi andranno in pensione dopo 14 anni di «servizio» e saranno sostituite da un nuovo biglietto, più piccolo e più colorato di quello attuale, con il ritratto di Marco Polo lo ha stabilito il ministro del Tesoro Andreatta con un decreto pubblicato lunedì sulla «Gazzetta Ufficiale». Sul «verso» del biglietto, al posto del Teatro alla Scala di Milano, sarà riprodotto il palazzo Ducale di Venezia. La nuova banconota — che dovrebbe entrare in circolazione tra qualche settimana — è però al centro di una polemica ancor prima di essere stata stampata: secondo il direttore della galleria che custodisce il dipinto dal

---

telex

Brigatista riciclava denaro del sequestro Costa
E' stato condannato a 8 mesi di reclusione e a 200.000 lire di multa il «pentito» Carlo Bozzo di 25 anni, studente, per il riciclaggio di 40 milioni di lire provenienti dal riscatto del rapimento di Piero Costa.

Trovata bomba in un camion della nettezza urbana
Una bomba a mano del tipo «Sipe», risalente alla prima guerra mondiale ma ancora efficiente, è stata trovata tra le eliche frantumatrici di un mezzo della nettezza urbana triestina. La bomba, che è stata solo scalfita dalle eliche, avrebbe potuto scoppiare durante il normale giro di raccolta delle immondizie.

Due persone arrestate dopo sparatoria a Napoli
Due persone delle quali non sono state ancora rese note le generalità — si tratterebbe di contrabbandieri — sono state arrestate nella zona di Santa Lucia, dopo una sparatoria che ha causato il ferimento di una giovane, Margherita Murè, di 22 anni, che era affacciata al balcone della sua abitazione.

Ponte sullo stretto: via libera a convenzione Fs-Anas
Presto sapremo se e come si farà il ponte sullo stretto di Messina. Il consiglio di amministrazione delle FS, che si è riunito sotto la presidenza del ministro Balzamo, ha infatti espresso parere favorevole allo schema di convenzione tra «FS», «ANAS» e la «Società Stretto di Messina».

Arrestato Longobardi, «boss» nuova camorra
Uno dei presunti «boss» della nuova camorra organizzata, Francesco Longobardi di 38 anni, è stato arrestato, dai carabinieri di Salerno. L'arresto è avvenuto in un albergo di Cetrato (Cosenza).

Inquinamento: quintali di pesci morti nel Pordenonese
Alcuni quintali di pesci pregiati (trote, temoli, anguille, barbi) sono morti nelle acque del fiume Meduna, nella destra del Tagliamento, a causa di un inquinamento, probabilmente di natura industriale. Sulle acque del fiume è comparso anche uno strato di schiuma spesso una decina di centimetri.

Scossa di terremoto in Friuli
Una scossa di terremoto con un'intensità di cinque gradi della scala Mercalli è stata registrata alle 12.55'56" nella zona di preone, ad ovest del monte Verzegnis, in Friuli. Nessun danno.

Medico in galera: prescrisse 48.500 fiale di morfina
Prescrivendo ricette abusive di fiale di morfina, un medico milanese trentenne è riuscito, nei soli primi sette mesi di quest'anno, ad incassare oltre 70 milioni di lire. Lunedì scorso il medico è stato arrestato: dall'inizio dell'anno aveva compilato 694 ricette (ciascuna per 70 fiale di morfina) all'ottantina di tossicomani suoi «clienti» fissi, che pagavano ogni volta da 100.000 a 150.000 lire.

Una denuncia Furibonda lite in casa Gucci

NEW YORK — Il creatore di moda Paolo Gucci ha sporto denuncia alla Corte suprema dello Stato a Manhattan contro cinque suoi parenti accusandoli di averlo colpito in testa con un registratore durante una riunione di famiglia per discutere sulle condizioni di lavoro. Gucci, che afferma di aver riportato una possibile commozione cerebrale, ha chiesto un risarcimento di circa 2 miliardi e mezzo
L'episodio è accaduto venerdì scorso a Firenze, dove Paolo Gucci si era recato per un incontro con cinque membri della sua famiglia che gestiscono i negozi di New York. Secondo l'avvocato di Gucci, questi era intervenuto alla riunione con un registratore
A questo punto, sostiene Paolo Gucci, i fratelli Giorgio e Roberto e il cugino Maurizio «lo avrebbero assalito coscientemente e maliziosamente, colpendolo con le mani, i pugni e infine con il registratore». Secondo Gucci, l'attacco era istigato da suo padre Aldo e zio Rodolfo.
Paolo Gucci ha detto nella denuncia di aver lasciato i negozi Gucci nel 1980 per diventare un creatore indipendente, ma era stato persuaso dalla famiglia a tornare

Due religiosi Aggediti a martellate: uno muore

VICENZA — Due religiosi dell'Ordine dei Servi di Maria del convento del Santuario di Monte Berico, a Vicenza, sono stati aggrediti ieri sera a colpi di martello: uno dei due è stato ucciso e l'altro ha riportato ferite gravissime.
Il fatto è accaduto poco dopo le 21. I due religiosi — Mario Lovato, di 71 anni, di Isola Vicentina e il fratello laico Grabriele Pigato di 65 anni di Mirabella Breganza — sono usciti dal convento per una breve passeggiata I che hanno imboccato via Cialdini, una stradina che la mezz'ora più tardi la stessa strada è stata percorsa da due fidanzati che hanno scorto padre Lovato e il Pigato a terra in un lago di sangue. Quando i religiosi sono stati soccorsi dagli agenti di polizia padre Mario Lovato era già morto per lo sfondamento del cranio causato da una serie di violenti colpi di martello.
Sul luogo dell'aggressione la polizia ha trovato un sacchetto di plastica con la pubblicità di un supermercato locale e dentro una sciarpa blu, poco lontani dal sacchetto anche due martelli macchiati di sangue usati per colpire i religiosi.

Il MESSAGGERO 21 luglio 1982

TRANSLATION   IL GIORNO Newspaper, July 21, 1982

PAOLO GUCCI HIT ON HIS HEAD WITH A TAPE RECORDER BY HIS RELATIVES.

July 21, New York

Paolo Gucci, fashion designer, reported five of his relatives to the Manhattan Supreme Court for having hit him on the head with a tape recorder during a family meeting. The dispute exploded Friday in Florence. The stores which Gucci has in New York were being discussed. "First they attacked me with fists, then with the tape recorder. The attack was instigated by my father Aldo, and by my uncle Rodolfo". Paolo Gucci has requested 18 billion 500 million Lire in compensation

continued on pg. 5:

VIOLENT SUIT IN THE GUCCI CLAN: PAOLO ASKS FOR OVER 18 BILLION LIRE

Paolo Gucci brought a suit against his family, Monday, in a New York State Court. He accuses his father Aldo, his brothers, Giorgio and Roberto, his cousin Maurizio and his uncle Rodolfo, of having cheated him out of 13 million 300 thousand dollars (about 18 billion 500 million lire). Paolo left the family company in 1980, because of "business differences" and became an independent designer. In February 1982, he returned as Vice President, but now he realizes that this position, which, contractually, should have yielded him an annual salary of $180,000 didn't give him any power within the family, not even the power to collect his salary.

His attorney, Stuart Speiser, says that Paolo "was not given any office, was not assigned any office personnel and his salary, as well as business expenses, were refused him.

The agreement, according to Speiser, was a simple facade in order to "neutralize him and make him appear ridiculous". The employees of the

company were instructed not to follow his orders, the clients were told
that Paolo didn't have the authority to conclude business matters, the
treatment he received in the family was "insulting and beyond the principles of human decency".

Not only, but at a Board of Directors meeting in Florence, this July 16,
Robert, Giorgio and Maurizio "intentionally and with premeditation,
assaulted and beat him". When Paolo brought a tape recorder in the
room, because he wasn't permitted to see the notes, says Speiser, the
three above mentioned persons threw it in his fact.

Abbye Hambra, spokesman for the family in New York, says that the
family is now in Florence and has no comment. Even Paolo is in
Florence "under the care of a doctor", says Attorney Speiser.

KINGSLEY NAPLEY

SOLICITORS

SIR DAVID NAPLEY
JOHN CLITHEROE   LAURENCE P. SHURMAN
FRANCIS WEAVER   DAVID M. SPEKER
CHRISTOPHER MURRAY
PETER PIMM
MICHAEL CAPLAN
RICHARD OSBORN
PAUL TERZEON
PAMELA C. N. COLLIS   ALBERT GEORGE

CONSULTANT
SIDNEY KINGSLEY, M.B.E.

107 - 115 LONG ACRE
LONDON WC2E 9PT

L.D.E. BOX 22

TELEPHONE 01- 240 2411
TELEX: 28786 KINNAPCO
FAX OP 2/3 01- 836 8357

ALSO AT
1 PLACE VILLE MARIE SUITE 1414
MONTREAL H3B 2B3
TELEPHONE: (514) 878 8484
TELEX: 055 62082

OUR REF PCNC/GDP/G.03455   YOUR REF   DATE 8th August 1985

Mr. Paolo Gucci,
Normans,
East Street,
RUSPER,
Nr. Horsham,
West Sussex

Dear Mr. Gucci,

I write further to my recent visit to interview your Mother to enclose a
copy of an Affidavit made by her whilst I was in Italy drafted on the
basis of the information provided by her to me. From what she told me it
is apparent that she does not consent to a divorce nor wishes one to take
place and had no prior knowledge of divorce proceedings. During recent
visits by your Father he denied that any divorce was taking place.

Your brother, Giorgio , has said that he would send me a copy of your
Mother's British and Italian passports in order to show her travels to
Britain over the last few years and to demonstrate that she has not been
spending lengthy periods in Britain recently.

The day after I saw your brother and your Mother, I had the opportunity
to discuss the position under Italian law with Avvocato Cefaly and I
enclose an attendance note of my discussion with him.

I should be grateful if you could liaise with Giorgio for an enquiry to
be made at the Anagrafe with a view to obtaining a copy of the Certificato
Di Matrimonio Con Annotazione Di Eventuale Separazione Dei Beni.

An application will now be made as a matter of urgency to set aside the
Decree Nisi of divorce that has been pronounced in the English Court
and obtain the dismissal of the Petition on the basis that the English
Court has no jurisdiction to entertain it.

In taking this step I am following your Mother's wishes. However, I should
inform you that if your Father were to be able to obtain a decree of
divorce in Italy and if he has made a declaration separating his goods
from those of your Mother (or if he has not acquired any goods since
1975) then her position so far as her financial position is concerned
under Italian law would be much worse than it would be under English law.
The divorce court in England has wide powers to make orders for
maintenance and capital provision. From what Avvocato Cefaly has told me

Contd...

- 2 -

it seems certain to me that any orders made by the Court in England on divorce would be more generous than those made by the Italian court. On the other hand, an English court would be in some difficulties in enforcing any order made by it if all of your Father's income is received abroad.

I understand that his shares are held through a Panamanian Company and it may well be that there would be difficulties in enforcing an order for maintenance no matter where the orders were made.

I did not discuss the financial implications of a divorce in Italy as opposed to a divorce in England with your Mother because:-

1.   I was not aware of the true position under Italian law when I saw your Mother;

2.   In any event I am not sure that she would be able to appreciate the financial implications.

Her instructions to me have merely been to the effect that she does not wish a divorce to take place. She does not appear to accept that she and your Father have truly separated although she has long been aware of the existence of Bruna Palumbo.

Because she does not wish a divorce to take place and because the powers of the English Court to enforce any orders for financial relief are not very good it seems to me that it would be in her best interests to prevent a decree absolute being pronounced in the English Court. If your Father then chooses to take Italian proceedings it will be up to the Italian lawyers to seek to block any proceedings for as long as possible (and which it appears they should be able to do fairly successfully).

I look forward to hearing from you with your comments.

Yours sincerely,

P.C.N. COLLIS

KINGSLEY NAPLEY

SOLICITORS

SIR DAVID NAPLEY
JOHN CLITHEROE LAURENCE P SHURMAN
FRANCIS WEAVER DAVID M SPEKER
CHRISTOPHER MURRAY
PETER PIMM
MICHAEL CAPLAN
RICHARD OSBORN
PAUL TERZEON
PAMELA C.N COLLIS ALBERT GEORGE

CONSULTANT
SIDNEY KINGSLEY, M B.E.

107-115 LONG ACRE
LONDON WC2E 9PT

L.D.E. BOX 22

TELEPHONE 01-240 2411
TELEX: 28786 KINNAPCO
FAX OP 2/3 01-836 8387

ALSO AT
I PLACE VILLE MARIE SUITE 1414
MONTREAL H3B 283
TELEPHONE: (514) 876 5464
TELEX: 055 62082

OUR REF PCNC/GDP/Misc.   YOUR REF   DATE 31st July 1985

Mr. Paolo Gucci,
Normans,
East Street,
RUSPER,
Nr. Horsham,
West Sussex

Dear Mr. Gucci,

I write further to our meeting of 29th July to inform you that I have obtained a photocopy of all documents on the Court's file and enclose a copy for your persual. I would refer to the documents and comment on them as follows:-

1. Petition

    This was filed on 4th December 1984 and states that your parents last lived together at 9 Gitton Road, Oswestry, Shropshire in the summer of 1956. Did your parents at any time live together at 9 Gitton Road? Can you remember the date when your mother obtained this property and whether or not she ever lived there? If she did not live there did she visit? If so, for what periods? You will see from the third paragraph that it is represented that your mother lived at 7 Gitton Road whereas I note from your uncle's letter that the property was sold by your mother some two years ago. From our meeting I understand that she has not visited this Country for some 4 or 5 years.

    You will note from the particulars that it is represented that your parents have never lived together since the summer of 1956. As I understand it your father did not leave your mother until 1976.

    The prayers for relief contain the usual prayers for a decree of divorce, an order for costs, and financial orders. It is, of course, ridiculous for your father to claim financial orders against your mother.

2. Acknowledgment of Service

    You will notice that part of this has not been completed. For instance, the answer to the question numbered 2 does not show

Contd...

the address at which your mother is alleged to have received the
Petition for divorce. You will see that the answer to question 6
provides her consent to a decree being granted although your
father could have dispensed with her consent bearing in mind that
there has been more than 5 years' separation. However, he has
chosen to petition on the grounds that the parties have been
apart for more than 2 years and for a decree to be pronounced on
this basis the consent of the other party must be obtained.
Where there has been 5 years' separation and this is pleaded in
the petition, it is not necessary to have the Respondent's
consent but, on the other hand, the Respondent can block the
pronouncement of a decree absolute until his or her financial
claims have been determined. It may be for the latter reason
that your father chose not to file a petition on the basis of 5
years' separation.

I do not understand the answer to question 7. You will see that
the Acknowledgment is undated and although the righthand bottom
box has been completed (as if there were a solicitor acting)
the solicitor's name is not stated and it seems unlikely therefore
that your mother has instructed solicitors in this Country.

3.   Affidavit by your Father in support of his Petition

Again you will see that it is alleged that the date of separation
was 1956 and that your mother has lived at 9 Gitton Road ever
since. You will see that your father's address at the date of
swearing of the Affidavit was shown as 27 Old Bond Street, ✗
London, W1. Your father identifies your mother's signature.
The signature is a little different from that shown on the
letters of authority to my Firm. ⟩

4.   Letter dated 6th June 1985 from H. Davies & Co.

You will see that your father appears to have decided not to
proceed with the divorce but then in a subsequent letter dated
24th June 1985 his solicitors inform the Court that he did wish
to proceed and subsequently a Decree Nisi was pronounced on 12th
July 1985. It does not appear that any application has been
made to abridge the usual 6 weeks' period between Decree Nisi
and decree absolute and the earliest date upon which Decree
Absolute might therefore be pronounced is 23rd August 1985. It
is obviously most important that some steps are taken prior to
that date to ensure that a Decree Absolute is not pronounced.

It appears to me that the Decree Nisi should be set aside by the Judge
who pronounced it (His Honour Judge Honig) on the grounds that the
Decree should not have been pronounced because:-

1.   The Court does not have jurisdiction to hear the Petition
because neither of your parents are domiciled or resident in
this Country (although your father's most recent address is

Contd....

- 3 -

shown as Old Bond Street, the residence requirement is 12 months. It might be open to him to argue that he is now domiciled here but that would, of course, be entirely contrary to his present application for American citizenship.)

2.   Service of the Petition was made on an incorrect address and your mother had no proper notice of it.

3.   Your mother's signature on the Acknowledgment appears to have either been obtained by deceipt or to be a forgery.

The application to the Judge is heard in open court and must be made on notice to your father (through his solicitors). The notice must be issued within 6 weeks of the Decree Nisi and served on your father's solicitors not less than 14 days before the day fixed for hearing. The date fixed for hearing must be before 23rd August and the notice should therefore be served on your father's solicitors by Friday next. Time is extremely short and any application must be supported by an affidavit either sworn by your mother or by one of her legal representatives setting out her understanding of the position and her knowledge of these proceedings (or absence of it).

Ideally I would like to go to Rome to interview her. If, after doing so it appears that her mental state is such that she is not in a position to provide me with any clear recollection I anticipate it will be necessary to take the advice of an Italian Lawyer as to any proceedings in Italy equivalent to seeking an order from the Court of Protection in this Country (which form of order I briefly mentioned at our meeting on Monday).

The less attractive alternative to my going to Italy would be for me to instruct an Italian Lawyer to visit your Mother in Rome, interview her, and then swear an affidavit as to what he is informed by her. I believe that this would be less satisfactory because there would be a time lapse whilst the affidavit was being drafted in Italy (approved by me here) and then sworn in Italy and sent back to England to be put before the English Court. Because of the time restrictions under which we are operating and because I believe it would be useful in any event for me to meet your mother and have an opportunity to discuss all matters with her generally it would be very much better if I could meet her personally.

I know that your mother is not fully aware of what has happened but it seems inevitable that at some stage she must be informed.

I should inform you that it is open to any person (other than a party to the proceedings) or the Queen's Proctor to show cause why a Decree Nisi should not be made absolute because of non-disclosure to the Court of material facts, and the Court may, if satisfied, rescind the Decree Nisi. Although it might be possible for either

Contd....

- 4 -

you or one of your brothers to provide evidence to the Queen's Proctor
that your mother has not lived in this Country, this does not overcome
the fact of her signature appearing on the Acknowledgment of Service in
respect of which an explanation from your mother personally is required.
If, however, you think that her health might be badly damaged if she
were to be informed of these proceedings I would be prepared to reconsider
the question of whether or not your mother should be troubled with this
matter.

In the light of the above advice I should be obliged if you could
contact me urgently to discuss the steps which should now be taken.

In the meantime, and in accordance with the Firm's usual custom, I should
be obliged if you could provide me with a cheque in the sum of £3,000
generally on account of costs bearing in mind that a considerable amount
of work in a short space of time will be required if your mother's
interests are to be protected.

I look forward to hearing from you.

Yours sincerely,

P.C.N. COLLIS

In the Divorce Registry   No 10913 of 1984.

Between

         Aldo Gucci   (Petitioner).

    and

         Olwen Elizabeth Price Gucci

                     (Respondent).

     I , Olwen Elizabeth Price Gucci , of Via Della Camilluccia , 510 Rome , Italy make oath and say as follows

1.   I am the Respondent herein and for the first time today have seen a copy of my husband's petition for divorce .

2.   I confirm that we were married on the 27ᵗʰ August 1927. and Following our marriage my husband and I lived in Florence until 1938 when we moved to Rome. Soon afterwards we moved to the matrimonial home at Via Della Camilluccia aforesaid . There is no produced and shown to me marked " OEPG 1 " a certificate of Italian nationality and of residence in Rome in respect of myself. I have had dual nationality since my marriage and have lived in Italy ever since the marriage.

3. I have visited my relatives in England (I was born near Oswestry) over the years but have never lived in England save that six years ago, during a visit to

2.

England I suffered from an attack of thrombosis and was obliged to spend about a year in England until I recovered. I have not been to England for about 2 or 3 years and think it unlikely that I will be well enough to travel there again. Because of my thrombosis I now have great difficulty walking.

4. My husband states that we last lived together at 9 Gitten Road, Oswestry, Shropshire in the Summer of 1956. I now own a property at 9 Gitten <u>Street</u> but did not, so far as I can recollect, own it in 1956. I bought it for my sister Muriel Price to live in and she still lives there. My husband and I never lived together at any property in Gitten Street and I do not recollect that he ever stayed at Gitten ~~prope~~ street.

5. I also bought a property at 7 Gitten Street but sold it a few years ago. It was bought as a holiday home and I stayed there for about 3 months each year but never lived there permanently. My home is at Via Delia Caminucia aforesaid and it has always been my intention to remain there.

6. I do not accept that the marriage has irretrievably broken down nor do I consent to a decree of divorce. My husband and I * have never discussed separation nor divorce. I have seen the acknowledgement of service filed in these proceedings. I recognise the

 * as set out at paragraph 7 below.

3.

signature as my own but have no recollection of signing the acknowledgment nor of having seen it before. My husband often asks me to sign documents relating to my house at Via Della Capulineia or to tax. I regret that I have signed such documents without reading them. It seems to me that I must have signed the acknowledgment (if it really is my signature) as a result of being asked to do so by my husband.

7. My brother, Ewart Price, telephoned me recently saying that he had been given papers sent to Oswestry by the Divorce Registry. This was the first that I knew of these proceedings. I saw my husband about 15 days ago and asked him about the proceedings. He said that it was nonsense, that there would be no divorce and that we were too old for such things.

8. I am 77 years old and regret that my health will not let me travel to London to explain the above personally to this Honourable Court.

~~Sworn this day of August 1985 before me~~

9. I note the address on the acknowledgment of service is Westbridge House, London Road. I do not own any property in England save 7 Cutler Street. This address is not familiar to me although it may be an address

4.

Known to my husband.

Sworn this 6ᵗʰ day of
August 1985 before me Oliwen Elizabeth Price
Gucci

AUTENTICA DI FIRMA
(Legge 4 gennaio 1968 n. 15 art. 26)

Certifico io sottoscritto dottor Sergio GALGANI, Notaio
in Monte Argentario, con studio in Porto Santo Stefano, ca=
poluogo del Comune di Monte Argentario, piazza del Valle n.1,
iscritto nel Ruolo del Distretto Notarile di Grosseto, che
la signora PRICE Oliwen Elizabeth GUCCI, nata a Westfelton
(Oswestry) - Inghilterra, il dieci novembre millenovecento=
sette, residente a Roma, via della Camilluccia n. 540, casa=
linga, della cui identità personale io Notaio sono certo,
da me Notaio ammonita ai sensi dell'articolo 26 della legge
4 gennaio 1968, numero 15, ha reso la sopraestesa dichiara=
zione e l'ha sottoscritta alla mia presenza.
In Porto Santo Stefano, capoluogo del Comune di Monte Ar=
gentario, nel mio studio, li sei agosto millenovecentoottan=
tacinque.

receipt of maintenance pursuant to an order and Mr. Gucci then died.

Avvocato Cefaly answered:-

1.   If they were still married Mrs. Gucci would, as his widow, receive one-third of his estate if he were to die intestate (the other two-thirds going to his children) or if he were to make a Will only one-third of his estate can be left as he chooses and the balance must go to his Wife and children.

2.   If they were divorced Mrs. Gucci would not receive anything out of his estate and the Court has no power to make secured provision.

So far as the quantum of maintenance is concerned, this is very difficult to assess in the case of the Guccis because Mr. Gucci is very rich. Avvocato Cefaly said that there was a sort of one-third rule applied but there are many factors considered by the Court.

2.   Division of matrimonial assets

Although the Court, on divorce, has power only to make maintenance orders, there is a separate jurisdiction relating to matrimonial assets. Prior to 1975 assets acquired before and after the marriage were viewed as quite separate and owned by the party who obtained them. In 1975 the law was changed to provide a presumption in favour of joint assets unless an agreement or declaration separating assets is made before the marriage or afterwards if the marriage was already in existence in 1975. PCC enquired whether Avvocato Cefaly knew if Aldo had made such a declaration. He said he did not but the declaration would have to be registered at the Town Hall. Avvocato Cefaly was himself going on holiday that day and would notbe able to check it. PCC said she would have to ask the Guccis to make arrangements for the records to be checked. The enquiries which should be made

2

ATTENDANCE NOTE   DATE: 7th August 1985

Re: Gucci

Attending Avvocato Cefaly at the Hotel when he came at the request of
Mr. Gucci to discuss the affairs of his mother.

PCC raised queries concerning the following:-

1.   A divorce in Italy.

      If the.separation between the Parties started before 1968 Mr.
      Gucci could directly ask for a decree of divorce.   If the
      separation started after that date Mr. Gucci would only be able
      to ask for a decree of judicial separation and for a divorce 5
      years thereafter.   This is the only ground for divorce.

      PCC enquired as to the definiation of separation under Italian
      law. Avvocato Cefaly said that from his knowledge of the family
      he believed that they separated, in reality, approximately 20
      years ago but if Mrs. Gucci wished to delay any Italian
      proceedings there was certainly a highly arguable point in this
      respect.

      Certainly it would be open to Mrs. Gucci to challenge that they
      were separated before 1968. Judicial proceedings in Italy
      tend to be very slow and this question could drag out
      proceedings considerably.

      On the making of a decree of judicial separation or divorce the
      Court has the power to make orders for maintenance in favour of
      wives. The Court has no power to make a capital settlement on
      a wife but such capital settlements are made by consent in
      consideration of wives giving up their claims for maintenance.
      (As per the position in England prior to the 1984 Act). PCC
      enquired what the position would be if Mrs. Gucci were in

would be in respect of the certificato di matrimonio con annotazione
di eventuale separazione dei veni. If such a declaration has been
made then Mrs. Gucci will not be entitled to any of her Husband's
wealth at divorce. If such a declaration has not been made,
however, any goods purchased by Mr. Gucci after 1975 would be
jointly owned with Mrs. Gucci.

Avvocato Cefaly said that the judicial process in Italy could take
5 to 10 years if enquiries were made as to Mr. Gucci's property
around the world. A decree of divorce is not pronounced until
the property situation is clarified.

3.   Court of Protection

Avvocato Cefaly said that he did not believe that Mrs. Gucci's
physical and mental state required the only form of order
available in Italy which is in respect of someone who is totally
unable to manage their own affairs. Mrs. Gucci was not in that
state. It was up to her family and lawyers to look after her.

PCNC

3

-5⊡ℑ37³o⅙ 4 ☖   0.040.00

IN THE DIVORCE REGISTRY   NO: |0913|34

In the Petition of ALDO GUCCI for dissolution of a
marriage shows that:-

1.   On 27 August 1927 the Petitioner was lawfully
married to Olwen Elizabeth Price Gucci (hereinafter
called the Respondent) the Respondent being then
Olwen Elizabeth Price at The Church of Our Blessed
Lady, Help of Christians and St Oswald, Upper Brook
Street, Oswestry in the District of Oswestry in the
County of Salop.

2.   The Petitioner and the Respondent last lived
together at 9 Gittin Road, Oswestry, Shropshire in
Summer 1956.

3.   The Respondent is domiciled in England and
Wales and is by occupation a housewife and resides
at 7 Gittin Road, Oswestry, Shropshire and the
Petitioner is by occupation a Company Director and
resides at 685 Fifth Avenue, New York City, USA.

4.   There are no children of the family now living
except: (i)   Giorgio Gucci - over 18 years
            (ii)   Roberto Gucci - over 18 years
           (iii)   Paolo Gucci - over 18 years

5.   No other child, now living, has been born to the
          Respondent during the marriage (so far as
is known to the Petitioner).

6.   There are or have been no other proceedings in
any Court in England and Wales or elsewhere with
reference to the marriage (or to any child of the
family) or between the Petitioner and Respondent with
reference to any property of either or both of them.

7.   There are no proceedings continuing in any
country outside England or Wales which are in respect
of the marriage or are capable of affecting its
validity or subsistence.

8.   The said marriage has broken down irretrievably.

9.   The Petitioner and the Respondent have lived
apart for a continuous period of 2 years immediately
preceeding the presentation of this petition and the
Respondent consents to a decree of dissolution of
marriage.

PARTICULARS

We had been quarrelling frequently for a considerable
time and we finally decided in Summer 1956 that the
marriage would never work and that we would live apart.
Accordingly, I moved out and we have never lived
together since that day.

<u>PRAYER</u>

The Petitioner therefore prays:-

1.   That the said marriage be dissolved.

2.   That the Petitioner may be ordered to pay the
      costs of this suit.

3.   That the Petitioner may be granted the following
      ancillary relief:-

      (a)   an order for maintenance pending suit
             a periodical payments order
             a secured provision order
             a lump sum order

      (b)   a property adjustment order

SIGNED   .... H. Davis & Co

The names and addresses of the persons to be served
with this petition are:-

Respondent:- Olwen Elizabeth Price Gucci of 7 Gittin
Road, Oswestry, Shropshire

The Petitioner's address for service is:- c/o
Messrs H Davis & Co of 105 Park Street, London W1Y 4AA

Dated this 4th day of December 1984

Acknowledgment of Service — Respondent Spouse   No. *10913*   of 19 &

IN THE DIVORCE REGISTRY

IF YOU INTEND TO INSTRUCT A SOLICITOR TO ACT FOR YOU, GIVE HIM THIS FORM IMMEDIATELY

Between   *Aldo Gucci*   Petition

and   *Olwen Elizabeth Price Gucci*   Responde

and   Co-Responde

READ CAREFULLY THE NOTICE OF PROCEEDINGS BEFORE ANSWERING THE FOLLOWING QUESTIONS

1. Have you received the   petition for divorce delivered with this form?   *Yes*

2. On what date and at what address did you receive it?   On the *16*   day of *December*   19 8

     at ....

3. Are you the person named as the Respondent in the petition?   *Yes*

4. Do you intend to defend the case?   *No*

5. ~~Do you admit the adultery alleged in the petition?*~~

6. Do you consent to a decree being granted?*   *Yes*

7. In the event of a decree nisi being granted on the basis of two years' separation coupled with the respondent's consent, do you intend to apply to the Court for it to consider your financial position as it will be after the divorce?   *No others that have from been made*

8. Even if you do not intend to defend the case, do you object to paying the costs of the proceedings?

If so, on what grounds?   *Yes*

9. ~~Even if you do not intend to defend the case, do you object to the claim in the~~ petition for custody of the children?

10. Do you wish to make any application on your own account for: (a)

     (a) custody of the children?   (b)

     ~~(b) access to the children?~~

11. [In the case of proceedings relating to a polygamous marriage] If you have any wife/husband in addition to the petitioner who is not mentioned in the petition, what is the name and address of each such wife/husband and the date and place of your marriage to her/him?   *N/A*

Dated this   day of   19

If a solicitor is instructed, he will sign opposite on your behalf *but if the answer to Question 5 or 6 is Yes, you must also sign here.*

Signed *Olwen Elizabeth Price Gucci*
Address
for service ....

     I / We are acting for the Respondent in this matter.

     Signed ....
     Address
     for service *Waltbridge House*
     London Road
     Sunninghill, Berks

Unless you intend to instruct a solicitor, give your place of residence, or if you do not reside in England or Wales, the address of a place in England or Wales to which documents may be sent to you. If you subsequently wish to change your address for service, you must notify the Court.

D5:

3

Aldo Gucci Pleads Guilty To Tax Evasion Charges

~\JR   By RICH WILNER /- 20-86

NEW YORK (FNS) — Aldo Gucci, former chairman of Gucci Shops, Inc., pleaded guilty Friday to conspiring to evade corporate and personal income taxes and agreed to pay $7 million in back taxes.

In an emotional appearance in federal court here, Gucci, 80, admitted not paying taxes on about $12 million pocketed over an 11-year period beginning in 1972.

Gucci, appearing tan and rested, broke down and wept when he read a prepared statement detailing his role in the conspiracy. "The diverted income was divided among myself, members of my family and others," he said.

Gucci and his unnamed conspirators diverted the monies through four devices, according to Assistant U.S. Attorney Stuart E. Abrams.

Stuart said a majority of the diverted funds purportedly were used for the expense of operating a buying office in Italy. The buying office checks drawn by Gucci Shops were made payable to "Gucci" and instead of being sent to Italy were deposited into personal bank accounts of the defendants, court papers said.

The conspiracy also allegedly included the use of a franchise fee, which was paid beginning in 1975 by the various franchise stores operated under an agreement with Guccio Gucci Sp.A.

The franchise fee, 10 per cent of net purchases from Guccio Gucci, was to be paid to a Hong Kong corporation known as F.D.C. Co., Ltd., according to court papers.

Stuart said the franchisees were instructed to mail their fees to a post office box in Union, N.J., where a Gucci employe would pick them up and mail them to Hong Kong.

Government prosecutors said that F.D.C., however, was owned by a sham corporation used by the Gucci family to conceal its ownership of Gucci Shops, prosecutors charged.

Also used in the conspiracy, court papers say, were design fees, supposedly to pay for fashion design consulting services, and management fees, paid to Garpeg Ltd., another sham company, Abrams said.

The assistant U.S. attorney said a total of $18 million was diverted, two-thirds of which went to Aldo Gucci. The remaining funds are the subject of a continuing investigation, Abrams said.

In a quiet courtroom, the founder of the 33-year-old Gucci Shops, dressed in a double-breasted, blue pinstriped suit, told a federal judge that he "knowingly and deliberately used the various methods" to divert the monies.

"While I did not personally prepare the tax returns either for myself or for Gucci Shops, Inc., I knew that those returns did not accurately report my income or the income of Gucci Shops, in that they omitted my share of the income diverted from Gucci Shops," Gucci said.

Departing from from his prepared text, Gucci said the acts didn't represent his "love for this country. My love for America."

Gucci then turned over a $1 million check to the Internal Revenue Service and agreed with prosecutors to pay an additional $6 million before sentencing, which is scheduled April 8 before Judge Vincent L. Broderick.

In a statement after the court proceeding, Domenico de Sole, president of Gucci Shops, said Gucci ceased to have an active role in the store after he resigned on Nov. 2, 1984.

"If there are any taxes due as a result of any wrongdoings, de Sole said, "they will be paid."

Gucci faces up to 15 years in prison and a $30,000 fine.

ß/NT 208   *pg 10*   *July 15, 1988*

enforcement

The US requests to the hong kong government

The US Justice department made a government-to-government request to the hong kong government for assistance in obtaining documents from the hong kong branches of Chase Manhattan Bank NA and Citibank NA and also from the accounting firms Ernst & Whinney and Arthur Young & Company. The US submitted two requests:

▶ One stated that it was in aid of a grand-jury investigation of possible criminal law violations (the 'criminal request').

▶ The other stated it was in aid of a non-criminal tax examination contemplating an adjustment to the amount of tax shown due on the returns plus interest and penalties (the 'civil request').

The requests were signed by US judges in new york city on august 31 1984 and september 6 1984, respectively, and were forwarded — not direct to hong kong, but — to the US Justice department in washington DC. The hong kong legal department acted on the requests by filing a petition in the hong kong court on february 4 1985. This more than 5 month delay may have been attributable to a delay by the US Justice department in transmitting the requests.

Shortly before the hong kong petition was filed, the US Justice department withdrew its 'civil' request (which the hong kong legal department had agreed to file). The hong kong legal department filed the 'criminal request' and in its accompanying petition asked the hong kong court to grant some — but not all — of the US requests. The petition sought all the documents the US wanted from the two accounting firms. But as to the two banks, the petition asked only for documents of the three principal companies which the IRS was interested in. The petition did not seek from the banks certain other documents the US wanted. (See 'fishing' p.79). The hong kong court granted the petition on february 6 1985.

Curiously, when the hong kong petition was filed the US Justice department officials knew that 3-months earlier the US had already received (on october 24 1984) the documents which the hong kong petition sought from the banks. Thus, the petition was operative only as to the accounting firms.

One interesting feature of the US requests is the absence of substantiating evidence. The unsworn requests summarize most of the information contained in six sworn affidavits of the IRS criminal investigator but only attach a copy of one of several pertinent documents which the US Attorneys had previously supplied to the two US judges during the IRS summons enforcement proceedings.

The two US requests are largely identical and are presented below as a consolidated version. Words enclosed below between ◊hollow arrows◊ appear only in the civil request. Words appearing only in the criminal request are enclosed below between ◆solid arrows◆.

    —Jud Harwood, editor

❝ United States District Court
Southern District of New York

◆In re grand-jury proceedings   M-11-116◆
◊In the matter of the tax liability of:
Aldo Gucci and Gucci Shops Inc.   M-19-820

Request for judicial assistance

The united states district court for the southern district of new york presents its compliments to the appropriate judicial authority in hong kong and requests international judicial assistance in obtaining ◊(1)◊ banking records and information regarding certain bank accounts from the hong kong offices of Chase Manhattan Bank and Citibank ◊(2) and financial statements and other accounting papers regarding FDC Co Ltd in the possession of the hong kong offices of Arthur Young & Co and Ernst & Whinney◊.

◊These records are needed for the purposes of civil proceedings which have been instituted before this court and for other civil proceedings which may be instituted if the evidence is obtained◊.

◆These records are needed for use in a criminal proceeding the institution of which is likely if the evidence is obtained◆.

Further detail regarding the assistance requested and the need for this assistance is set-out in full in the attached 'application of the united states' made to this court by the United States Attorney for this judicial district. This assistance is essential to insure that justice is done.

We offer you our assurance of reciprocal judicial assistance. In this connection, the courts of the united states are authorized — by title 28 united states code §1782 — to use all their power to assist foreign and international tribunals. Attorneys of the united states government will present requests of foreign and international tribunals to the courts of the united states for execution.

The united states district court for the southern district of new york is prepared to reimburse your court for all costs incurred in executing the instant request and extends to the judicial authorities of hong kong the assurance of its highest consideration.

Date: New York New York
    ◆August 31 1984
         /s/John F. Keenan
         United States District Judge◆

    ◊September 6 1984
         /s/Leonard B. Sand
         United States District Judge◊ ❞

Judge Sand was the judge in the *Marc Rich + Co AG* case who fined the swiss company $50,000-per-day for not delivering documents located in switzerland (which the swiss government had ordered it not to deliver) even though the US Justice department refused to ask the swiss for the document and even though the swiss agreed to deliver them if asked. (See issue 55 of *Taxes International* (may 1984)).

This curious contrast in judge Sand's behavior be-

ЛЛ

B/MT 208
enforcement

PG 11

July 15, 1986

The Gucci investigation by Jud Harwood

tween Marc Rich + Co AG and Gucci illustrates an important aspect of international document-gathering. US investigations are undertaken by the executive — not the judicial — branch of government. The judge's signature on the request is thus misleading. The US judge does not initiate a request; does not ask for the documents for his/her own use; and does not vouch for any of the facts transmitted by the request. In Gucci, the US judges merely confirmed that a grand-jury investigation was underway (the criminal request) and that the IRS had filed a civil suit to enforce a summons (the civil request).

Below is the text of the two US applications attached to the two foregoing requests. They are presented in a consolidated form using ◊hollow arrows◊ (civil request) and ◆solid arrows◆ (criminal request) as discussed at the bottom of the first column on the previous page.   —Jud Harwood, editor

❝ United States District Court
Southern District of New York

◆In re grand-jury proceedings   [M-19-116]◆
◊In the matter of the tax liability of: [M-19-82]◊
Aldo Gucci and Gucci Shops Inc.

Application of the united states for the court to request the assistance of the judiciary of hong kong

Description of assistance requested

The united states of america — by its attorney, Rudolph W. Giuliani (United States Attorney for the southern district of new york) and ◊Jonathan A. Lindsey◊ ◆Stuart E. Abrams◆ (assistant United States Attorney) — applies to the court pursuant to ◊28 USC §1781◊ ◆rule 57(b)◆ of the 'federal rules of criminal procedure'◆ for the issuance of a request for the assistance of the judiciary of hong kong in performing the following judicial acts:
◊[Civil request text:]
▶ (1) Ordering that Chase Manhattan Bank, hong kong, produce the following:
▷ (a) All records pertaining to any checking accounts (including A/C #74-34-02976-0, A/C #20-74-25-00038-8, A/C #74-34-03116-2, and A/C #949-1-343514), saving accounts, and/or certificates of deposit in the name of and/or under the signatory authority of FDC Co Ltd and Garpeg Ltd for the period september 1 1978 through january 31 1982 and in the name of and/or under the signatory authority of Aldo Gucci for the period january 1 1979 through december 31 1981, including but not limited to:
1. Signatory cards.
2. Statement of account.
3. Ledger cards or transcripts of account.
4. Deposit tickets and corresponding deposit items.
5. Checks drawn.
6. Withdrawal items, including any certified or cashier's checks or money-orders.
7. Cash transit letters.
8. Wire transfers.
9. Bank checks purchased (records regarding Aldo Gucci only).

▷ (b) All records pertaining to any loans and/or mortgages in the name of either FDC Co Ltd or Garpeg Ltd during the period september 1 1978 through december 31 1981 and in the name of Aldo Gucci during the period january 1 1979 through december 31 1981, including but not limited to:
1. Applications for loans or mortgages.
2. Financial statements submitted.
3. Loan/mortgage reduction schedules reflecting dates of payments and amounts of payments.
▷ (c) Originals and/or photocopies of the bank's correspondence from, to, or on behalf of, either FDC Co Ltd or Garpeg Ltd during the period september 1 1978 through december 31 1981 and from, to, or on behalf of, Aldo Gucci during the period january 1 1979 through december 31 1981.
▷ (d) Originals and/or photocopies of the bank's credit file on either FDC Co Ltd or Garpeg Ltd for the period september 1 1978 through december 31 1981 and on Aldo Gucci for the period january 1 1979 through december 31 1981.
▷ (e) All records pertaining to the purchase and/or sale of any securities during the period september 1 1978 through december 31 1981 for, by, or on behalf of, either FDC Co Ltd or Garpeg Ltd and for, by, or on behalf of, Aldo Gucci during the period january 1 1979 through december 31 1981.
▷ (f) All records pertaining to any safe deposit boxes in the name of either FDC Co Ltd or Garpeg Ltd for the period september 1 1978 through september 30 1981 and in the name of Aldo Gucci for the period january 1 1979 through december 31 1981, including but not limited to:
1. Applications submitted.
2. Records of entry.
▶ (2) Ordering that Citibank, hong kong, produce the following:
[Editor's note: The application repeats the foregoing requests, substituting for 'FDC Co Ltd' the words 'Vanguard International Manufacturing Ltd' and substituting for the Chase checking account numbers in the first paragraph these Citibank checking account numbers: #3063-7969 and #3063-9067].◊
◆[Criminal request text:]
▶ (1) Ordering the hong kong branches of the Chase Manhattan Bank and Citibank to produce records of transactions for all accounts in the name of and/or under the signatory authority of Aldo Gucci, Edward Stern, Mario Savarino, Kerry Obonai, Garpeg Ltd, FDC Co Ltd, Vanguard International Manufacturing Ltd, Anglo-American Manufacturing Ltd, Retailing Wholesales Promotions Ltd, Gika International Ltd, and Anfars A°. Such documents should include but not be limited to signature cards, ledger sheets, bank statements, cancelled checks, deposit and withdrawal records, wire transfers, and correspondence relating to such accounts and transactions.
▶ (2) Ordering the hong kong branches of the accounting firms of Arthur Young & Co and Ernst &·Whinney to produce records pertaining to FDC Co Ltd. Such documents should include but not be limited to financial statements, accounting workpapers, books of account, and correspondence relating to FDC.◆
[Resuming with both requests consolidated:]
▶ (3) Taking the sworn statements of the representatives of Chase Manhattan Bank and Citibank ◆Arthur Young & Co, and Ernst & Whinney◆ regarding the requested documents referred to in paragraphs (1) and (2) to establish the following:

/V/M/T ~o8   *YG/2*   *July 15, 1980* *confidential*

Full text: The 2 US requests to hong kong   The Gucci investigation by Jud Harwood

▷   (a) That the documents are true and exact copies of original records presently in the custody of Chase Manhattan Bank and Citibank ◆Arthur Young & Co, and Ernst & Whinney.◆

▷   (b) That the originals of these copies are kept and retained in the ordinary course of the businesses of Chase Manhattan Bank and Citibank ◆Arthur Young & Co, and Ernst & Whinney◆, and that it is the regular practice of these businesses to keep and retain records of this type.

◆Nature of the investigation◆
▷Statement of facts
◊   In furtherance of an Internal Revenue Service investigation seeking to determine the correct federal income tax liabilities of Aldo Gucci and Gucci Shops Inc., and whether they may have violated the federal tax (or 'internal revenue') laws of the united states, the united states has instituted civil proceedings before this court to enforce Internal Revenue Service summonses served upon Chase Manhattan Bank and Citibank seeking records relevant to that investigation. A federal grand-jury for the united states district court, southern district of new york, is also conducting proceedings under the authority of this court to determine whether Aldo Gucci, Gucci Shops Inc., and others have committed criminal violations of the criminal laws of the united states.◆
◆   The United States Attorney for the southern district of new york is conducting an investigation under the authority of this court to determine whether Aldo Gucci, Gucci Shops Inc., and others have committed criminal violations of the tax (or 'internal revenue') laws and other provisions of the criminal laws of the united states.◆

The Gucci family is widely known as dealers in expensive leather goods and other items. The Gucci business was founded 78 years ago in florence italy, by Guccio Gucci. After his death his three sons, Aldo, Rodolfo, and Vasco, have carried-on the business. Aldo Gucci is the sole surviving son.

Gucci's american business is conducted by Gucci Shops Inc. — a new york corporation with office at 689 Fifth Avenue, New York New York. Aldo Gucci is the chairman of Gucci Shops. Until the early 1970's the stock of Gucci Shops was owned individually by several members of the Gucci family. Thereafter, however, the stock of Gucci Shops was transferred to the following companies: Vanguard International Manufacturing Ltd, Anglo American Manufacturing Researches Ltd, Retailing Wholesales Promotions Ltd, Gika International Ltd, and Anfars AG. According to information the ◊Internal Revenue Service◆ ◆government◆ has obtained, each of these companies serves no function other than to act as nominee or 'front' for members of the Gucci family.

In 1975 a corporation — FDC Co Ltd — was formed in hong kong. FDC is owned by Vanguard and Anglo American, two of the ◆'front'◆ companies that are stockholders in the Gucci Shops. The first meeting of the board of director of FDC was held at Gucci Shops' office in new york. The three directors of FDC were Edward Stern, Marie Savarine (treasurer of Gucci Shops), and Kerry Obonai (a japanese national who is manager of Gucci Shops in hong kong). Mr Stern and ms Savarine resigned as directors of FDC in august 1983, after the Internal Revenue Service began investigating Gucci Shops' relationship with FDC. ◆The Internal Revenue Service believes◆ ◆We believe◆ that FDC is a mere alter ego of Gucci Shops and the Gucci family.

According to a letter dated october 20 1975 from Edward Stern (accountant for Gucci Shops) to Aldo Gucci, arrangements were made for Gucci Shops to transfer large sums of money to FDC, supposedly in payment for 'design services' provided by FDC to Gucci. A copy of the letter is attached hereto as appendix-A. However, evidence obtained by the ◊Internal Revenue Service◆ ◆government◆ indicates that FDC performed no such services. ◆Specifically, a financial statement for FDC for 1977 shows that FDC had no salary expenses or other expenses that necessarily would have been incurred if FDC had in fact been performing design services.◆ ◊The Internal Revenue Service believes◆ ◆We believe◆ that FDC was created for the purpose of siphoning-off funds properly attributed to Gucci Shops in order to artificially reduce Gucci Shops' united states income tax liability and that the payments by Gucci Shops to FDC were made solely to generate ◊improper◆ ◆fraudulent◆ tax deductions for Gucci Shops.

FDC is also ◆believed to be◆ involved in another scheme that ◊may have been◆ ◆was◆ used to evade taxes on income properly attributable to Gucci Shops. Franchisees of Gucci Shops were required — apparently as a condition of obtaining a franchise — to make large payments to FDC. These payments totalled approximately one million US dollars per year. The franchisees were instructed to mail the payments to FDC to a post office box in union city new jersey, that had been opened by Marie Savarine (treasurer of Gucci Shops). The payments were apparently later sent to hong kong for deposit into FDC's bank accounts, accounts over which Aldo Gucci had signatory authority. ◊The Internal Revenue Service believes◆ ◆We believe◆ that these payments constituted income to Gucci Shops and that the income was routed to FDC to disguise this fact and to artificially lower Gucci Shops' tax liability.

Gucci Shops also ◊may have◆ used another hong kong company — Garpeg Ltd — as a vehicle to mask its income and to generate fraudulent income tax deductions. Garpeg is a hong kong company the stock of which is owned by Vanguard, Retailing Wholesales, Gika International, and Anfars—the same companies that hold the stock of Gucci Shops and ◊are believed to◆ act as alter ego of the members of the Gucci family. Two of the directors of Garpeg are Edward Stern and Kerry Obonai, who are also affiliated with FDC and Gucci Shops. Gucci Shops regularly made large payments to Garpeg, allegedly for 'management services'. Here, too, the ◊Internal Revenue Service◆ ◆government◆ has obtained evidence that Garpeg performed no such services.

It appears that FDC and Garpeg ◊may have◆ served a further function by enabling Aldo Gucci — a united states resident — to evade payment of the tax properly due on his personal income. As a united states resident, Aldo Gucci is required to report his world-wide gross income to the Internal Revenue Service. Mr Gucci has reported relatively small amounts of income for a person of his status (under $100,000 per year), and ◊has not reported◆ ◊did not report◆ any income derived from FDC, Garpeg, Vanguard, or the other companies. There is reason to believe that the money diverted to these companies was actually used for mr Gucci's personal benefit and hence should have been reported by ◊him◆ ◆Aldo Gucci◆ as income. For example: mr Gucci has two residences in the united states: in fort lauderdale florida and in beverly hills california. Title to mr Gucci's home in florida is in the name of Vanguard and title to his home in california is in the name of Garpeg.

According to the information received thus far, FDC.

Q/MT 208   PG 13   July 15, 1986

enforcement

The Gucci investigation by Jud Harwood

Garpeg, and Vanguard maintained bank accounts at hong kong branches of Chase Manhattan Bank and Citibank, and Aldo Gucci, Edward Stern, Maria Savarine, Kerry Obonai, and others had signatory authority on the accounts. ◊The other companies described herein also may have had accounts with these banks.◊ These bank records will show the flow of funds from Gucci Shops to FDC and Garpeg, and ultimately to Vanguard and the other companies that are ◊believed to be◊ the alter egos of the Gucci family.

◊The government also has received information that at various times accounting services for FDC have been performed by hong kong affiliates of Arthur Young & Co and Ernst & Whinney. The financial information from these firms will demonstrate that FDC did not perform design services that would justify the payments it received from Gucci shops.◊

◊The offenses

As noted above, Gucci Shops is a new york corporation that is required by law to file united states corporate income tax returns. The grand-jury is investigating whether Gucci Shops filed false tax returns in which it fraudulently deducted from its income the payments made to FDC and Garpeg and whether Gucci Shops filed false corporate tax returns by failing to report the fees that its franchisees paid to FDC when those fees were in fact taxable income of Gucci Shops.

The grand-jury is also investigating whether Aldo Gucci attempted to unlawfully evade his personal income tax liability by means of the payments to FDC and Garpeg.

United states income tax returns also require disclosure of whether the taxpayer had signatory authority over any bank accounts in a foreign country. Mr Gucci stated under penalties of perjury on his tax returns that he did not have signatory authority over any foreign bank accounts. The investigation has already shown that mr Gucci's tax returns were false in this respect since mr Gucci did have signatory authority over bank accounts in the name of FDC and Garpeg in hong kong, and it is likely that criminal proceedings will be instituted if authenticated copies of the records of the accounts can be obtained.

For your assistance, the text of the united states criminal statutes involved in this matter is reproduced in pertinent part in appendix B attached hereto.◊

◊Need for assistance

The Internal Revenue Service is investigating the allegations described above to determine if civil or administrative action against Aldo Gucci or Gucci Shops Inc would be appropriate. The Internal Revenue Service has instituted civil proceedings before this court to compel Chase Manhattan Bank and Citibank to produce copies of certain documents relevant to the resolution of these charges.

As described above, all of the requested bank records are needed to show the flow of funds from Gucci Shops to FDC, Garpeg, and then to Vanguard and the other 'front' companies in order to determine whether Aldo Gucci and Gucci Shops Inc correctly reported their income and paid federal taxes thereon for the years under investigation.

By opinions and orders dated:
▷ march 23 1984 (Garpeg v. United States 84 Civ. 0437 (RWS))
▷ march 27 1984 (United States v. Chase Manhattan Bank M-18-304 (GLG)) and
▷ july 6 1984 (Vanguard International Manufacturing Inc v. United States 83 Civ. 6884, 84 Civ. 436 (RWS) and

Garpeg Ltd v. United States 83 Civ. 6885, 84 Civ. 435 (RWS))
this court ordered Chase and Citibank to comply with the summonses. While Chase and Citibank have produced certain documents from their new york files, they have advised the IRS that they could not fully comply with the summonses because of outstanding injunctions in hong kong.

On july 10 1984 this court adjudged Chase to be in civil contempt of court for its failure to produce Garpeg records and assessed a penalty of $10,000 per day until the documents are produced. (Garpeg v. United States 84 Civ. 0437 (RWS)).

On august 16 1984 this court held Chase in contempt for its failure to produce FDC records and imposed a fine of $5,000 per day of noncompliance. (United States v. Chase Manhattan Bank M-18-304 (GLG)).

Imposition of these penalties has been stayed, and the contempt orders are now on appeal. If the hong kong judiciary can provide the needed records cited in the summonses, the need for further proceedings may be obviated.◊

◊Need for assistance requested

As described above, the requested bank records are needed to show the flow of funds from Gucci Shops to FDC, Garpeg, and then to Vanguard and the other 'front' companies. In addition, signature records of the bank accounts are needed to prove that Aldo Gucci filed under penalties of perjury tax returns that were false in that the tax returns stated Aldo Gucci did not have signatory authority over any foreign bank accounts. The records of the accounting firms are needed to confirm that FDC did not perform services for the payments it received from Gucci Shops.◊

Conclusion

Accordingly, the united states of america applies to this court to issue a request to the judiciary of hong kong for the assistance described herein.

◊Date: August 31 1984◊
New York New York
◊Date: September 6 1984◊

Respectfully submitted,

Rudolph W Giuliani
United States Attorney for the
Southern District of New York

◊By: /s/Stuart E. Abrams

Stuart E. Abrams
Assistant United States Attorney◊

◊By: /s/Jonathan A. Lindsey

Jonathan A. Lindsey
Assistant United States Attorney
Office of the US Attorney
United States Courthouse Annex
One St Andrew's Plaza
New York New York 10007
Telephone: ([1/]212) 791-1961◊

”

Q/KTT 208   Pg 14   July 15, 1986   enforcement

❝ Appendix-A:

[Each of the two US government requests attached as appendix-A a copy of the following letter:]

[From:]
Edward H. Stern
Certified Public Accountant
685 Fifth Avenue
New York New York 100[—]
212-221-3774

[To:]
Dr Aldo Gucci   October 20 1975
Gucci Shops Inc
689 Fifth Avenue
New York, New York 10022

Re: FDC Co Ltd

Dear Dr Gucci:

In accordance with your instructions, I had several meetings, in hong kong, with mr Kerry Obonai and mr Anthony K. P. Yung, concerning the organization and operation of FDC Co Ltd.

Both of these gentlemen have been informed of the purposes for which the corporation was organized.

They were instructed and have started proceedings to issue the 2500 shares of the corporation capital stock equally in the names of Vanguard International Manufacturing Ltd and Anglo American Manufacturing Researches Ltd.

The organization's corporate minutes have been revised to reflect this fact.

Four invoices were made out to Gucci Shops Inc, 689 Fifth Avenue, New York City 10022, which in total represent a 20% commission on all ready-to-wear invoices issued to Gucci Shops Inc, during the calendar year 1974, by italian suppliers.

All invoices of FDC are being mailed from hong kong to the Gucci Shops Inc.

In order to have substantiation for the services for which such invoices were rendered and to document the underlying need for the company, it will be necessary for FDC Co Ltd to send a variety of fashion designs and sketches to new york city to Gucci Shops Inc for approval or rejection. This is only to build-up some sort of record for our future needs.

The more numerous and varied such sketches and designs are, the better will be the possibility for substantiation of this as an expense by Gucci Shops Inc.

It is my wish and desire to build an overwhelming set of facts, with adequate supporting documentation, to explain the expense, and the information herein requested will be of great service in this respect.

At the conference with mr Yung, we decided that a firm contract for the type of service rendered by FDC should be drawn as between FDC and Gucci Shops Inc and such contract should specify the basis upon which the commission is to be billed and the percentage of such commission.

I ask that you request counsel for the corporation to draw-up such a contract for signature by the parties involved.

In the course of my discussions with mr Yung, I raised the issue of the amount of corporation taxes to be paid to hong kong on the corporation profits. It developed that — similar to new york state law — if most of the work of the design and sketching for FDC was performed outside of

hong kong, there is a good possibility that all the profits generated by this corporation, in hong kong, would be completely exempt from all income taxes.

To arrive at such a result, it will be necessary for bills for services rendered to be sent to FDC in hong kong, from a source outside of hong kong.

If such a program is possible, then payment would have to be made from hong kong to the source from which such billing is made.

Mr Yung will await a decision from us on this matter before making the application for income tax exemption.

Mr Yung confirmed the fact that dividends — representing profits made by FDC — may be paid to the stockholders and the funds exported from hong kong without any income tax consequences to the stockholders.

Mr Obonai asked about compensation for himself for services given to FDC and I informed him that arrangements for such compensation would have to be made directly with you.

Mr Obonai had retained the services of a young man to work for FDC but, since the type of the operation has been changed, he has placed this young man on the payroll of Gucci Ltd hong kong.

A bank account for FDC Co Ltd has been established at the Chase Manhattan Bank in hong kong. Checks on that account may be signed by any one of either mrs Savarino, mr Obonai, or myself.

I have brought back with me a check book on the account which will be kept in new york city.

Mr Yung is arranging with the solicitors for the company — Deacons — to provide for the limitations upon the dispositions of the capital stock of the corporation, similar to the restrictions which are being placed on the capital stock of Gucci Ltd.

I hold myself in readiness to discuss any and all of the matters contained in this report, at your convenience.

Please accept my consideration for your attention.

Respectfully submitted,

/s/Edward H. Stern

Certified Public Accountant

Appendix-B:

[These excerpts from US law were attached as appendix-B to the criminal request:]

▶ Title 18, United States Code, section 371 provides in pertinent part:

"§371. Conspiracy to commit offense or to defraud united states. If two or more persons conspire either to commit any offense against the united states, or to defraud the united states, or any agency thereof in any manner or for any purpose, and one or more of such persons do any act to effect the object of the conspiracy, each shall be fined not more than $10,000 or imprisoned not more than five years, or both."

▶ Title 26, United States Code, section 7201 provides in pertinent part:

"§7201. Attempt to evade or defeat tax. Any person who willfully attempts in any manner to evade or defeat any tax imposed by this title or the payment thereof shall, in addition to other penalties provided by law, be guilty of a felony and, upon conviction thereof, shall be fined not more than $10,000, or imprisoned not more than 5 years, or both, together with the costs of prosecution."

▶ Title 26, United States Code, section 7206 provides in pertinent part:

Q/MT 208   PG 15   JuLy 15, 1986

enforcement

The Gucci investigation by Jud Harwood

"§7206. Fraud and false statements. Any person who—

(1) **Declaration under penalties of perjury.**—Willfully makes and subscribes any return, statement, or other document, which contains or is verified by a written declaration that it is made under the penalties of perjury, and which he does not believe to be true and correct as to every material matter or

(2) **Aid or assistance.**—Willfully aids or assists in (or procures, counsels, or advises) the preparation or presentation under (or in connection with any matter arising under) the internal revenue laws of a return, affidavit, claim, or other document, which is fraudulent or is false as to any material matter (whether or not such falsity or fraud is with the knowledge or consent of the person authorized or required to present such return, affidavit, claim, or document

shall be guilty of a felony and, upon conviction thereof, shall be fined not more than $5,000, or imprisoned not more than 3 years, or both, together with the costs of prosecution."

Here is the order of the hong kong court:

In The Supreme Court Of Hong Kong
High Court
Miscellaneous Proceedings   MP 324/1985

In the matter of section 77B of the evidence ordinance, chapter 8 of the laws of hong kong and
In the matter of order 70 of the rules of the supreme court and
In the matter of criminal proceedings likely to be instituted before the united states district court, southern district of new york

Before master Crawshaw of supreme court in chambers

Order

Upon the application by the 'Crown counsel of legal department' and upon reading the affidavit of Robert Alexander Osborne filed herein on the 4th day of february 1985 and the documents exhibited thereto — comprising the letter of request of the united states district court, southern district of new york dated the 31st day of august 1984 — and that such court is desirous of obtaining the testimony of the following person(s) namely:

(1) The manager, The Chase Manhattan Bank NA, Alexandra House, Central District, Hong Kong, or other responsible officer of the said bank;

(2) The manager, Citibank NA, 18 Whitfield Road, Causeway Road, Hong Kong, or other responsible officer of the said bank;

(3) The accountant acting or formerly acting for FDC Co Ltd, Arthur Young & Co, Great Eagle Centre, Causeway Bay, Hong Kong; and

(4) The accountant acting or formerly acting for FDC Co Ltd, Ernst & Whinney, 10 Harcourt Road, Central District, Hong Kong.

It is ordered that the said witnesses do attend before master _____ in chambers at the supreme court of hong kong, sitting at queensway hong kong, one of the examiners of the court, who is hereby appointed examiner herein on ___day, the ___ day of ___ 1985 at ___ o'clock in the ___noon, or such other day and time as the

said examiner may appoint and do submit to be examined upon oath or affirmation upon the said request touching the testimony so required as aforesaid.

It is also ordered that the below-mentioned persons do produce at the said examination the below-mentioned documents; namely:

▶ (1) The manager, The Chase Manhattan Bank NA, or other responsible officer of the said bank to produce the following documents in relation to the following accounts held at the aforesaid bank:

Accounts:
(a) FDC Co Ltd, account number/s unknown.
(b) Garpeg Ltd, account number/s unknown.
(c) Vanguard International Manufacturing Ltd, account number/s unknown.

Documents required in each case:
(i) Signature cards.
(ii) Ledger sheets and bank statements.
(iii) Cancelled cheques.
(iv) Deposit and withdrawal records.
(v) Wire transfer(s).
(vi) Correspondence relating to the account.

▶ (2) [The text of item (1) is repeated, substituting 'Citibank NA' for 'The Chase Manhattan Bank NA'].

▶ (3) The accountant acting or formerly acting for FDC Co Ltd, Arthur Young & Co, to produce the following documents in respect of the records pertaining to the said company:

Documents required:
(i) Financial statements.
(ii) Accounting workpapers.
(iii) Books of account.
(iv) Correspondence relating to the said company.

▶ (4) [The text of item (3) is repeated, substituting 'Ernst & Whinney' for 'Arthur Young & Co'].

And it is further ordered that the said examiner do takedown in writing the evidence of the said witnesses, according to the rules and practice of the supreme court of hong kong pertaining to the examination of witnesses; and do cause the said witnesses to sign the deposition in his (the said examiner's) presence; and do sign the deposition taken in pursuance of this order; and when so completed do transmit the cause together with this order and letter of request to the said court desiring the evidence of such witnesses.

And it is further ordered that the Crown solicitor do have leave to make further application for such orders as may give effect to the said request of the united states district court, southern district of new york.
Dated the 6th day of february 1985.

(J. Betts)
Acting Registrar

Indorsement. If you — the within named [bank officials and accounting firms] — neglect to obey and fail to attend before master _____ of the supreme court of hong kong at the time and place herein mentioned, [you] will be liable to process of execution for the purpose of compelling you to obey the same.

(R. A. Osborne)
Counsel for Crown Solicitor

For the text of §77B of the hong kong 'evidence ordinance', see page 77 of this issue of Taxes International.   —Jud Harwood, editor

Gucci Admits Evading $7 Million in Income Taxes

NYT 15/1/86

Continued From Page 1

and "ceased to have an active role in the company at that time." It noted that his plea involved an earlier period and primarily concerned his personal taxes.

The statement quoted the company's president, Domenico De Sole, as saying that if Mr. Gucci's activities resulted in any taxes being owed by Gucci Shops, "they certainly will be paid."

The charges against Mr. Gucci were filed yesterday by Rudolph W. Giuliani, the United States Attorney in Manhattan. Civil penalties and interest for overdue taxes may be added.

Mr. Gucci pleaded to one charge of conspiracy to defraud the Government and two charges of tax evasion. The conspiracy charge said he had failed to report about $11.8 million of income on which he owed about $7.3 million in taxes from 1977 to 1982. Of that amount, the tax-evasion charges specified that he owed $2 million for 1979 and $1.5 million for 1980.

The charges added that a total of $18 million was improperly diverted since 1972, but that some of the money did not go to Mr. Gucci.

According to the conspiracy charge, Mr. Gucci and unnamed co-conspirators "used fraudulent devices to divert income from Gucci Shops Inc. to Aldo Gucci and other members of the Gucci family."

It also said: "The devices employed included, among other things, the use of sham foreign corporations to hold the stock of Gucci Shops Inc. and other companies controlled by the Gucci family; the use of sham foreign corporations to submit bills to Gucci Shops Inc. for nonexistent services and to receive diverted corporate income; the creation of bills and invoices to justify

The New York Times / Marilyn Church
Aldo Gucci, left, and his lawyer, Milton S. Gould, in court yesterday.

payments made by Gucci Shops Inc. that were in fact diverted to Aldo Gucci and other members of the Gucci family, and the presentation of such bills and invoices to auditors from the United States Internal Revenue Service."

Noting that "the Gucci family has been the owner of a well-known business engaged in the sale of leather goods" for many years, the charges said the business was founded by Mr. Gucci's father, Guccio Gucci, in Florence, Italy.

They added that the founder's three sons formed Gucci Shops Inc. in 1953, with headquarters at 685 Fifth Avenue, at 54th Street, and later opened shops in other cities. Two of the three sons died in recent years.

Gucci Admits Evading $7 Million in Income Taxes

By ARNOLD H. LUBASCH

Aldo Gucci, the former head of Gucci Shops Inc., pleaded guilty yesterday to criminal charges for failing to pay more than $7 million in Federal income taxes.

Mr. Gucci, whose name has come to evoke elegance and wealth, waived his right to an indictment and trial. He admitted not reporting more than $11 million in personal income from his business, which sells fashionable leather goods in New York and other cities.

As part of the plea agreement, he gave a $1 million check to the Government and must pay the rest of more than $7 million in taxes before sentencing, according to Howard Wilson, chief of the Criminal Division of the United States Attorney's office.

Three Charges

Judge Vincent L. Broderick, who accepted the guilty plea in Federal District Court in Manhattan, set April 8 for the sentencing. Mr. Gucci pleaded guilty to three criminal charges, each carrying up to five years in prison and a $10,000 fine.

Mr. Gucci is 80 years old and has homes in New York and Beverly Hills, Calif., as well as Rome, Federal prosecutors said.

Standing before the judge, Mr. Gucci expressed his love for this country in an emotional tone. Although he is not an

WAS THIS COPY OF THE TIMES delivered to you? Home and office delivery is available in many U.S. cities. Get details by calling toll-free 1-800-631-2500.—ADVT.

American citizen, he noted that he has lived in the United States since 1977.

He admitted that various devices had been used to "divert income from Gucci Shops Inc." in the United States to himself and members of his family from 1977 to 1982, without his reporting it as taxable income. The amount, he said, exceeded $11 million.

'Foolish and Improvident'

"While I was generally aware of the situation," he told the judge, "the details of these various methods of income diversion were devised by an accountant, and I was not involved in the creation of these methods."

The prosecutor in charge of the case, Stuart E. Abrams, said later that the accountant in the scheme was dead. Mr. Abrams declined to name the accountant. He also declined to say who else might be a target of the continuing investigation.

Milton S. Gould, the lawyer for Mr. Gucci, described the guilty plea as the culmination of long negotiations with the Government. He said Mr. Gucci had ended a "foolish and improvident" practice devised by others.

In a statement, Gucci Shops said Mr. Gucci had resigned as chairman in 1984

Continued on Page 36, Column 4

NYF
JAN
18
1 86

18/1/86

INSIDE

Foreigners Flee Aden

Hundreds of Russians and other foreigners were evacuated by ship from Southern Yemen as fighting continued in the capital, Aden. Page 4.

Kohl Cautious on Libya

Chancellor Helmut Kohl warned that overt action against Libya could generate a wave of Arab solidarity that would hurt Western interests. Page 3.

Spain Recognizes Israel

Spain and Israel formally established relations — almost four decades after the founding of the state of Israel — at a ceremony in The Hague. Page 3.

Home Building Surges

Construction of new housing surged 17.5 percent in December, the biggest increase in 3½ years, but the total for 1985 fell 1 percent. Page 33.

United States of America vs.

United States District Court for
SOUTHERN DISTRICT OF NEW YORK

DEFENDANT

ALDO GUCCI

25 WEST 54th STREET
NEW YORK, NEW YORK

DOCKET NO. ——▶ 86 CR 58-01 (VLB)

JUDGMENT AND PROBATION/COMMITMENT ORDER

AUSA-STUART ABRAMS

In the presence of the attorney for the government
the defendant appeared in person on this date ——

DATE OF OFFENSE
JANUARY 1972-84

MONTH	DAY	YEAR
SEPTEMBER 11, 1986		

COUNSEL

|___| WITHOUT COUNSEL   However the court advised defendant of right to counsel and asked whether defendant desired to have counsel appointed by the court and the defendant thereupon waived assistance of counsel.

| X | WITH COUNSEL |___ MILTON GOULD, ESQ. & STUART A. SMITH, ESQ.___
(name of Counsel)

COUNTS 1, 2, and 3.

PLEA

| X | GUILTY, and the court being satisfied that
there is a factual basis for the plea,

|___| NOLO CONTENDERE |___| NOT GUILTY

There being a finding/verdict of { |___| NOT GUILTY. Defendant is discharged
{ |___| GUILTY.

DOCKETED AS
A JUDGMENT 86,2088
ON 9/19/86

FINDING & JUDGMENT

Defendant has been convicted as charged of the offense(s) of knowingly did combine, conspire and agree with others to defraud the United States of America by impeding, obstructing and defeating the lawful functions of the Internal Revenue Service. Count 1. (Title18 United States Code, Section 371) wilfully and knowingly did evade and defeat a large part of the income tax due and owing to the United States of America by filing with the Internal Revenue Service false and fradulent tax returns. Counts 2 and 3. (Title 26, United States Code, Section 7201.)

The court asked whether defendant had anything to say why judgment should not be pronounced. Because no sufficient cause to the contrary was shown, or appeared to the court, the court adjudged the defendant guilty as charged and convicted and ordered that: The defendant is hereby committed to the custody of the Attorney General or his authorized representative for imprisonment for a period of

SENTENCE OR PROBATION ORDER

ONE (1) YEAR and ONE (1) DAY; Fined:TEN THOUSAND ($10,000.)DOLLARS on Count 1.
THREE (3) YEARS; Fined:TEN THOUSAND ($10,000.)DOLLARS and Cost of Prosecution on each Counts 2 and 3.
Custodial sentence on Counts 2 and 3 to run concurrent with each other. Execution of custodial sentences on Counts 2 and 3 is suspended and defendant is placed on Probation for a period of FIVE (5) YEARS, subject to the standing Probation order of this Court. Probation to begin at expiration of sentence on Count 1.
TOTAL FINES: THIRTY THOUSAND ($30,000.), plus Cost of Prosecution.

SPECIAL CONDITIONS OF PROBATION

Conditions of Probation: 1)defendant will make full restitution. 2)defendant will cooperate with the Government on its continuing investigation. 3)defendant will for the first year of probation devote himself on a full time basis to community service to be worked out by the defense attorneys with Probation Department and approved by the Court. 4)defendant will surrender passport to defense attorneys today. (9/11/86)
Defendant is continued on present bail until October 15, 1986, at which time he is to surrender to the facility designated by the Bureau of Prisons.

ADDITIONAL CONDITIONS OF PROBATION

In addition to the special conditions of probation imposed above, it is hereby ordered that the general conditions of probation set out on the reverse side of this judgment be imposed. The Court may change the conditions of probation, reduce or extend the period of probation, and at any time during the probation period or within a maximum probation period of five years permitted by law, may issue a warrant and revoke probation for a violation occurring during the probation period.

COMMITMENT RECOMMENDATION

The court orders commitment to the custody of the Attorney General and recommends,

a federal prison adjacent to Egland Air Force Base near Pensocola, Florida,

MICROFILM

It is ordered that the Clerk deliver a certified copy of this judgment and commitment to the U.S. Marshal or other qualified officer.

SEP 19 1986   9 00 AM

FILED
SEP 18 1986

SIGNED BY

| X | U.S. District Judge

|___| U.S. Magistrate

VINCNET L. BRODERICK   Date 9/11/86

OCT 1 1985

30,000   30,000

CENTRAL
DIST. COURT
PROBATION

10/14/86

FINAL PAYMENT

When probation has been ordered the defendant shall comply the terms of the probation order...

Maximum probation period (per indictment or information) which may be imposed on defendant eligible for sentencing under the Youth Corrections Act 18 U.S.C. § 5005 et seq., is one year for conviction of a misdemeanor or six months for conviction of a petty

JUDGMENT MARKED SATISFIED AND ENTERED IN THE

MONEY JUDGMENT BOOK

RETURN

I have executed the within Judgment and Commitment as follows:

Defendant delivered on _____ to _____

Defendant noted appeal on _____

Defendant released on _____

Mandate issued on _____

Defendant's appeal determined on _____

Defendant delivered on _____ to _____

at _____, the institution designated by
the Attorney General, with a certified copy of the within Judgment and Commitment.

_____
United States Marshal

By _____
Deputy Marshal

G

```
 1    UNITFD STATES DISTRICT COURT,

 2    SOUTHERN DISTRICT OF NEW YORK

 3    ---------------------------------

 4    United States of America

 5         v.                                    86 Cr. 58 (VLB)

 6    Aldo Gucci,

 7              Defendant.

 8    ---------------------------------

 9                                  October 14, 1986
                                    2:30 p.m.
10

      BEFORE:
11
                   HON. EDWARD WEINFELD,
12
                                    District Judge
13

      APPEARANCES:
14
                   Rudolph W. Giuliani,
15                      United States Attorney
                   Stuart Abrams,
16                      Assistant United States Attorney

17                 Peter Moran,
                        Litigation & Legal Advice Staff
18                      Immigration & Naturalization Service

19                 Shea & Gould,
                        Attorneys for Defendant
20                 Stuart A. Smith,

21                      of counsel

22

23

24

25
```

md   2

1   THE COURT: Who is representing Mr. Gucci?

2.   MR. SMITH: My name is Stuart Smith.

3   THE COURT: Proceed.

4   MR. SMITH: Thank you, your Honor.

5   I filed this motion on October 7, 1986.   It is a

6   motion under 8 USC 1251(b) for a recommendation to the

7   Attorney General that the defendant not be deported on the

8   basis of his conviction in this case.

9   The sentencing judge was Judge Broderick.   Judge

10   Broderick, I have been advised, has been away on vacation

11   and will not return until early November 1986.

12   THE COURT: Did you make this motion before

13   Judge Broderick?

14   MR. SMITH: Yes, I did.

15   THE COURT: Does he have it under advisement?

16   MR. SMITH: By the time I had filed it, he had

17   gone.   I filed it with chambers.   His chambers advised me --

18   THE COURT: When was sentence imposed?

19   MR. SMITH: Sentence was imposed on September 11,

20   1986.

21   THE COURT: Under the statute, you had thirty

22   days.

23   MR. SMITH: Yes.

24   THE COURT: When does the thirty days expire?

25   MR. SMITH: At the close of business today, because

md

3

1   I am advised by the Immigration & Naturalization Service

2   that --

3   THE COURT: When did you make your motion?

4   MR. SMITH: October 7th.

5   THE COURT: Why did you wait until the zero

6   hour? The statute is clear that there is only one judge

7   that can grant the relief.

8   MR. SMITH: Quite frankly, I was preoccupied with

9   a number of matters dealing with his probation.

10   THE COURT: Is that an excuse?

11   MR. SMITH: No. But we did file it within the

12   thirty-day period.

13   THE COURT: If you filed it with Judge Broderick,

14   it is sub judici by him, is it not?

15   MR. SMITH: Yes. But let me explain the

16   chronology.

17   Judge Broderick's chambers advised me immediately

18   he wouldn't be back in chambers until November 3rd at the

19   earliest. I then asked Judge Broderick's chambers to

20   forward the motion, being aware of the thirty-day time

21   limit, to Judge Sweet, who was the Part 1 judge last

22   week. Also, in the interim I had entered into a

23   stipulation with the United States Attorney saying that we

24   agreed that the entry of any order by Judge Broderick upon

25   his return to chambers recommending to the Attorney General

md   4

1   that the defendant not be deported would be honored by the

2   United States Immigration & Naturalization Service, and would

3   be given full force and effect.

4   Judge Sweet endorsed that as so ordered on

5   October 10th.

6   I am prepared at some later time, if it became

7   necessary, to argue Judge Sweet's order v believe preserved

8   the opportunity for Judge Broderick to address the merits

9   of my motion, but having been advised by the Immigration

10   & Naturalization Service that they view the thirty-day time

11   limit as strict and unbendable, it appeared to me the best

12   course of action to take, this still being within the time

13   limits, was to ask the court today, today being the thirtieth

14   day, to grant my motion, subject to reconsideration by

15   Judge Broderick.

16   I think this is a --

17   THE COURT: What jurisdiction do I have to

18   grant the motion? It is subject to a determination by

19   Judge Broderick under the statute. What does the statute

20   provide?

21   MR. SMITH: The statute provides the provisions

22   of Subsection A (4) -- that is the general definition of

23   what is a deportable crime -- respecting the deportation of

24   an alien convicted of a crime or crimes shall not apply,

25   and this is the pertinent language, if the court sentencing

nd

5

1   such alien for such crime shall make at the time of first

2   imposing judgment or passing sentence, or within thirty

3   days thereafter --

4   THE COURT: How does another judge have

5   jurisdiction?

6   MR. SMITH: I would suggest to the court that the

7   court has jurisdiction over this matter, that the

8   statutory phrase --

9   THE COURT: That means you can go to any judge?

10   MR. SMITH: Precisely. Becuase I think this is

11 an important right that Congress has granted aliens in

12 this particular position. I don't think that Congress

13 meant that this right was to be cut off.

14   THE COURT: I don't know of any statute that is

15 more strictly applied that the provision in this section.

16   MR. SMITH: I agree with your Honor that --

17   THE COURT: I wrote an opinion on that, did I

18 not?

19   MR. SMITH: I don't know whether you wrote an

20 opinion, but I have surveyed the opinions, and there is

21 case law to the eeffect that an order cannot be entered

22 nunc pro tunc.

23   I would suggest that --

24   THE COURT: Once the thirty days pass, no

25 judge, including the sentencing judge, has jurisdiction.

n.d

1   MR. SMITH: Given that fact. But while we are

2   in the thirty-day period the statutory phrase: If the

3   court sentencing such alien for such crime -- I believe that

4   those statutory words can be construed as meaning the

5   court, meaning the United States District Court for the

6   Southern District of New York.

7   I think your Honor sitting in this general motion

8   part can grant this motion, subject to reconsideration by

9   Judge Broderick.

10   We are not asking the court to address the merits

11   of this motion. I think that Judge Broderick is the appropri-

12   ate judge to make that determination. He is familiar with

13   the presentence report, he is familiar with the defendant,

14   he is familiar with what the defendant has been charged

15   with, and I would suggest to the court that simply because

16   the sentencing judge is on vacation should not be the basis

17   for the defendant's rights to be cut off.

18   THE COURT: Except the sentencing judge knew,

19   or his chambers certainly knows, that you filed the

20   application.

21   MR. SMITH: That is true, the sentencing judge

22   did know that. However, Judge Broderick is in France, and

23   is unreachable. I spoke to chambers about the possibility

24   of reaching him, and his chambers doesn't know where he is.

25   He is on vacation.

md

I don't think that happenstance should be the basis of cutting off the defendant's statutory rights. The courts have often said that deportation is a drastic remedy. I think even Judge Learned Hand, in one of the early decisions of this court, in construing the thirty-day rule --

THE COURT: He is the one who wrote the first opinion on this.

MR.SMITH: I think the Supreme Court in the Costello case described deportation as a drastic remedy.

Here is a statute that Congress has given defendants in this position who are aliens the right to ask the sentencing judge to do this. I don't think anybody in this room can ascertain what Judge Broderick had in mind. I would suggest, as I have said in my papers on the merits, that Judge Broderick did not want to subject the defendant to deportation. He sentenced him to a year and a day followed by a period of full-time community service for a year. That's full-time community service in the Southern District of New York.

I don't think that the Immigration & Naturalization Service's position that the defendant should be automatically subject to deportation is consistent with Judge Broderick's sentence.

I must say that in speaking to Judge

md   E

Broderick's chambers about this, the law clerk advised me
that from time to time she has heard Judge Broderick
imposing sentence on aliens specifically say that they are
going to be subject to deportation.

Judge Broderick did not say that in this case.
All he did was to impose a jail term, suspend sentence on
two other counts, and impose fines, and impose a year of
full-time community service to be worked out between defense
attorneys and the probation department, subject to approval
of the court.

I think that that is enough at this juncture for
all of us to be able to conclude that it appears that
Judge Broderick did not want to have the defendant subject
to automatic deportation, but I am not asking --

THE COURT: Why didn't you make a motion at the
time of sentence? Why did you wait until the zero hour
to make your motion?

MR. SMITH: Quite frankly, the fact of this
statute I became aware of later in the month, and I think
the fact that I waited until early October is not fatal
in this particular case because we are still within the
thirty days, and I think the court has the authority, and
has the power under the statute, no matter how it is
construed, to grant the motion, subject to reconsideration
by Judge Broderick. I think that would be the fair and

md

1   appropriate thing to do, given the fact that I think that

2   there is considerable doubt as to how Judge Broderick felt

3   about this matter, and I don't think anybody is prepared to

4   say finitely what Judge Broderick would do in this case,

5   but I think that Judge Broderick ought to have the

6   opportunity to rule on the merits of this motion.

7   THE COURT: When did you file the papers with

8   Judge Broderick's chambers?

9   MR.SMITH: October 7th.

10   THE COURT: He was here at that time, wasn't he?

11   MR. SMITH: I don't think so, because I was

12   given a call by chambers and was told he was not here, and

13   I discussed with chambers how I might proceed, and they were

14   at a loss as to how I should proceed.

15   I then called somebody in the Attorney General's

16   Office in Washington, and in the interim spoke to the

17   Assistant United States Attorney, and we devised this

18   stipulation procedure under which the United States Attorney,

19   on behalf of the United States and the Immigration &

20   Naturalization Service, agreed with me that Judge Broderick

21   could address the merits of this motion upon his return to

22   chambers.

23   THE COURT: What information do you have as to

24   when Judge Broderick is coming back?

25   MR. SMITH: I have been told by chambers early

md   10

November 1986. That might be the first day.

    THE COURT: That is inconsistent with what you say, that you filed the papers and you were told at that time that he would be away for three weeks.

    MR. SMITH: No, I never said that he would be away for three weeks. I just said they told me --

    THE COURT: Let me get the facts right. When did you file the motion?

    MR.SMITH: I filed the papers on Tuesday, October 7th.

    THE COURT: What were you told then?

    MR. SMITH: I was told then Judge Broderick was away and would return in early November. I do not in fact know what day Judge Broderick will return, but I know that November 3rd is the first business day in November.

    THE COURT: Who represents the United States Attorney's Office?

    MR. SMITH: ·The United States Attorney's Office is represented by Stuart Abrams, Assistant United States Attorney. I spoke to him earlier.

    THE COURT: Are you Mr. Abrams?

    MR. ABRAMS: Yes, your Honor.

    Your Honor, the sequence, as far as our office is concerned --

    THE COURT: Pardon?

md   11

MR. ABRAMS: I would like to lay out the
sequence as far as our office is concerned.

I heard from Mr. Smith, I believe it was the
day he filed the motion, that he was filing the motion.
I know that these motions usually are handled directly by
the Immigration & Naturalization Service and not our
office, and I told Mr. Smith that.

He explained to me the problem as far as Judge
Broderick's absence, and I did make an attempt to find
someone at INS on the case, but I was unable to do so.
I told Mr. Smith from my perspective I didn't see any
reason it couldn't be adjourned until Judge Broderick
returned.

In fact, I was apparently wrong in saying that,
and the next day I heard from someone at INS saying the
position of the government was that it was jurisdictional.

THE COURT: I think your position was a very
fair one, yet the INS takes the position that it is a
jurisdictional problem.

MR. ABRAMS: I understand that. Someone is here
from INS, and I think they are prepared to argue the
government's position on this case. As I understood, they
are essentially the one who will address these motions.

THE COURT: Who represents the INS?

MR. MORAN: Good afternoon, your Honor. My name

1   is Peter Moran. I represent the INS.

2   It is the government's position that since

3   Saturday was the 11th of September that this is day

4   thirty.

5   THE COURT: Since what?

6   MR. MORAN: I'm sorry.

7   Since Saturday last was the 11th of October this

8   is the thirtieth day.

9   THE COURT: What was the day of sentence?

10   MR. MORAN: September 11th. So Saturday last,

11   October 11th, would have been the actual day thirty, but

12   since --

13   THE COURT: When was the motion made, October

14   what?

15   MR. MORAN: Seventh. It was within the thirty

16   days.

17   THE COURT: Of course it was made timely, and

18   Judge Broderick could have acted within the time.

19   MR. MORAN: I am not sure myself, as counsel for

20   the defendant stated, whether or not Judge Broderick was

21   in fact available at that time. I will agree with counsel

22   that it is the government's position that it does not have

23   to be the sentencing judge, and as a result I am asking you

24   today to act on this motion, becuase if it is not acted

25   upon today it will be the position of the Immigration

1   Service that any --

2   THE COURT: Are you saying that I have the power

3   to act?

4   MR. MORAN: I believe so, your Honor, because

5   you are the sentencing court as described in the statute,

6   the Southern District.

7   THE COURT: I am not the sentencing court. Are

8   you saying any judge of the court?

9   MR. MORAN: I believe any judge of the Southern

10   District, since that is where the matter was and is, can

11   act on this motion, yes.

12   THE COURT: Until when do I have to decide this?

13   MR. MORAN: Today. It will be the position of

14   the government that any --

15   THE COURT: Then I would like to know the

16   facts, if you concede I have the authority. I was under the

17   impression it was only the sentencing judge as distinguished

18   from the sentencing court, and you are saying it is the

19   sentencing court.

20   MR. MORAN: I will state to the court I haven't

21   done research on that exact point.

22   THE COURT: Why don't I hear from the petitioner

23   his argument as to why he thinks the order of the court

24   should be entered denying deportation to the authorities?

25   Who has a copy ofthe presentence report?

MR. SMITH: It is in the probation department, and I assume it is in Judge Broderick's chambers.

If I may, your Honor, assuming agreement among the lawyers that your Honor does have the authority to enter an order today, I would like to address the merits of my motion, although I would like to state at the outset that I think that if the court has any doubts about the merits of my motion the proper course --

THE COURT: I don't know the first thing about your motion because this jurisdictional issue was raised. The Immigration Service tells me I have the authority to act here.

MR. SMITH: I would tell the court at the outset, given the press of time and the court's own schedule, that I would think the court might feel more comfortable granting the motion subject to reconsideration by Judge Broderick when he comes back.

THE COURT: I think your adversary would argue it has to be decided today.

Is that correct?

MR. MORAN: That is correct, your Honor.

MR. SMITH: I don't think that is the case. May I cite to the court the Second Circuit decision which I think is persuasive on the point. It is a case called Halo v. Esperdy, 397 F. 2d 211.

md

In that particular case the trial judge, or the

sentencing judge, did enter the order within the thirty-day

period. However, he failed to advise the Immigration &

Naturalization Service of the entry of the order.

They took the position in that case that the

judge's order was a nullity, and it went up to the Second

Circuit on the question as to whether the judge, having

failed to advise the Immigration & Naturalization Service,

since the statutory procedure contemplates that before the

judge enters the order the INS will have an opportunity to

speak to the merits of the matter, the Second Circuit

in a unanimous opinion by Judge Feinberg, with the panel of

judges of Ward, Hayes and Feinberg, held the order was

valid and could be subject to reconsideration upon the

INS making its submission.

I would suggest to the court in the same way

here your Honor .could enter the order granting the motion

under 1251(b), and it could be made specifically subject to

reconsideration by Judge Broderick. I think on the authority

of that case there wouldn't be any problem about the

validity of your order or the validity of Judge Broderick's

reconsideration.

THE COURT: Your adversary would. argue once I

granted it Judge Broderick couldn't do anything about it.

MR. SMITH: I suspect they would argue that, but

md   16

1   I would suggest the authority of this case suggests that is

2   not so.

3   THE COURT: Can I stay any deportation by the

4   authorities subject to a determination by Judge Broderick?

5   MR. SMITH: I think you would have the authority.

6   THE COURT: Would I have that authority, since

7   he knows the facts of the case and I don't?

8   MR. SMITH: Exactly. That's my point. My point

9   is that since this is the thirtieth day, if counsel

10   would all agree that you have the authority to enter the

11   order today, Judge Broderick is obviously much more

12   familiar with the facts of this case, he took the plea, he

13   has read the presentence report, and I think that your entry

14   of the order today, subject to Judge Broderick's reconsidera-

15   tion, would prevent the defendant's rights from being cut

16   off in this case in a manner that I don't think Congress

17   contemplated when it proscribed that the sentencing court

18   can do this within thirty days.

19   Since this is the thirtieth day, and you are a

20   judge of the sentencing court, I would suggest that there

21   is appropriate authority here to do that.

22   With that out of the way, I would like, if you

23   feel it appropriate, to address the factual merits of my

24   motion if the court would like to have some idea of what this

25   case is about in terms of the merits of the propriety of

md

1   even a temporary order.

2   THE COURT: Why not address yourself to the

3   merits, if your adversary thinks I am the one to make the

4   disposition?

5   What would be your position if I said I would

6   stay a deportation pending a determination by Judge

7   Broderick?

8   MR. MORAN: Your Honor, the problem there is

9   that even if you were to deny this motion it would still

10   place the burden on the Immigration Service to initiate

11   deportation proceedings, so that's one level a decision has

12   to be made.

13   THE COURT: You have the advantage of having

14   the order of the court then. What would be the basis to

15   impose the deportation then?

16   MR. MORAN: I think the assumption goes too

17   far, your Honor, because of the fact that the defendant,

18   Mr. Gucci, in this matter has been a permanent resident

19   for such a long time that he can ask for termination of

20   deportation proceedings should they ever be initiated

21   because of Section 212 (c) of the Act, because he has had

22   his residency for more than seven years.

23   THE COURT: It seems to me you are trying to

24   carry water on both shoulders now.

25   If your insistence is that the time expires

18

md

1   today, and if your position is correct that it is the

2   sentencing court as distinguished from the sentencing judge

3   that has the power, then it should be disposed of today.

4   MR. MORAN: Absolutely.

5   THE COURT: I am suggesting that instead of this

6   court disposing of it, since I didn't try the case, I

7   don't know the facts. I would have to hear your argument,

8   it makes more sense to me that there be a consent that

9   deportation be stayed, or any action by the Service be

10   stayed, until Judge Broderick makes his ruling.

11   If you want me to make the ruling, I will make

12   it, but I must say in all fairness if I am going to

13   err I am going to err on the side of leniency.

14   MR. MORAN: I appreciate the court's candor.

15   THE COURT: Then you are through once I make

16   a decision.

17   MR. MORAN: Once you make a decision, if it is

18   favorable to the motion.

19   THE COURT: Let me hear the merits. Tell me

20   how long he has been here, his background, what his

21   family is, has he been convicted of any other crime. Give

22   me all the information you can.

23   MR. SMITH: Defendant is 81 years old.

24   THE COURT: How old?

25   MR. SMITH: 81 years old. Actually, 81-1/2.

md   19

1   He will be 82 years old next May.

2   THE COURT: How many years has he been in this

3   country?

4   MR. SMITH: He has been in this country off and

5   on since 1953, when he established the Gucci business in

6   New York.

7   THE COURT: Is this the Gucci --

8   MR. SMITH: This is the leather goods business.

9   THE COURT: I have heard about him.

10   MR. SMITH: Sometime in December 1976, he applied

11   for and received permanent residence in the United States.

12   This tax case represents the only time he has ever gotten

13   into any problems with the law in any country in the world.

14   I think the probation report will fairly reflect this,

15   because he was assigned the highest personal saliency

16   factor for purposes of submitting the report to Judge

17   Broderick.

18   On January 17, 1986 -- let me back up a bit.

19   This tax investigation started in January of

20   1983, or early 1983, when summonses were issued. I got into

21   this case in the spring of 1984, and I think that Mr. Abrams,

22   who handled the investigation for the United States

23   Attorney, will attest to the fact that since we have

24   represented Mr. Gucci that he has cooperated fully with

25   the government in disclosing the details of this case.

md

Before we were involved in this case there was a good deal of obstruction and opposition to the enforcement of summonses on Hongkong banks. Once we got into the case all that obstructionism and opposition came to an end, and ultimately it resulted in a guilty plea from Mr. Gucci before Judge Broderick to one count of conspiracy to impede the lawful functions of the Internal Revenue Service with respect to the collection of corporate income taxes, and two counts of personal income tax evasion for the years 1980 and 1981.

Since the time of that guilty plea, Mr. Gucci, under our recommendation and representation, has filed all of his back tax returns, and has filed, in my view, accurate back tax returns, amended tax returns, for 1977 through 1981, and original tax returns for 1982, 1983 and 1984. That was pursuant to a memorandum of understanding entered into between the defendant and the United States.

Tomorrow the defendant is going to surrender to begin his prison term at Eglund Air Force Base Prison Camp in Florida. Tomorrow, also, Mr. Gucci will be filing his 1985 tax return. It is sitting in my office waiting to be sent to the Internal Revenue Service. That would complete his filing obligations with the Internal Revenue Service to date.

1   THE COURT: How much has he paid in back taxes?

2   MR. SMITH: He has paid thus far six million

3 dollars, I believe, and has entered into an agreement with

4 the Internal Revenue Service to pay another million dollars

5 by December 31, 1986.

6   Thereafter, the agreement calls for the payment

7 of a million dollars per quarter from 1987 to 1988, until

8 his obligations are completely discharged.

9   THE COURT: Is that six million dollars payble

10 in installments?

11   MR. SMITH: The six million dollars, your Honor,

12 one million dollars was paid upon the entry of the plea in

13 January 1986.

14   THE COURT: Has that been paid?

15   MR. SMITH: Yes.

16   THE COURT: How was the balance payable?

17   MR. SMITH: It has been paid over the calendar

18 year.

19   THE COURT: It has been paid?

20   MR. SMITH: Yes.

21   THE COURT: The six million dollars has been paid?

22   MR. SMITH: Yes.

23   After tomorrow, Five million dollars has been

24 paid as of this moment. As of tomorrow, another million

25 dollars will have been paid, pursuant to an agreement with

md   22

1   the Internal Revenue Service. On December ·31, 1986, another

2   million dollars will have been paid. That represents

3   practically the sum total of the taxes that were at issue

4   in this case.

5   There is interest and some penalties. They will

6   be discharged over the calendar year of 1987, and if there

7   are any left over in 1988.

8   The defendant also has paid his fines that were

9   imposed by Judge Broderick.

10   THE COURT: What fines?

11   MR. SMITH: It was the maximum of $10,000 per

12 count. He paid that $30,000.

13   I think that Mr. Abrams would attest to the

14 fact that since the entry of the plea in this case the

15 defendant was allowed to travel abroad until his sentencing.

16 He never was anywhere where defense counsel were not aware of

17 where he was and where he could be reached.

18   The government, I think, recognizing the fact

19 that the defendant is basically a law-abiding person,

20 and was a situational offender in this particular case,

21 is an honorable person who intends to honor all his

22 obligations to the United States, not only the financial

23 but also in connection with the serving of this jail

24 sentence.

25   After he comes out of jail he will be subject to

md   23

a year of full-time community service to be worked out

between the defense attorneys and the court.

I think that Judge Broderick intended for the

defendant to be present in this country during that

period and beyond for purposes of supervising his probation.

I might also add that from a personal point of

view the defendant has a daughter here in the United

States who is living in New York. Her husband lives here

as well. She is a young woman who is 23 years old. She

has a two year old or a year and a half old baby, with

whom the defendant has a very close relationship.

He does not want to have to leave the United

States involuntarily. He has made this country a second

home in terms of --

THE COURT: How long ago do you say he first

entered the United States?

MR. SMITH; He first entered the United States

in 1953. He traveled back and forth to the United States.

THE COURT: Is he a permanent resident of the

United States?

MR. SMITH: He became a permanent resident of

the United States in December 1976, and he has been a

permanent resident since that time.

He has very strong roots in this country. He can

be equally viewed culturally as an American as well as an

24

Italian. I think he has made important contributions

this country in terms of his business and in terms of

employment of people.

He still has significant business interests in

this country.

I think that it would be unfair, at really the

end of his life, to subject him to compulsory deportation.

THE COURT: Was there any discussion of the

community service which he was required to perform as part

of his sentence?

MR. SMITH: No, there has been none.

THE COURT: Does the judgment of conviction

make any reference to it?

MR. SMITH: The judgment of conviction, of which

I think your Honor or your chambers has a copy, simply

says full-time community service for one year, and my dis-

cussions -- I have had one brief discussion with the

defendant's probation officer, Mr. Loughran of the

probation department here in this court, and he indicated

to me that we would work out while the defendant is

incarcerated some community service plan to be approved by

Judge Broderick.

The defendant is ready to perform that

obligation. He wouldn't even think of trying to evade it

one jot or tittle, and I think under those circumstances,

25

plus the fact that the defendant really has to continue
to be in this country in order to liquidate certain assets
of his in order to pay back the Internal Revenue Service,
the assets to some extent involve real estate, to some
extent involve an art collection, and it really is in the
interests of the United States, it seems to me, to say
nothing of the defendant, for him to be allowed to stay
in this country, which is his second home, in order to
discharge those obligations not only to the court in terms
of the sentence imposed by Judge Broderick, but to the
Internal Revenue Service.

      I think that it would be counter productive at
this stage of the proceedings to subject the defendant to
compulsory deportation when the defendant's continued
presence has not only been required by Judge Broderick
pursuant to the terms of the sentence but is really part
and an inherent part of the defendant's ability to make
restitution to the United States, which is also a condition
of probation.

      THE COURT: Let me hear from the other side.

      MR. MORAN: Your Honor, speaking to the facts of
this case, if I might, not just simply legal argument --

      THE COURT: First, what is your name?

      MR. MORAN: My name is Peter Moran.

      THE COURT: All right, Mr. Moran.

1   MR. MORAN: Thank you, your Honor.

2   THE COURT: Let me understand your position here.

3   You say I do have power?

4   MR. MORAN: Yes, sir.   As the sentencing court,

5   as part of the sentencing court.

6   THE COURT: The provision in the statute as to

7   the sentencing court does not refer to the judge who

8   imposed sentence but a judge of the court that imposed

9   sentence, and in a court composed of different judges

10 any one of the judges has a right to make that

11 determination?

12 MR. MORAN: Yes, your Honor.

13 THE COURT: You say it must be made by midnight

14 tonight?

15 MR. MORAN: Yes, your Honor.   The reason I make

16 that argument basically is to fulfill --

17 THE COURT: I accept your argument, though I am

18 not sure I agree with it.

19 MR. MORAN: Thank you.

20 Your Honor, in this case Mr. Gucci was convicted

21 in January of this year of a conspiracy that started in

22 1972.   That's before he became a permanent resident of

23 the United States.   So this was an ongoing conspiracy over

24 a period of years that this particular defendant was

25 convicted.

THE COURT: How does that change the picture
whether the conspiracy started a year ago or ten years
ago?

MR. MORAN: He was in the United States seeking
in a sense the protection of the United States, and in 1976
he sought and received permanent residence which could be
a big step toward naturalization as a citizen of the
United States, so that at that time even he was violating
the laws of the United States and was not in effect
acceptable as a permanent resident.

THE COURT: You accept the fact he violated the
law by reason of his conviction on his plea of guilty.
The question is why should a man at that stage, with roots
in the United States, with members of his family here,
under a sentence whereby he is to make additional payment
of one million dollars -- when?

MR. MORAN: I think counsel said to 1988.

THE COURT: How is the government going to
collect that money if it deports him?

MR. MORAN: What I am arguing today to the court
is that there is a provision in the statute by which a
person convicted of a crime involving moral turpitude is
a deportable alien.

The government, I believe, should be allowed to
pursue its due court of trying to deport Mr. Gucci. Counsel

md   28

said something to the effect --

   THE COURT: That is subject to the power of the

court to deny deportation. That is exactly why we are

here.

   MR. MORAN: Exactly.

   THE COURT: The decision does not rest with the

Immigration Service if a proper application is approved by

the court.

   MR. MORAN: What we are talking about here is

counsel's motion to deny the use of this conviction in a

deportation proceeding. The deportation wouldn't by any

stretch of the term be automatic. He is entitled to a

hearing. Assuming an order to show cause is issued by the

Immigration Service against Mr. Gucci that absolutely

entitles him to a hearing before an Immigration judge

tantamount to an administrative hearing.

   THE COURT: Why should he go through that

process if he can satisfy the court that he is entitled to

relief? What is the purpose of that?

   MR. MORAN: There is another type of relief he

can ask. He can ask for 212 (c) relief, which is under the

Immigration & Naturalization Act, which enables a person

who has seven years as a resident -- and the only reason he

can make this particular application to this court now is

the fact that he is a permanent resident -- if he were not

md

1 a permanent resident it wouldn't apply to him.

2   THE COURT: How would the government collect

3 the million dollars?

4   MR.MORAN: Take his assets.

5   THE COURT: Take it how?

6   MR. MORAN: Sue him for his assets. It is two

7 avenues. The government is not precluded from getting

8 any moneys that are due to it by the fact that he has

9 been deported.

10   We can also stay deportationsyhould that ever

11 come to pass. I am not saying -- what I am asking this

12 court to do is to deny this motion, to allow the Immigration

13 Service to decide if in fact an order to show cause will

14 issue, which hasn't been decided, and then if it is issued

15 Mr. Gucci can make appropriate application for termination

16 of the proceedings by virtue of the fact htat he has seven

17 years.

18   THE COURT: That's a long red-tape proceeding,

19 with due respect to the Immigration Service.

20   MR. MORAN: It also enables him a lot of

21 protections which are not being discussed today by counsel.

22   THE COURT: Isn't it of some significance that

23 part of the sentence required the defendant, upon his

24 release, to render community service? How could he render

25 community service if he is deported?

md   30

1   MR. MORAN: Again, that could be something

2   the Immigration Service would be glad --

3   THE COURT: That's why I think Judge Broderick

4   should be the one to decide it, and if you don't accept my

5   suggestion to stay deportation --

6   MR. MORAN: A stay of deportation is not

7   appropriate because he has not been ordered deported.

8   All a denial of the motion would do, it would enable the

9   administrative process as to whether or not he would be

10   served with an order to show cause to take effect, and then

11   he could make an appropriate request.

12   Also, your Honor, again, it is the position of

13   the Service it is too late for Judge Broderick to come

14   back from vacation and act on this. Should you grant this

15   motion, it is the position of the Immigration Service that

16   we cannot use this.

17   THE COURT: You cannot what?

18   MR. MORAN: If you grant the motion, we cannot

19   use this conviction as a charge in bringing deportation

20   proceedings against Mr. Gucci.

21   THE COURT: Of course you can't, if I grant this

22   motion.

23   MR. MORAN: Therefore, because the elapsed time

24   occurs at midnight today, or close of business, however

25   you wnat to look at it, somebody has to act on this

31

md

1 motion today.

2   THE COURT: All right.

3   It is your postiion the United States Attorney's

4 Office entered into a stipulation which seemed to me a

5 very fair-minded stipulation, but you contend the United

6 States Attorney had no right to enter into that

7 stipulation?

8   'MR. MORAN: Yes. And I also would refer the

9 court to Mr. Stuart Smith's representations to the oourt

10 earlier today that in fact it was done in error without an

11 ability to consult with the Immigration Service, and no

12 such stipulation can control the Immigration Service.

13   I would like to bring one other thing to your

14 attention. Counsel made representations about what the

15 intent of Judge Broderick was. There was never a motion to

16 Judge Broderick under this section of the Act, so I don't

17 think any inference as to what he wanted can be drawn from

18 the sentence.

19   THE COURT: I understand there was a motion

20 pending.

21   MR. MORAN: There was, but he never saw it.

22   THE COURT: What difference does it make if he

23 didn't see it? It was filed in his chambers. That's a

24 motion made to a judge.

25   If I am away for a week, and there is a motion

md   32

1   filed in my chambers that is a motion before me.

2   We are discussing technicalities here.

3   MR. MORAN: Counsel represented to the court

4   because of the sentence that Judge Broderick had given

5   Mr. Gucci that he meant certain things by it, and I don't

6   think that that is an appropriate representation.

7   THE COURT: I don't know what he meant, and

8   I have no judgment as to what he meant.

9   MR. MORAN: Thank you.

10   THE COURT: But it is clear to me that having

11 imposed a condition of parole, I think it was, upon his

12 release, that he was to render community service -- I don't

13 have the judgment before me -- he clearly contemplated

14 that the man would have to stay here in order to render

15 community service.

16   MR. MORAN: I will state categorically to the

17 court if an order of deportation is ever found against

18 Mr. Gucci during the period of time that he is to serve

19 in the community service it will not be affected. He will

20 be allowed to fulfill that sentence of the court.

21   THE COURT: The court will dictate a brief

22 memorandum, and elaborate upon it when it has a better

23 opportunity to review all the papers.

24

25

md

1   This is an application by Aldo Gucci, who was

2 sentenced by Judge Broderick on September 11, 1986, for

3 violation of income tax laws, the sentence being a period

4 of a year and a day.

5   The court does not have before it the judgment

6 of conviction, but counsel has stated that part of the

7 sentence required that upon release the defendant render

8 community service for a period of one year, which by itself

9 suggests that the defendant is required to remain in this

10 country.

11   An application was made before Judge Broderick

12 for relief under the provisions of 8 USC, Section 1251 (b)

13 under which a sentencing court may recommend that a

14 defendant not be deported as authorized under that

15 section.

16   Such an application has to be made within thirty

17 days of the date of sentence. The application in this

18 instance was made on October 7th, shortly before the

19 expiration of thirty days, by which time the representation

20 is made to this court that Judge Broderick was not available,

21 was out of the country.

22   This court has long been of the view that the

23 application within the thirty days had to be made to the

24 sentencing judge. However, the attorney representing the

25 Immigration Service states and represents to the court

md   34

that this provision applies to any judge of the sentencing

court, and any judge may make the disposition, and counsel

is of the view that this court presently sitting is the

one that has the authority to make the determination.

The court is further advised that the power to

make a decision expires at midnight tonight.

On the information submitted, the application

is for a stay of deportation of the defendant, and such

application is granted.

The court regrets the Immigration Service

did not accept the suggestion that a stay be consented to

to await the return of Judge Broderick so that he could

make the final dispostion, particularly in view of the

fact that he is familiar with all the basic facts that

must have come before him in the presentence report.

I will go over this and for a more extended

opinion.

Mr. Abrams, let me say on behalf of the court

I commend your office for the position that you took

when you signed that stipulation that was so ordered

by Judge Sweet.

I thought it was a very fair-minded position

that the government took, unlike the position that the

Immigration Service has advanced here.

MR. SMITH: Thank you, your Honor.

35

md

1   THE COURT: Don't thank the court for its

2   judgment.

3   ---------

4

5

6

7

8

9

10

11

12

13

14

15

16

17

18

19

20

21

22

23

24

25

SUSAN JANE FRALE
TRADUTTRICE
VIA DEL BISARNO, 3 - TEL. 8.810.295
50126 FIRENZE

"La Repubblica" - Tuesday, 4th November 1986

Milan, the company headquarters are searched

MAURIZIO GUCCI ACCUSED OF EXPORTING CAPITAL

by our correspondent.

Florence - Maurizio Gucci, company chairman, has been accused of exporting capital. On magistrate's orders, Customs revenue police searched company headquarters in Milan and Maurizio's home. It appe that numerous documents were sequestrated and are now being examinec

The initiative of the Florentine Public Prosecutor's office is somehow linked to a long statement presented by by Paolo Gucci against his cousin. Two weeks' ago, Paolo was cross-examined as witness for about four hours. Rumour has it that they are tryinc to remap the Panamese companies created by the Guccis during the sixties: Vanguard International Manufacturing, Anglo American Manu-facturing, Cika International and Anfars Ag.

Now the gucci case seems to be even more complicated: M. is being investaigated by the Milanese magistrature for false evidence, forging public acts and fraud, for the ?apocryphal (false) signatures affixed to the shares (50% of the company) which he inherited on his father's death whereas another investigation has been started by the Roman Public Prosecutor's office.

It then goes on to say how it was Paolo who sparked off these enquiries.

The part highlighted:

During a violent argument that arose during a family gathering, Paolo Gucci in fact presented his first statement demanding two billion lire from his brothers, father and cousins who has "intntionally wounded him".

PROCURA DELLA REPUBBLICA - FIRENZE

N. 4181/86 R.G.

ORDINE DI ACCOMPAGNAMENTO

Il Procuratore della repubblica di Firenze
in persona del sostituto Dottor Ubaldo NANNUCCI

Visti gli atti del procedimento penale a carico di

- MAURIZIO GUCCI, nato a Firenze il 26/9/1948 e domiciliato a Milano,
  Galleria Passarella n. 1;

- DOMENICO DE SOLE, nato a Roma il 1/1/1944, ed ivi residente in Via
  dell'Umanesimo n. 299;

- SANDRO SAGGIONO, nato a CaNNOBBio (NO) il 21/3/1943, e residente a
  Milano, Corso Sempione n. 33

I M P U T A T I

(come da fogli allegati)

Visti gli artt. 252, 254 e 261 C.P.P.:

- rilevato che il mandato di cattura è facoltativo;
- considerato che vi è fondato motivo di ritenere che il mandato di comparizione possa rimanere senza effetto perchè gli imputati sono soliti trascorrere lunghi periodi di tempo all'estero e risultando perciò difficile il loro rintraccio;

O R D I N A

a Ufficiali di Polizia Tributaria della Guardia di Finanza di Firenze di
condurre i nominati davanti a noi, nel nostro Ufficio, alle ore 9,00 DEL
GIORNO 17 GIUGNO 1987 usando anche la forza in caso di rifiuto.

Firenze, 11.6.1987

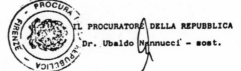

IL PROCURATORE DELLA REPUBBLICA
Dr. Ubaldo Nannucci - sost.

Maurizio GUCCI

Domenico DE SOLE

I M P U T A T I

A) del delitto di cui agli artt. 1, c. II, L. 30 aprile 1976, n°159,
81, C/V 110 C.P., per avere in concorso tra loro, essendo Maurizio
GUCCI cittadino valutariamente residente in Italia, costituito sen
za l'autorizzazione prevista dalle norme in materia valutaria, at
tività all'estero. costituendo la società STANDARD INVESTIMENT AND
TRADING CO - di Panama; acquistando nel dicembre '83, pper la somma
di 400.000.= $, un veliero a tre alberi denominato CREOLE che in-
testavano alla predetta società di comodo rappresentata da Domenico DE SOLE, stretto collaboratore del GUCCI e faceddovi di poi ese
guire lavori di restauro in Italia nel corso degli anni 1983, 1984
e 1985 per complessive £. 5.330.000.000.= circa.

Sandro SAGGIOMO

B) del delitto di cui agli artt. 1, c. II, L. 30 aprile 1976, n°159,
110 c.p. per avere, dopo che Maurizio GUCCI - cittadino valutariamente residente in Italia - e Domenico DE SOLE avevano costituito,
con le modalità descritte al papo precedente e senza l'autorizzazione prescritta, l'attività costituita dal veliero "Creole", con
corso nell'accrescere tale attività, partecipando, qquale persona
di fiducia di Maurizio GUCCI, alle operazioni di restauro con fun
zioni di direttore dei lavori e supervisore, nonché di persona in
caricata di autorizzare i pagamenti durante il corso dei lavori;
così concorrendo ad accrescere il valore dell'attività predetta fi
no a circa 7 miliardi di lire.

TRANSLATED FROM
ITALIAN

- OFFICE OF THE PUBLIC PROSECUTOR - FLORENCE

ORDER OF ACCOMPANIMENT

The Public Prosecutor in Florence
designated Doctor Ubaldo Nannucci
Having seen the acts of the penal proceedings against
- MAURIZIO GUCCI, born in Florence, the 26.9.1948 and resident in Milan,
        Galleria Passarella no. 1;
- DOMENICO DE SOLE, born in Rome, the 1.1.1944 and there residing in
        Via dell'Umanesimo no. 299 ;
- SANDRO SAGGIOMO , born at Cannobbio (Novara), the 21.3.1943 , and
        resident in Milan, Corso Sempione no. 33

THE ACCUSED
(as per attached sheets)

Having seen the articles nos. 252, 254 and 261 C.P.P. (Italian abbrev-
iation for Code of Penal Proceedure)
- it is noticed that the warrant of arrest is optional;
- it is considered that there is a strong reason to believe that the
        warrant of appearance may remain without effect
        because the accused are normally spending long
        periods of time abroad, making their location
        difficult;

IT IS ORDERED
TO· the Ufficiali di Polizia Tributaria della Guardia di Finanza (customs
officials within the police force) in Florence, to bring the accused
before the Public Prosecutor, in our office, at 9 o'clock the 17th day
of June 1987, also using force in case of refusal.

Florence, 11.6.1987

The Public Prosecutor
Dr. Ubaldo Nannucci - designated.

Maurizio GUCCI

Domenico DE SOLE

ARE ACCUSED

A) of the crime as in articles 1, c. II, L. 30th April 1976,
   no. 159, 81 C/V 110 C.P.,
   Between them, Maurizio Gucci being an Italian resident citizen,
   subject to Italian taxation laws, entered into foreign activities
   without the due authorisation required by the monetary regulations,
   by forming the company Standard Investment and Trading Co. of Panama;
   buying in December 1983, for the sum of $ 400,000, a three-masted
   sailing ship called CREOLE which was registered to the above company,
   formed for convenience and represented by Domenico De Sole, close
   collaborator of Gucci, and undertaking arrangements for restoration
   works in Italy during the course of 1983, 1984 and 1985 for an
   approximate sum of 5,330,000,000 Italian lire.

Sandro SAGGIOMO

B) of the crime as in articles 1,c. II, L. 30th April 1976, no. 159, 110 c.p.
   for having taken part in increasing such an activity, as a person
   trusted by Maurizio Gucci, to the restoration works with functions
   of director of works, supervisor, and as a person responsible for
   the payments during the course of the works, contributing to increase
   the value of the above mentioned activities to a value of approximately
   7 billion Italian lire, after Maurizio Gucci, Italian resident citizen
   subject to Italian taxation laws, together with Domenico De Sole
   had carried out the activities involving the sailing ship 'Creole'
   with the methods described in the above paragraph and without due
   authorisation.

Il manager accusato di illecita costituzione di capitali all'estero

Una nuova tempesta in casa Gucci ordine di cattura contro Maurizio

FIRENZE — Tempesta in casa Gucci. Maurizio, maggior azionista dell'omonima azienda di pelletteria, è stato colpito da ordine di cattura per illecita costituzione di capitali all'estero. Il manager è in Svizzera per affari, ma per la giustizia italiana è latitante. Le manette sono invece scattate attorno ai polsi di Giovanni Vittorio Pilone, membro del consiglio d'amministrazione della società. E' sfuggito all'arresto anche un terzo imputato, Sandro Saggiano, cognato di Pilone.

A PAGINA 15 IL SERVIZIO DI PAOLO VAGHEGGI

Presto una legge in Parlamento?

Sono tutti d'accordo, la patente a 16 anni

● A PAGINA 20

Portfolio

Oggi si vincono quattro milioni

● IL CONCORSO
A PAGINA 41

☐ la Repubblica
mercoledì 24 giugno 1987

La Repubblica   Wednesday, the 24th June

The manager accused of making illegal capital abroad

A.NEW TEMPEST IN THE GUCCI FAMILY - ORDER OF ARREST AGAINST MAURIZIO

FLORENCE - Storm in the Gucci family. Maurizio, mojor shareholder of the
leather company carrying the same name, has been hit by an order of arrest
for making illegal capital abroad. The manager is in Switzerland on
business, but as far as the Italian justice is concerned, he has absconded.
The handcuffs have been put upon Giovanni Vittorio Pilone, member of the
administration board of the company. Also the third man accused, Sandro
Saggiomo, Pilone's brother- in- law has eluded arrest.
          On page 15 is the article by Paolo Vagheggi.

N.B. In this article Sandro Saggiomo is referred to as Sandro Saggiano.

Mercoledì 24 giugno 1987

CRONACHE ITALIANE

CORRIERE DELLA SERA 5

Ordine di cattura contro l'industriale della moda e due suoi stretti collaboratori (uno già arrestato)

È stata Grecia a tradire Maurizio Gucci

I guai sono derivati da questo pacillo di sogno, venduto da Niarkos per un miliardo e addebito con altri 5 miliardi - Il denaro era stato speso occultamente, secondo il giudice, capitali all'estero - La fine in famiglia ha rotto il trucco - Il presidente, attualmente e Lugano, è accusato dai parenti di aver acquisito le azioni della società con il falso

Maurizio Gucci, ricercato dal Giudice di Firenze

FIRENZE — Grecia the ...

Wanda Lattes

Panorama

Catania, Cossiga dà la grazia al frate ergastolano

Patente a 16 anni anche in Italia? Favorevole la Motorizzazione civile

Fatto catturare dai genitori l'assassino del carabiniere

CORRIERE DELLA SERA   Wednesday 24th June 1987

ITALIAN CHRONICLES

Warrant of arrest against the fashion industrialist and two of his
collaborators (one already arrested)

IT WAS CREOLE THAT BETRAYED MAURIZIO GUCCI

The troubles were brought by this dream yacht, sold by Niarkos for 1
billion Italian lire and refitted for another 5 billion. According to the
Judge, the money was spent in order to transfer a capital abroad. The
family quarrel has uncovered the trick. The president, currently in
Lugano, is accused by his relatives of having acquired shares in the
company by fraud,.

FLORENCE — Creole. An inspiring name for a boat, a name that calls to
mind visions of Southern Seas and superb idleness, women with swaying hips
and luxurious encounters between the palm trees.Who would have ever said
to Mr. Maurizio Gucci, gentleman of distinguished looks, president of
the Guccio Gucci Spa, that just this little boat, beautiful but not
very much used, (enjoyed), would have had the power to lock the handcuffs
around his wrists, if only yesterday morning he had been at his residence
in Milan, rather than absent from Italy on a providential trip to Lugano ?
          The designated Public Prosecutor of Florence, Ubaldo Nannucci,
has in fact issued a warrant of arrest against Maurizio Gucci, for the
illicit constitution of capital abroad for the specific reason of purchasing
and refitting the Creole, a three masted sailing vessel of great class,
bought last year, it seems, by a company formed for convenience which,
according to the prosecution, would lead to Maurizio Gucci. The boat
which belonged to nonother than Niarkos, was purchased for a sum of
around 1 billion lire, but in order to become worthy of his dreams and
also to be seaworthy, it absorbed another 5 billion lire.
You can say that one has the right to spend his money as he wishes,
but this right ceases when the money is found outside your homeland,
in the hands of a company which appears to be of convenience.
So the designated Nannucci has issued the warrant of arrest, not only
against the 40 year old Maurizio, but also against two of his close
collaborators resident in Milan. One of the most unfortunate, is the
57 year old Venetian Vittorio Pilone, Maurizio's right hand, detained
in the prison of Sollicciano, at Scandicci near Florence, where he
has already been interrogated, in the presence of his defending lawyer

Nino d'Avirro. The other, more fortunate, is abroad, he is 64 year old
Sandro Saggiomo. Only a very naive person would fail to notice the
connection between the facts related to the boat and the series of
bad events which for some time have been ruining the Gucci name, synom-
inous of many years of elegance. The family is unquestionably a dynasty
of unsurpassed creators of handbags, suitcases, scarves, shoes and
many other objects of clothing and for the home.
The connection appears explicit:, and is in the dossier presented in
the autumn of last year to the Attorney General of the Court of Appeal
in Rome, also forwarded to the Guardia di Finanza (customs officials
within the police force) andto the various information bodies.
Here , however, a clear reference was made to the yacht owned by Niarkos.
On the 21st October 1986 it was heard .by Doctor Nannucci, in Florence,
that the very same Paolo Gucci, is notoriously in a bitter dispute
with all his relations. The judicial system in Italy runs slowly, but
it runs, and on the basis of investigations carried out in five or six
months, the designated Nannucci is now holding the " sword of Damocles "
over the head of the handsome Maurizio. But Maurizio the most Milanese
of all the Gucci's, who has the office above the shop in Via Montenapoleone and always lives between San Babila and Saint Moritz, does
not have only this money matter open. Rather it seems that the news
of the warrant of arrest, which should have remained secret, has come
to light because the still young manager did not appear before the
Milanese magistrate, to whom he owed explanations regarding another
complicated matter.
    In fact Maurizio, who is the president of Guccio Gucci Spa, as
he owns more than 50% of the company shares, is accused by his uncle
Aldo and his cousins Roberto and Paolo of having acquired possession
of these shares, not just thanks to a donation made by his father Rodolfo
before he died, but rather due to a series of forged signatures of the
old man, carried out by one of his lady collaborators to "pass on "
the ownership of the shares.
    At this point of the story, it is necessary to sum up the
characteristics of the dynasty and clarify the motives of these fierce
rivalries. The founder of the family Guccio, born in 1881 and deceased
in 1953 started in his business of luxurious handbag maker, three of his
five sons, Vasco, who has not left any heirs, then Rodolfo, the eldest
a successful actor in "white phone " films, and finally Aldo, the youngest
and still alive, dedicated to the company from his early years and currently
also involved in unpleasant matters with the american tax department,
From Rodolfo, Maurizio was born; from Aldo, between 1928 and 1962 four
sons were born of whom Roberto and Paolo are closely involved in the

intricated mountain of scarves and handbags commercialised throughout the world.

The current judicial events are three, but behind them lie tons of official documents and dozens of lawyers. The main event relates to the ownership of the company shares; Aldo, Paolo and Roberto maintain that the majority of Maurizio has been badly acquired, and Maurizio on the other hand, is letting loose investigators and accusations against his claimed crime of forgery.

The second event originated from the rivalry of Paolo, confronting alone the whole company: elegant, pale, polite, Paolo has confirmed not to be in agreement with the methods of running the company and has claimed independence in the use of the company trade mark. Amongst other things he has presented a mountain of documents about the irregularities committed, in his view by his cousin and president Maurizio. Amongst these the story of the boat, and here we are at the third event ----the Creole of the handcuffs.

Just for the record, it must be said that within four days there should be a meeting of the board of the company, to which in the meantime mortgages for hundreds of billions of lire have been taken out, caused by disloyal accusations, unpaid taxes and so on. But recently on 18th June in Lugano, Maurizio has been able to speak about the necessity to improve the Gucci image. The company in fact is doing very well: the turnover has increased from 227 to 234 billion lire, only in Florence the Gucci shops of Via Tornabuoni are at the centre of continuous international coming and going.

Wanda Lattes.

Firenze, ricercato Maurizio, il maggior azionista della società

Scatta l'ordine di cattura
Per un veliero da sogno i Gucci nella tempesta

di PAOLO VAGHEGGI

FIRENZE — Per cinque mesi gli agenti del nucleo di polizia tributaria della Guardia di Finanza hanno controllato scrupolosamente i documenti riguardanti la compravendita di «Creole», un tre alberi che le riviste specializzate definiscono «la più bella barca del mondo», di proprietà di Maurizio Gucci. Alla fine hanno inviato un voluminoso rapporto al sostituto procuratore Ubaldo Nannucci che ha sollecitato un ordine di cattura per illecita costituzione di capitali all'estero. Da ieri Maurizio Gucci, maggior azionista della Guccio Gucci, manager di successo, è, per la giustizia italiana, un latitante.

Il provvedimento era nell'aria. Appena una settimana fa Maurizio per presentare il bilancio del '86 aveva convocato una conferenza stampa al Grand Hotel di Lugano. In Svizzera non ha nulla da temere: i reati valutari non comportano estradizione. Le porte del carcere si sono invece aperte per un suo uomo di fiducia: Giovanni Vittorio Pilone, 57 anni, membro del consiglio di amministrazione della Gucci. Come Maurizio è riuscito a evitare l'arresto in terza imputata, Sandro Saggiano, 64 anni, cognato del Pilone.

Di notizie ufficiali e ne sono poche. Le indiscrezioni che han comunicato a circolare ieri mattina hanno irritato sia il sostituto incaricato dell'inchiesta sia il nucleo di polizia tributaria che si trincerano dietro un «no comment». Le «Fiamme gialle» pro...

Una società di "comodo"

Il primo a fame le spese è stato Aldo Gucci, figlio di Guccio, il fondatore di questo impero dove...

so, o in occasione dell'assemblea ordinaria dell'azienda convocata per il 29 giugno. Proprio in vista di questa scadenza l'ex presidente aveva rivolto un appello ai parenti inviandoli a deporre le armi. Sono anni che all'interno della famiglia Gucci si è scatenata una guerra feroce per il controllo della società che dà il suo nome ha fatturato 233 miliardi. Non si è badato ai colpi: fratello contro fratello, padre contro i figli.

Ora tocca a Maurizio, nei panni da tempo per le false firme di cui è accusato sulle azioni ereditate dal padre Rodolfo, il 50 per cento del pacchetto. L'inchiesta fiorentina però nota intorno al «Creole» e ad una società che gli inquirenti ritengono di comodo», finita. La barca apparteneva ad un altro personaggio piuttosto noto: il miliardario greco Stavros Niarchos. Secondo le poche voci che circolano fu acquistata per un miliardo tra dove fu «ristrutturata». Spesa dei lavori seguiti da Sandro Saggiano: sei miliardi. Lo splendido veliero, che attualmente sarebbe ormeggiato a Palma di Maiorca...

Intercettazioni e pedinamenti per seguire le mosse dei parenti-nemici

Nella Saga, detectives e spioni

FIRENZE - C'è anche una «spy story», nella saga dei Gucci ma non è finita bene per un gruppo di detectives milanesi incaricati di sorvegliare un testimone eccellente di questo caso: Roberta Cassol, per molti anni le dele collaboratrice di Rodolfo Gucci, il padre di Maurizio. «Intercettai» casualmente dai carabinieri mentre piazzavano delle microspie pochi giorni fa sono stati processati a Milano e pesantemente condannati: 14 mesi di reclusione a Teresio Pastori, ti-

tolare del negozio Gucci di via Montenapoleone. Proprio quest'ultimo aveva contattato gli spioni per scoprire movimenti e abitudini della Cassol.

La donna era stata ascoltata dalla magistratura per verificare l'autenticità delle firme di girata apposte sulle azioni in eredità da Maurizio Gucci. La Cassol non aveva avuto dubbi: non erano di Rodolfo.

Le aveva imitate un'altra dipendente dell'azienda Liliana Colombo. È così per...

È finito invece in cella il braccio destro del manager, Giovanni Vittorio Pilone. L'accusa sostiene che lo sviata ha trasferito capitali all'estero. Nelle indagini coinvolto anche un costruttore. Il tre alberi 'incriminato' è il 'Creole'.

Maurizio Gucci (caption)

...serial tipo Dallas.

È una famiglia di «nemici» per la pelle, come è stata inoculatamente definita, e tanto è cominciato con una vera e propria rissa. Quattro anni fa al Gucci si ritrovarono in una villa fiorentina per dirimere una lunga vertenza che divideva Paolo Gucci dagli altri componenti del clan. Paolo, intenzionato a creare un proprio marchio, arrivò con un registratore. La discussione degenerò. Fratelli e cugini ed il padre Aldo, così scrisse Paolo, in un esposto presentato alla corte federale di New York lo assalirono coscientemente, maliziosamente, colpendolo con le mani, i pugni infine l'hanno graffiato». La denuncia che in Usa si occupa della riscossione delle imposte. Di ultimo Aldo Gucci fu condannato a un anno di reclusione.

La guerra però divenne definitivamente fratricida alla morte di Rodolfo, il padre di Maurizio. Quest'ultimo aveva acquisito il controllo della società allcandosi prima con Paolo e successivamente con Giorgio. Due brevi matrimoni finiti in burrasca. La rottura degli accordi tra Maurizio e Paolo e quella che ha consolidato l'intervento della magistratura. Paolo Gucci non è riuscito a creare una propria azienda, è stato fermato dal pretore di Roma. Ma in qualche modo si è vendicato. Ha varcato la soglia delle procure di Firenze, Roma, Milano. Ha consegnato ai giudici...

La riunione del 1983

Il 1987, che doveva essere l'anno del rilancio, si sta rivelando come quello dei grandi guai, delle paure. Le inchieste pendenti sono ormai 18 e la Gucci story sta facendo impallidire anche i...

bisogna dimenticare che sul patrimonio di Maurizio Gucci sono state iscritte ipoteche per 599 miliardi a garanzia delle sanzioni che lo Stato presume di dover infliggere perché il Gucci si ritrovasse. A tre ordini di cattura emessi dal sostituto Nannucci. L'unico arrestato è però Giovanni Vittorio Pilone, coinvolto anche nell'inchiesta per le false girate.

Per Maurizio Gucci un brutto colpo. A Lugano aveva parlato di un nuovo piano in realizzare l'immagine dei Gucci. Ma ora non potrà neppure partecipare all'assemblea di lunedì che si annuncia decisiva per il controllo dell'azienda. Avrà anche ben poca voce in capitolo. Il suo pacchetto azionario è sotto sequestro per decisione della magistratura milanese, custodito dagli avvocati Casella e Poli. E non è intestato a una società che secondo gli inquirenti, è riconducibile a Maurizio Gucci. Durante la compravendita sarebbero avvenuti degli illeciti valutari. Dopo...

...te evasione delle imposte di successione. Ma a questo punto — la storia risale all'estate del 1983 — sono entrati in scena gli spioni.

Ingaggiati dal direttore del negozio di Milano i segugi della Fidelitas, un'agenzia investigativa privata, hanno cominciato a sorvegliare notte e giorno la Cassol per svelare eventuali segreti contatti con i parenti-nemici di Maurizio. Causa la scarsità di risultati però non sono bene di controllare an...

...non tramonta mai il sole, finito in carcere a New York per evasione fiscale.

La Repubblica   Wednesday 24th June.

Cronaca - Chronicle

Florence, Maurizio, the major shareholder of the company is wanted.
Maurizio Gucci's right hand man is imprisonned instead. The prosecution
maintains that the stylist has transferred a capital abroad. In the
investigation a constructor is also involved. The " incriminated "
three masted boat is the Creole.

THE ORDER FOR ARREST IS SPRUNG - FOR A DREAM BOAT THE GUCCI'S ARE IN A
STORM

By Paolo Vagheggi

Florence - For five months the customs agents have thoroughly examined the
documentation related to the purchase of the Creole, a three masted sailing
boat which according to specialised magazines is defined as " the most
beautiful boat in the world." It is the property of Maurizio Gucci. At the
end the customs agents sent a voluminous report to the designated Public
Prosecutor Ubaldo Nannucci and the magistrate has issued a warrant of arrest
for illicit transfer of capital abroad. From yesterday, Maurizio Gucci,
major shareholder of Guccio Gucci and successful manager is, as far as the
Italian justice is concerned, a fugitive.
The provision of this warrant was in the air. Only a week ago Maurizio, in
order to present the company accounts, had called a press meeting at the
Grand Hotel in Lugano. In Switzerland he has nothing to worry about: the
currency crimes do not carry an extradition order. The prison doors have
been opened instead for his right ·hand man Giovanni Vittorio Pilone,
57 years old and member of the board of administration of Gucci. As with
Maurizio, the third man accused, Sandro Saggiomo, 64 years old and Pilone's
brother - in - law has succeeded in avoiding arrest.
There is very little official news. The indiscretions that have been in
circulation since yesterday morning, have irritated the designated Public
Prosecutor responsible for the inquest as well as the customs agents who have
replied to enquiries with " no comment ". "Fiamme gialle" (yellow flames, logo
worn by the customs. agents), probably hoped to capture Maurizio Gucci
yesterday in Milan where he was expected to attend a court case, or on the
occasion of the ordinary general meeting of the company called for the 29th
June. In view of this expiry date the former president appealed to the relatives
encouraging them to lay down their arms. A fierce war has raged for years

amongst the Gucci family for the control of the company whose turnover last year was 233 billion Italian lire. No punches were spared, brother against brother, father agaist sons.

A COMPANY OF " CONVENIENCE "

The first person to suffer the consequences was Aldo Gucci, son of Guccio, the founder of this empire where the sun never sets, who ended up in a New York jail for tax evasion.

Now it is Maurizio's turn, in trouble from the time the forged signatures on the shares inherited from his father Rodolfo, which represent 50 % of the company shares. The Florence inquèst however rotates around the Creole and a company which the investigators believe to be of " convenience," in other words fictitious, The boat used to belong to another rather well - known person; the Greek billionaire Stavros Niarchos. According to the few rumours which circulate, the boat was bought for 1 billion lire and immediately transferred tda Ligurian shipyard where it was "restructured." The ammount spent for the works carried out by Sandro Saggiomo was 6 billion lire. The splendid s·iling boat, which presently seems to be moored at Palma di Majorca, is in the name of a company which, according to the investigators, leads to Maurizio Gucci. During the purchase transaction illegal exportation of capital would have taken place. From this the three Warrants of arrest were issued by the designated Nannucci. However only Giovanni Vittorio Pilone has been arrested being also investigated regarding the forged signatures.

For Maurizio Gucci this is a bad shock. In Lugano he referred to a plan to " raise the Gucci image." But now he wont even be able to take part in Monday's meeting which will be decisive for the control of the company. He will also have very little say. His shares have been seized following a decision by the Milanese magistrate, and now are in the hands of Messrs Casella and Poli, solicitors. It must not be forgotten that some 599 billion lire have been mortgaged as a warranty to the sanctions that the state presume to inflict because the inheritance tax department has discovered irregular declarations of valuables and has singled out possessions, in Italy and abroad, the existence of which had not been declared.

The Reunion of 1983

1987 was supposed to be the year of the relaunch, is proving to be the year
of great adversity and fear. There are already 18 pending inquests and the
"Gucci story" is creating even more impact than soap operas like Dallas.
It is a family of "deadly enemies", as it was ironically defined and everything started with a real fight. Four years ago the Gucci family met in a
villa in Florence in order to dispel a long standing controversy which was
dividing Paolo Gucci from the other members of the clan. Paolo, determined
to create his own trade-mark, arrived with a tape recorder. The discussion
deteriorated. Brothers, cousins and father Aldo, as Paolo described in a
document filed with the Federal court of New York, attacked him "intentionally
and maliciously," hitting him with hands, fists and finally with the tape
recorder. The accusation put in motion the agents of the Internal Revenue
Service, the U.S.A. agency which deals with tax collection. At the end
Aldo Gucci was sentenced to 1 year in prison.

The war really became fratricidal with the death of
Rodolfo, father of Maurizio. Maurizio had acquired the control of the
company making an alliance with at first Paolo and subsequently with
Giorgio, two short partnerships which ended in quarrels. The breaking of
the agreements between Maurizio and Paolo was the cause of the magistrate's
intervention. Paolo Gucci did not succeed in creating his own company and
has been stopped by the police magistrate in Rome. But in some way he took
his "revenge". He crossed the threshold of the Public Prosecution in Florence,
Rome and Milan and delivered to the judges hundreds of documents. In Tuscany
the investigations about the "Creole" started and the former president is
now shipwrecked.

Interceptions and tailings to discover the moves of the enemy relatives
A STORY OF DETECTIVES AND SPIES

Florence - There is a "spy story" in the Gucci family saga which did not have
a happy ending because a group of Milanese detectives were instructed to
watch a very important witness in the case ; Roberta Cassol, for many years
the trusted collaborator of Rodolfo Gucci, Maurizio's father. The detectives
who were accidentally intercepted by the police while planting micro
bugging devices, have been prosecuted a few days ago in Milan and heavily
sentenced; fourteen months imprisonment for Teresio Pastori, proprietor of
the agency Fidelitas, twelve months each imprisonment to three technicians
and seventeen months imprisonment to Antonino Taffara, director of the
Gucci shop in via Montenapoleone. It was Mr. Taffara who contacted the spies in
order to discover the movements and habits of Roberta Cassol.

The woman was heard by the magistrate in order to verify the authenticity
of the signatures shown on the shares inherited by Maurizio Gucci. Cassol
did not have any doubt: they were not Rodolfo's signatures.

Another employee of the company, Liliana Colombo, had forged them. And
this was the beginning of Maurizio's troubles. The forgery was covering
up the evasion of succession taxes. But at this point, back to the summer
of 1985 - the spies entered the scene.

Hired by the director of the shop in Milan, the detectives from
Fidelitas, a private investigation agency, started a day and night
surveillance of Cassol in order to uncover possible secret contacts
with Maurizio's enemy relatives. Due to the poor results achieved they
decided also to bug the telephone. They were stopped by the police while
in the act of planting the bugging devices.

INDEX

359